DICTIONARY OF WIT AND WISDOM

DICTIONARY OF WIT AND WISDOM

Compiled by Gerd de Ley

Translations by
David Potter

Introduction by
James Geary

TENTH STREET PRESS

THIS EDITION

Copyright © 2017 Gerd de Ley

Published by Tenth Street Press 2017
Cover design by Axel for Tenth Street Press

ISBN-10: 0-6481676-0-7
ISBN-13: 978-0-6481676-0-0

PRINTED IN THE U.S.A.

This book is sold on the condition that it shall not, by way of trade or otherwise, be lent, re-sold or circulated by any traditional or electronic means or have any original content contained herein reproduced in any form without prior written consent from the publisher.

TENTH STREET PRESS Ltd.
MELBOURNE LONDON
www.tenthstreetpress.com
contact@tenthstreetpress.com

CONTENTS

Introduction 9
A 11
B 33
C 53
D 83
E 101
F 115
G 133
H 151
I 165
J 179
K 183
L 185
M 197
N 217
O 225
P 233
Q 261
R 263
S 277
T 309

U	325
V	329
W	335
X	345
Y	347
Z	349

Introduction

Dictionaries are, by definition, not definitive. We cannot really say with complete precision what something is. Words are too mercurial, and our own perceptions too partial, for that. Insights slip and slide; connotations come and go. We can never dip into the same meaning twice because words, and the thoughts they carry with them, are always flowing on. The 'last word' on any subject cannot be spoken because language itself withholds it. The best we can do are approaches, approximations. So, for me, the most accurate definition of 'definition' is by English novelist Samuel Butler, who wrote: "A definition is the enclosing of a wilderness if idea within a wall of words." This definition comes close to definitiveness by recognizing its own inadequacy, by acknowledging that the most fertile ideas inevitably outgrow any attempts to confine them by defining them.

To open Gerd de Ley's magnificent dictionary is to enter a garden of definitional delights where, within the space of a few imperfect words, we encounter the wildest reaches of the human mind and heart.

James Geary
Author of "The World in a Phrase: A Brief History of the Aphorism" and "Geary's Guide to the World's Great Aphorists"

A - the camping tent of the alphabet.
Ramon Gomez de la Serna
AAAA - a new organization for drunks who drive. Give them a call and they'll tow you away from the bar.
Martin Burden
AAAAAA - American Automobile Association Against Alcohol Anonymous (for those who are driven to drink).
Lawrence Brotherton
aardvark - alphabetically advantaged animal.
William Flis
abacus - profanity used by Scandinavian singers.
Chris Cox
abalone - an expression of disbelief.
Tony Thoennes
abandon - the Mafia leader who is not allowed to go anywhere.
Phil Hudson
abasement - an act of faith when a man decides he is not God.
Oliver Wendell Holmes
abbreviate - the cheese we had yesterday.
Hank Levinson
(to) abdicate - to give up all hope of ever having a flat stomach.
Tom Witte
abdomen - the reason why man does not easily take himself for a god.
Friedrich Nietzsche
ability - the art of getting credit for all the home runs someone else hits.
Casey Stengel
abnormal person - any one who behaves differently from you.
O.A. Battista
A-bomb - an abode filled with bees.
Victoria Tarrani
(see also: neutron bomb, tactical nuclear weapon)
abortion - the Chinese method of birth control.
Mike Barfield
above - down when standing on your head.
Harry Mulisch

absence - the best defence.
Nils-Fredrik Nielsen
absentee - a missing golfing accessory.
Gunjan Saraf
absent-mindedness - often evidence of deep thought and goodness. Stupid and malicious people always have presence of mind.
Charles-Joseph de Ligne
absolute morality - the regulation of conduct in such a way that pain shall not be inflicted.
Herbert Spencer
absolute truth - the thing that makes people laugh.
Carl Reiner
abstainer - the kind of man you wouldn't want to drink with even if he did.
George Jean Nathan
abstract art - a product of the untalented, sold by the unprincipled to the utterly bewildered.
Al Capp
abstract noun - one you can't see when you look for it.
Milton Berle
absurd - every opinion that differs from ours.
Augusto Gil
absurdity - hell's miracle.
Dean Anthony Granitsas
abundance - the scourge of prosperity.
Werner Mitsch
abut - the highpoint for a leg man.
H. Gordon Havens
academic - someone who studies the passion-stains on the bedsheets.
Irving Layton
accelerato - the Italian word for a train stopping at every station and going very slowly in between, so as not to overshoot.
Clive James
accent - something other people have.
Colin Bowles
acceptable risk - a risk to others.
Chaz Bufe
acceptance - the courage of the losers.
Frans de Wilde
accident - a child conceived long after your husband's vasectomy.
Cy DeBoer

accomplishment - the full-blown rose of effort.
Merry Browne
accordion - a piano with suspenders.
Piet Grijs
accountability - holding teachers, public officials and private business responsible for their misdeeds.
Thomas Sowell
accountancy - one of the most difficult professions for people trying to find dates.
Frances Pyne
accountant - a person you can seldom count on.
Ramon Gomez de La Serna
accounting - a-one, a-two, a-three, a-four...
Douglas Helsel
acedia - the malady of monks.
Charles Baudelaire
achievement - the amount of success you allow yourself.
Richard Wilkins
acquiescence - daily suicide.
Honor de Balzac
acre - small dog of mixed parentage.
John S. Crosbie
acrimony - what a man gives his divorced wife.
Robert Myers
acrobat - a guy who goes around with a chap on his shoulder.
Milton Berle
acting - the ability to keep an audience from coughing.
Ralph Richardson
action - the antidote to despair.
Joan Baez
(see also: precipitous action)
activist - everyone who encourages people to think.
Michael Thomas Ford
activity - the only road to knowledge.
George Bernard Shaw
(see also: furious activity)
act of God - something which no reasonable man could have expected.
A.P. Herbert
act of love - the enjoyment is quite temporary; the cost is quite exorbitant; the position is simply ridiculous.
Philip Dormer Stanhope

actor - a guy who if you ain't talkin' about him, ain't listening.
George Glass
(see also: best actors, coarse actor, movie actors, talented actor, veteran)
actor-manager - one to whom the part is greater than the whole.
Ronald Jeans
actress - someone with no ability who sits around waiting to go on alimony.
Jackie Stallone
(see also: character actress, scream queen)
actuary - someone who cannot stand the excitement of chartered accountancy.
Glan Thomas
acupuncture - a jab well done.
Jerry Ulett
Adam - the luckiest man - he had no mother-in-law.
Sholom Aleichem
adamant - the very first ant in the Garden of Eden.
Keith Martin
Adam's rib - the first phallus.
Francis Picabia
adaptability - power of resistance and assimilation.
Mahatma Gandhi
adaptation - the strength of the weak.
Wolfgang Herbst
addiction - a friendship without a friend.
Connie Palmen
adresses - items given to us to conceal our whereabouts.
Saki
adjective - the banana peel of the parts of speech.
Clifton Fadiman
adjucation - a legal game in which courts try to find where legislatures have hidden justice.
Edmund H. Volkart
administration - a public limited company with an unlimited irresponsibility.
Jean Amadou
admiral - a general with sealegs.
Delfeil de Ton
admiration - jealousy in an evening dress.
Fernand Lambrecht

adolescence - the time when children start trying to bring up their parents.
Richard Armour
adolescents - grown-ups under supervision.
Sarah Bourgeois
(see also: teenager)
adults - children who earn money.
Kenneth Branagh
adultery - doing the right thing with the wrong person.
Colin Bowles
(see also: cuckoldry)
adulthood - childhood without despair.
Jean-Guy Rens
adult western - one in which the hero still loves his horse, only now he's worried about it.
Henny Youngman
adventure - risk plus purpose.
Robert McClure
adversity - the first path to truth.
Lord Byron
advertisements - the most truthful parts of a newspaper.
Thomas Jefferson
(see also: art of advertisement)
advertiser - someone who makes women unhappy with what they have. *Earl Puckett*
advertising - the science of arresting the human intelligence for long enough to get money from it.
Stephen Leacock
advertising agency - eighty-five per cent confusion and fifteen per cent commission.
Fred Allen
advertising man - yessir, nosir, ulcer.
Robert Myers
advice - what we ask for when we already know the answer but wish we didn't.
Erica Jong
(see also: art of advice, giving advice, good advice, unsolicited advice)
aerobic exercises - exercise to the brink of cardiac arrest.
Russell Ash
aerobics - gay folk dancing.
Bruce Smirnoff

aesthete - a forlorn, arty person who professes to worship beauty, but never seems to find the right church.
Edmund H. Volkart
aesthetic value - often the by-product of the artist striving to do something else.
Evelyn Waugh
affcot - the sort of fart you hope people will talk after.
Douglas Adams & John Lloyd
affectation - the vain and ridiculous attempt of poverty to appear rich.
Johann Kaspar Lavater
affection - the mortal illness of lonely people.
Gary Indiana
affluence - the greatest of all contraceptives.
Indira Gandhi
(see also: true affluence)
affluenza - a psychiatric disturbance arising from an excess of money.
Gaty Dunford
afraid - a country with no exit visas.
Audre Lorde
Africa - God's country, and he can have it.
Groucho Marx
(see also: Zimbabwe)
African - a nigger that votes our way.
Ambrose Bierce
Afrikaans - a language that sounds like Welsh with attitude and emphysema.
A.A. Gill
after dinner speech - an occupation monopolised by men - women can't wait that long.
Steve Miller
after dinner speaker - a person who eats a meal they don't want so they can get up and tell a load of stories they can't remember to people who've already heard them.
Mitch Murray
afternoon snack - the pause that refleshes.
Mary B. Michael
After-Ski - most men think it means Before-Bed.
Monique Lacour
age - a high price to pay for maturity.
Tom Stoppard
(see also: middle age, old age, serenity of age)

(to) age - to learn to endure yourself.
Hans Kudszus
aged man - a paltry thing, a tattered coat upon a stick.
William Butler Yeats
agent - a guy who's sore because an actor gets 90% of what he makes.
Alva Johnson
(see also: intelligent agent)
aging - a non-curable disease.
Seneca
agitation - the marshalling of the conscience of a nation to mold its laws.
Robert Peel
agitator - a statesman who shakes the fruit trees of his neighbour - to dislodge the worms.
Ambrose Bierce
aggression - the mother of all sports.
Toon Verhoeven
agnostic - just a fat slob who is too lazy to go to mass.
Conor Cruise O'Brien
agnosticism - the philosophical, ethical and religious dry-rot of the modern world.
F.E. Abbot
agreeable person - a person who agrees with me.
Benjamin Disraeli
agreement - an altogether tiresome constituent of conversation.
Michel de Montaigne
Aids - the big disease with the little name.
Prince
aoli - the nearest thing the French have to HP sauce.
John Lanchester
air-conditioning - an efficient and widely used method for spreading disease.
John Ralston Saul
Air France - a good name for an airline but a bad name for a deodorant.
Danny Bravman
airline food - gastronomic murder, preceded by culinary torture.
Egon Ronay
airplane - a tin can filled with other people's farts.
Frankie Boyle

airplane travel - hours of boredom interrupted by moments of stark terror.
Al Boliska
air pollution - a mist-demeanour.
Geoff Tibballs
Alabaster - an illegitimate Arab.
Milton Berle
alarm clock - an object used to wake up people who don't have children.
Mel Allen
alarms - an octopus.
Gunjan Saraf
alas - early Victorian for oh, hell.
Oliver Herford
Alaska - an ideal place for a golf course - mighty few trees and damn few ladies' foursomes.
Rex Lardner
Albania - the sort of place you get into as late as possible, bring your own food, go to bed, get up, go for a walk, play the game and get out.
Jack Charlton
Albanian - a language that sounds comic with all its pffts, pees, wees, pings and fitts.
Cecil Beaton
alcohol - the anaesthesia by which we endure the operation of life.
George Bernard Shaw
alcoholic - someone you don't like who drinks as much as you do.
Dylan Thomas
(see also: drunk)
alcoholic psychosis - D.T.'s in a dinner suit.
Kin Hubbard
alcoholism - the only disease in the world which tells you you haven't got it.
Kevin Kennedy
Alderney - a great spinach omelette off the coast of France.
Miles Kington
ale - man, ale's the stuff to drink
For fellow whom it hurts to think.
A.E. Housman
algebra - a form of low cunning.
William James

Ali Bi - Turk with a broad-minded attitude to sex.
Gerd de Ley
alibi - proof that you were somewhere else when you committed the crime.
Jimmy Durante
alimony - a contraction of "all his money."
Helen Hoke
allegory - a piece of garden statuary.
Ramon Gomez de La Serna
allergy season - Mother Nature's way of telling me flowers have more sex than I do.
Basil White
allies - tomorrow's enemies.
Edmund H. Volkart
alligator - an animal that looks like a handbag filled with harmonicas.
Richard Brautigan
allowance - what you pay your kids to live with you.
Milton Berle
almanac - annual manual.
Stan Kegel
almost - a word that sticks in the throat like failure.
David McCallum
alms - the small coins given away by the rich from what they stole from the poor.
Fritz Francken
aloha - an all-purpose Hawaiian phrase meaning 'hello', 'goodbye', 'I love you', and 'I wish to decline the collision damage waiver'.
Dave Barry
alone - nobody plus one.
Rob Godthelp
aloof - top of a Chinese house.
Alan Burke
alphabet - one of the most surprising phenomena. How else can you explain that you can write so much rubbish with so few letters?
Sim
Alps - objects of appallingly bad taste.
Oscar Wilde
alternative - a person born during his parent's wedding ceremony.
John S. Crosbie

Alton Towers - the poor man's Disney, the sort of place you send a child who's dying of something not that serious.
Jimmy Carr
altruist - a reasonable egotist.
Rémy de Gourmont
altruism - another name for egoism.
Holbrook Jackson
aluminum - a jive metal.
George Carlin
alumni - a group of college graduates who attend football games on Saturday to find reasons to fire the coach on Monday.
Jimmy Cannon
Alzheimer's - another way of stopping smoking.
Pierre Légaré
amateur - a guy who won't take a cheque.
Paul Gallico
amateur in politics - the person who is always sure he knows the result of the next General Election.
Enoch Powell
ambassador - someone who sends coded telegrams home with information that was in the newspaper three days earlier.
Roger Peyrefitte
ambidextrose - able to pour corn syrup onto pancakes with either hand.
Larry T. Green
ambiguity - the devil's volleyball.
Emo Philips
ambition - a poor excuse for not having sense enough to be lazy.
Charlie McCarthy
ambitious car driver - a murderer with malice aforethought.
Léon Bloy
ambivalence - watching your mother-in-law drive over a cliff in your new Cadillac.
David Mamet
(to) amend - to rewrite a law in such a way as to further obscure its already confused meaning.
Edmund H. Volkart

America - the only country that went from barbarism to decadence without civilization in between.
Oscar Wilde
(see also: arts in America, California, Delaware, Florida, Long Island, Miami, Nebraska, New Orleans, New York, Niagara Falls, Oklahoma City, Philadelphia, Omaha, Pittsburg, Reno, San Francisco, Seattle, South Carolina, Texans, United States, USA, Washington)

American artist - the unwanted cockroach in the kitchen of a frontier society.
John Sloan

American consumerism - buying things we don't need, with money we don't have, to impress friends we don't have time for.
Leo Horrigan

American democracy - the inalienable right to sit on your own front porch, in your pyjamas, drinking a can of beer and shouting out 'Where else is this possible?'
Peter Ustinov

American diplomacy - something like watching somebody trying to do joinery with a chainsaw.
James Hamilton-Paterson

American food - a plenitude of peanut butter and a dearth of hot mustard.
Patrick Dean

American football - committee meetings separated by outbreaks of violence.
George F. Will

American government - a rule of the people, by the people, for the boss.
Austin O'Malley

American male - the world's fattest and softest; this might explain why he also loves guns - you can always get your revolver up.
Gore Vidal

American politics - a form of socialism for the rich.
Gregory Nunn

American presidency - a Tudor monarchy plus telephones.
Anthony Burgess

Americans - deeply religious people. You can tell by the way they drive.
Alex Ayres

American society - a sort of flat, freshwater pond which absorbs silently, without reaction, anything which is thrown into it.
Henry Brooks Adams

American television - a world in which the audience speaks to the artist instead of the other way round.
Ralph Schoenstein
amnesia - nature's way of saying, "Forget it!".
Robert Orben
ampu-tater - a medical specialist who removes gangrenous appendages from French fries.
Gary Hallock
Amsterdam - a paltry, rubbishy Venice.
William Hazlitt
amusement - the happiness of those who cannot think.
Alexander Pope
anagram - a small measure of weight.
Audrey Cowper
anal - half of analysis.
Marty Indik
anal sex - the best drain cleaner.
Marc Pairon
anarchism - a game at which the police can beat you.
George Bernard Shaw
anarchy - the purpose of those who have nothing to lose.
Ernst R. Hauschka
anatomy - something everyone has, but which looks better on a girl.
Bruce Raeburn
anchor (person) - a bland, well-coiffed TV entertainer who is paid more to read the news than ten reporters are paid to report it.
Rick Bayan
anecdote - a joke in evening-dress.
Paul Jacobs
anger - one letter short of danger.
Robert Anthony
angling - an innocent cruelty.
George Parker
Anglo-Irishman - a Protestant with a horse.
Brendan Behan
Anglo-Saxon - a German that's forgot who was his parents.
Finley Peter Dunne
anguish - proof of the soul.
Patrick Hunt
animal - something invented by plants to move seeds around.
Terrence McKenna

animal lover - a humane person who is happy when the bull kills the torero.
Gabriël Laub
animal testing - a terrible idea; they get all nervous and give the wrong answers.
Stephen Fry
anno domini - the most fatal complaint of all in the end.
James Hilton
annual income - more than you admit to the tax man, less than you tell your friends and certainly less than you spend.
Yvonne Kroonenberg
anonymity - the biggest gift in life.
Alan Titchmarsh
anonymous letter - a special kind of letter. I only received one once and it was signed.
Jean Cocteau
anorexia - just another word for nothing left to lose.
Joy Behar
anorexics - what cannibals eat when they are on a diet.
Pierre Légaré
answer - the best way of killing a question.
Wim Triesthof
(see also: good answer)
Antarctica - Snowman's land.
L.L. Levinson
antediluvian - one who is against the support of Paris museums.
Marvin Goodman
ante-post bet - a way of prolonging life. A man holding an ante-post voucher never dies before the race itself is over.
Jeffrey Bernard
anthologies - just pre-digested food for the brain.
Rebecca West
antidotes - what you take to prevent dotes.
Art Linkletter
anti-feminist - the man who is convinced that his mother was a fool.
Rebecca West
antipasta - a hatred of Italian food.
Willie Meikle
antipasto - weight-watchers.
Bernard H. Cohen
antique - yesterday's kitsch at today's prices.
Jacques Tati

anti-semitism - the socialism of fools.
August Bebel
antithesis - the narrow gate through which error is fondest of sneaking to the truth.
Friedrich Nietzsche
ants - insects that attend picnics for a living.
Kenny Everett
anxiety - the interest paid on trouble before it is due.
William R. Inge
apartment - a place where you can be apart.
Audrey Niffenegger
apathy - the glove into which evil slips its hand.
Bodie Thoene
ape - the only other animal that kisses.
Robert Myers
apéritif - a set of dentures.
Spike Milligan
aphorism - the 'amen' of an experience.
Hans Kudszus
(see also: maxim, orism)
apology - the only thing that will allow you to get the last word with a woman.
Danny Cummins
(see also: stiff apology)
app - boredom avoidance tool with opposite long-term effect.
Matt Haig
appeal - when you ask one court to show it's contempt for another court.
Finlay Peter Dunne
appeaser - one who feeds a crocodile hoping it will eat him last.
Winston Churchill
appetizers - little things you keep eating until you lose your appetite.
Richard Armour
appetite - luxury edition of hunger.
Anita
applause - a frequently-used television sound, usually recorded in advance.
Herman de Coninck
apple - fall fruit.
Hans-Horst Skupy
apple butter - a goat that hates MacIntoshes.
Johnny Hart

appreciation - a plant that grows mainly on gravestones.
Robert Lembke
apprenticeship - hire learning.
Leopold Fechtner
apricots - bed for baby apes.
Kevin Goldstein-Jackson
April - the cruelest month, breeding lilacs out of the dead land, mixing memory and desire, stirring dull roots with spring rain.
T.S. Eliot
April 1 - the day upon which we are reminded of what we are on the other three hundred and sixty-four.
Mark Twain
April showers - taxpayers' tears.
Arnold H. Glasow
aquadextrous - possessing the ability to turn the bathtub faucet on and off with your toes.
Rich Hall
aquarium - lava lamp with faeces.
David Corrado
Arab - a Greek on a camel.
Colin Bowles
arcade - Noah's assistant.
Stan Kegel
archaeologist - someone whose career is in ruins.
Hal Roach
archeology - science without a future.
Georges Elgozy
archery - the study of arrow dynamics.
Joseph Leff
architect - someone who forgets to put in the staircase.
Gustave Flaubert
architecture - the art of how to waste space.
Philip Johnson
(see also: modern architecture)
archive - where Noah kept his bees.
Geoff Tibballs
argument - the longest distance between two points of view.
Dan Bennett
aria - Italian for 'a song that will not end in your lifetime'.
Dave Barry
aristocracy - asses who talk about horses.
Heinrich Heine

aristocrat - a democrat with his pockets filled.
Josh Billings
arithmetic - numbers you squeeze from your head to your hand to your pencil to your paper until you get the right answer.
Carl Sandburg
armed conflict - the ideal euphemism for war.
Gerd de Ley
armful of chairs - something some people would not know whether you were up them with or not.
Barry Humphries
armistice - peace on credit.
Fritz Francken
arms - adult toys.
Jean Follain
army - a place where you get up early in the morning to be yelled at by people with short haircuts and tiny brains.
Dave Barry
aroma - a smell described by a bore.
Henry Beard
arrest - what you take when you are tired.
Leopold Fechtner
arrival - the start of a departure.
Robert Sabatier
arrogance - the humility of the uncertain.
Milton Berle
(see also: complete arrogance)
arsonist - a man with a burning desire.
Ethel Meglin
art - making something out of nothing and selling it.
Frank Zappa
(see also: abstract art, culinary art, dramatic art, fine art, good art, great art, work of art)
art criticism - a form of intellectual flatulence.
Richard Greene
art critics - failed artists, like most artists.
Paul Citroen
artery - the study of painting.
Mike McKinley
art for art's sake - the philosophy of the well-fed.
Cao Yu
art history - the nightmare from which art is struggling to awake.
Robert Fulford

arthritis - twinges in the hinges.
G.B. Howard
artichoke - a vegetable of which one has more at the finish than at the start of a dinner.
Lord Chesterfield
artificial insemination - procreation without recreation.
Rick Bayan
artificial intelligence - the art of making computers that behave like the ones in movies.
Bill Bulko
artist - a person who thinks more than there is to think, feels more than there is to feel, and sees more than there is to see.
John Oliver Hobbes
(see also: American artist, fine artist, great artist, primitive artist, real artists)
artistic temperament - a disease that afflicts amateurs.
G.K. Chesterton
art of acceptance - the art of making someone who has just done you a small favour wish that he might have done you a greater one.
Russell Lynes
art of advertisement - untruthfulness combined with repetition.
Freya Stark
art of advice - to make the recepient believe he thought of it himself.
Frank Tyger
art of conversation - to leave unsaid the wrong thing at the tempting moment.
Dorothy Nevill
art of flying - to throw yourself at the ground and miss.
Douglas Adams
art of government - taking as much money as possible from one party of the citizens to give to the other.
Voltaire
art of living - knowing how to enjoy a little and to endure much.
William Hazlitt
art of love - knowing how to combine the temperament of a vampire with the discretion of an anemone.
E.M. Cioran
art of management - the art of taking credit for other people's work.
Germaine Greer

art of medicine - amusing the patient while nature effects the cure.
Voltaire
art of politics - to get someone to change their mind without humiliating them.
Lorna Fitzsimons
art of taxation - so plucking the goose as to obtain the largest amount of feathers with the least possible amount of hissing.
Jean-Baptiste Colbert
art of teaching - the art of awakening the natural curiosity of young minds for the purpose of satisfying it afterwards.
Anatole France
art school - a place for young girls to pass the time between high school and marriage.
Thomas Hart Benton
arts in America - a gigantic racket run by unscrupulous men for unhealthy women.
Thomas Beecham
art theatre - a place where the theatre is clean - the pictures are filthy.
Henny Youngman
as a matter of fact - an expression that precedes many an expression that isn't.
Laurence J. Peter
asceticism - a refined and complicated form of sensuality.
Gerrit Komrij
ashtray - something for a cigarette butt when there is no floor.
Robert Myers
asking - polite demanding.
Howard Brookner
aspect - what you get when you bend over in a chicken run.
Ian Barker
assembly line - the notion that if a job is worth doing, it's worth repeating 9,614 times a day.
Rick Bayan
assassin - one who takes life easily.
Laurence J. Peter
assassination - the extreme form of censorship.
George Bernard Shaw
assets - baby donkeys.
Kevin Goldstein-Jackson

asshole - the most commonly employed word in an argument, often used correctly by both sides.
Chaz Bufe
assimilate - to pretend to be a donkey.
Paul Pence
ass kissing - see "How to Succeed in Business Without Really Trying."
Chaz Bufe
associate producer - the only guy in Hollywood who will associate with a producer.
Harry Tugend & Jack Yellen
assumption - the mother of screw-up.
Angelo Donghia
asters - the most grateful flowers.
Janosch
asthma - a disease that has practically the same symptoms as passion except that with asthma it lasts longer.
Bill Sadgarden
astrology - what makes economic forecasting seem reasonable.
J.K. Galbraith
astronaut - a man who doesn't have to bring along something for his wife.
Robert Lembke
astronomer - a night watchman.
Michael Driscoll
atheism - a non-prophet organization.
George Carlin
atheist - someone who refuses to give God the benefit of the doubt.
C. Buddingh'
(see also: Glaswegian atheist, real atheist)
Atlanta - Siberia with mint juleps.
Ferenc Molnàr
Atlantic City - all that and a bag of poker chips.
Michael Musto
atom bomb - an explosive device under which all people are cremated equal.
Joel Rothman
atomic war - herald of total peace.
Ron Kritzfeld
atrophy - what you get for winning a marathon.
Ed Parrish

attentive wife - one of the best hearing aids a man can have.
Groucho Marx
attic - a tall storey.
Merlyn Baby
attorney - a rhetorical bird that flies around in ever-decreasing concentric circles until it winds up with its head up its ass.
J.H. Goldfuss
attractive - just not beautiful enough.
Theo Mestrum
auctioneer - someone who never lies unless it's absolutely necessary.
Josh Billings
audience - play watched from the stage.
Les Coleman
audit - a tax debate.
Robert Orben
Australia - a land of harsh rules, which everyone breaks.
Jilly Cooper
(see also: Melbourne)
Australian - someone who is too drunk to feel his sunburn.
Colin Bowles
Australian-based - a person of diminished aspiration who has been successfully bribed with grants and awards to resist the lure of expatriation.
Barry Humphries
Australian flag - Britain at night.
Jerry Seinfeld
Australian foreplay - consists largely of the words 'Are you awake?'
Barry Humphries
Australian gentleman - someone who gets out of the bath to piss in the sink.
Peter Darbo
Austria - Switzerland speaking pure German and with history added.
J.E. Morpurgo
author - the mother of a book.
Johan Daisne
(see also: best author, writer)
authority - a high hat under which every donkey can hide his ears.
Antoon Vloemans

autobiography - an obituary in serial form with the last instalment missing.
Quentin Crisp
auto-eroticism - necking in cars.
Peter de Vries
auto insurance - the only kind of insurance for which the premiums get higher the younger you are.
O.A. Battista
automatic - means that you can't repair it yourself.
Mary H. Waldrip
automobile - a machine that runs up hills and down people.
Syman Hirsch
autumn - a second spring when every leaf is a flower.
Albert Camus
autopsy - a dying business.
Peter Darbo
avalanches - things that happen to other people, in the resorts you never go to.
Mark Heller
avant-garde - French for off-Broadway garbage.
Dick van Dyke
avant-garde music - to fart against a gong and to amplify this sound electronically.
François Glorieux
avant-gardism - an addiction that can be appeased only by a revolution in permanence.
Harold Rosenberg
avarice - the vice of declining years.
George Bancroft
average man - a guy who spends his whole life trying to prove to everybody that he isn't.
Harvey Kurtzman
average Ph.D. thesis - nothing but a transference of bones from one graveyard to another.
James Frank Dobie
aversion - platonic hatred.
Jan Vercammen
aviation - proof that given the will, we have the capacity to achieve the impossible.
Eddie Rickenbacker
avoidable - what a bullfighter tries to do.
Norm Gilbert

awards - the badges of mediocrity.
Charles Ives
Azusa - a town where a drugstore sells straw hats for horses.
Groucho Marx

B

baby - a loud noise at one end and no sense of responsibility at the other.
Ronald Knox
(see also: crying baby, having a baby, wet baby)
baby boom - birthquake.
Robert Myers
babysitter - someone you pay by the hour to eat all your food and let your kids do what they want.
Jasmine Birtles
baby swing - a safe place to put the baby unless she has a brother.
Joyce Armor
Bacchus - the Greek god of drunken football chants.
Bren Tierney
bachelor - a man who never makes the same mistake once.
Ed Wynn
(see also: Mexican bachelor)
bachelorhood - one way of keeping all that alimony money for yourself.
Gene Perret
Bacillus - Roman god of germs.
Carol Drew
back - the prairie of the anatomy.
John B. Keane
backwash - what the nurse gives you in the hospital.
Douglas Drill
bad breath - yak scent.
Charles G. Waugh
bad conscience - the illness man was bound to contract once he found himself imprisoned in society and peace.
Friedrich Nietzsche
bad critic - a fellow who has the faculty of reading books backwards.
Ramon Gomez de la Serna
bad English - a much more international language than good English.
Herman de Coninck

bad officials - the ones elected by good citizens who do not vote.
George Jean Nathan
bad poet - a nightingale that whistles out of his arse.
Christian Friedrich Hebbel
bad reference - almost as hard to find as a good employee.
Robert Half
bad temper - a sign of inferiority.
Alfred Adler
bad review - something like baking a cake with all the best ingredients and having someone sit on it.
Danielle Steel
bad taste - simply saying the truth before it should be said.
Mel Brooks
bad woman - the sort of woman a man never gets tired of.
Oscar Wilde
bagel - an unsweetened doughnut with rigor mortis.
Beatrice Freeman
bagpipes - the missing link between music and noise.
E.K. Kruger
baker's dozen - twelve of today's doughnuts and one of yesterday's.
Johnny Hart
balance - the enemy of art.
Richard Eyre
balanced diet - a cookie in each hand.
Barbara Johnson
balderdash - a rapidly receding hairline.
Paul Kocak
balding - God's way of showing you are only human... He takes off your head and puts it in your ears.
Bruce Willis
(see also: going bald)
baldness - nudism on a higher level.
Frank Sinatra
ball - man's most disastrous invention, not excluding the wheel.
Robert Morley
ballet - an opportunity for arms and legs to talk.
Jan Schepens
(see also: dance)
balloon - bad breath holder.
Demetri Martin
ballot box - a most inadequate mechanism of change.
Bill Sadgarden

ballots - the rightful and peaceful successors to bullets.
Abraham Lincoln
ballroom dancing - a dreary, neuralgic cocktail of starch and Babycham set to music.
James Christopher
Bambification - the mental conversion of flesh-and-blood living creatures into cartoon characters possessing bourgeois Judeo-Christian attitudes and morals.
Douglas Coupland
Bamboo - what you get when you cross Bambi with a ghost.
Randall Woodman
bananas - a waste of time. After you skin them and throw the bone away, there's nothing left to eat.
Charley Weaver
bank - a prestigious establishment that in the end will lend us our own money.
Willy Reichert
banker - a pawnbroker with a manicure.
Joey Adams
banking - the second oldest profession but more profitable than the oldest profession.
Flann O'Brien
bankruptcy - a legal proceeding in which you put your money in your pants pocket and give your coat to your creditors.
Joey Adams
banquet - dinner during which you must be aware of indigestion brought about by speeches.
Gerd de Ley
barbarians - those who consider other people as barbarians.
Michel de Montaigne
barbarism - the absence of standards to which appeal can be made.
José Ortega y Gasset
barbecue - the plural of burning wounds.
Johan Anthierens
barber - an authority on everything except how to cut hair properly.
William H. Roylance
bargain - something you can't use at a price you can't resist.
Franklin P. Adams
baritones - the born villains in opera.
Leonard Warren

barium - pure of tombstone.
Jonathan Miller
barnacle - bloodsucker bestowed below the belly-bottom of a boat.
Stanley Anderson
baroque music - the kind where the audience doesn't notice when the players fall asleep.
J.H. Goldfuss
barque - noise made by dyslexic dogs.
Jan Hyde
barrage - tavern insanity.
Joseph Leff
barrister - a word in the dictionary that comes between bankrupt and bastard.
Stephen Phillips
bartender - a splendid person who practices psychiatry on the cheap by keeping his mouth closed, his ears open, and the glass filled.
Edmund H. Volkart
baseball - a game which consists of tapping a ball with a piece of wood, then running like a lunatic.
H.J. Dutiel
(see also: saturnine)
baseball game - simply a nervous breakdown divided into nine innings.
Earl Wilson
basic research - what I am doing when I don't know what I am doing.
Werner von Braun
basketball - staying in after school in your underwear.
Ring Lardner
basketball player - a person who plays on court and pays in court.
Joseph Martino
bastard - lower class love child.
Tina Spencer Knott
bath - lying in your own dirt.
Ruby Wax
bathing suit - a garment cut to see level.
Jacob Braude
bathroom - where your child doesn't need to go until you're backing your car out of the driveway.
Joyce Armor

bathroom scale - something you step on in the morning, and all it does is make you angry.
Milton Berle
bay - a huge expanse of water surrounded by restaurants and hotels.
Alfredo La Mont
beach - a place where a woman goes today when she has nothing to wear.
Milton Berle
beard - ornamental excrement which grows beneath the chin.
Thomas Fuller
beatnik - Santa on the day after Christmas.
John S. Crosbie
Beaujolais - a nice wine that makes women happy when men drink it.
Henry Clos-Jouve
beautiful - adjective applied to the daughter of any woman prominent in the weekly illustrated newspapers.
J.B. Morton
beautiful dress - one which follows the body, and only the body.
Cristobal Balenciaga
beautiful quotation - a diamond on the finger of a man of spirit and a stone in the hand of a fool.
Joseph Roux
beautiful woman - one who loves me.
Sloan Wilson
beauty - the shadow of God on the universe.
Gabriela Mistral
beauty shop - a business venture which is founded on the motto: "a thing of beauty is a job forever".
Lee Daniel Quinn
bed - a bundle of paradoxes: we go to it with reluctance, yet we quit it with regret.
Charels Caleb Colton
bedrock - a popular dance performed while lying down.
Douglas Drill
beer - an intoxicating golden brew that re-emerges virtually unchanged an hour later.
Rick Bayan
beer baron - a malty millionaire.
Robert Myers
beggar - someone who is looking for sponsors.
Fons Jansen

beginning - the time for taking the most delicate care that balances are correct.
Frank Herbert
behaviour - a mirror, in which everyone shows his image.
Johann Wolfgang von Goethe
being busy - the best excuse for not working.
Kenneth Tynan
being funny - just about the toughest way to earn a living.
Des MacHale
being ill - one of the greatest pleasures of life, provided one is not too ill and is not obliged to work until one is better.
Samuel Butler
being in love - a fertile form of madness.
Theo Mestrum
being in love with yourself - never having to say you've got a headache.
Ellie Laine
being old - getting up in the middle of the night as often as George Clooney, but not for the same reason.
Mel Brooks
being smart - what keeps some people from being intelligent.
Thomas Sowell
being widowed - God's way of telling you to come off the Pill.
Victoria Wood
belcanto - power training for the vocal cords.
Fernand Lambrecht
beleagured - stuck in the semipros.
William Safire
Belgium - a country invented by the British to annoy the French.
Charles de Gaulle
belief - nothing more than the acceptance of something you don't know.
Aster Berkhof
(to) believe - to know for certain that you have doubts.
Freek de Jonge
bells - the clergy's artillery.
Joseph II
belly - nothing more than a small container of excrement.
Guido van Heulendonk
belly laugh - your own gag.
Groucho Marx
bench mark - the worn place on a judges pants.
Johnny Hart

benefactor - a person who makes two smiles grow where one grew before.
Chauncey Depew
benign - what you can't wait to do when you're eight.
Jeffrey Rich
best - the enemy of the good.
Voltaire
(see also: better)
best actors - those who feel the most and show the least.
Jean-Louis Trintignant
best art - the art of making money.
Andy Warhol
best author - he who is ashamed to become one.
Friedrich Nietzsche
best director - the one you don't see.
Billy Wilder
best doctor - the one you run for and can't find.
Denis Diderot
best-dressed woman - one whose clothes wouldn't look too strange in the country.
Hardy Amies
best executives - those with the sense enough to pick up the right people for the job, and then let them get on with it.
Paul Miller
best friend - the one who brings out the best in you.
Henry Ford
best government - that which governs least.
John L. O'Sullivan
bestiality - a poke in a pig.
Andrew Austin
best liar - he who makes the smallest amount of lying go the longest way.
Samuel Butler
bestseller - a book on which the publisher earns a lot of money.
Louis Paul Boon
best teacher - the one who suggests rather than dogmatizes, and inspires his listener with the wish to teach himself.
Edward Bulwer-Lytton
best travel - that which one can take by one's own fireside, in memory or imagination.
George Eliot
betrayal - the only truth that sticks.
Arthur Miller

better - the arch-enemy of 'Good'.
Charles de Montesquieu
better ideas - the only sure weapon against bad ideas.
Whitney Griswold
Beverly Hills - a place where, if an actor's wife looks like a new woman - she probably is.
Joey Adams
(see also: Hollywood, movie star)
be yourself - about the worst advice you can give to people.
Mark Twain
Bible - an Irish book because it says that it all began at the beginning.
Dave Allen
(see also: New Testament)
biblethumper - someone who's all preaches and scream.
Louis A. Safian
bicentennial - sexually confused 100-year-old.
Paul Drechsler
bidet - a little headless horse with as many behinds as you could possibly imagine.
Miguel Zamacoïs
bigamist - a man who has the bad taste to do what conscience and the police keep the rest of us from doing.
Finley Peter Dunne
bigamy - a form of insanity in which a man insists on paying three board bills instead of two.
Gideon Wurdz
big business - only small business with an extra nought on the end.
Robert Holmes Court
big city - a cold, lonely place. At least that's what it's like on the days I forget to wear clothes.
Scott Griffin
big companies - small companies that succeeded.
Robert Townsend
big dictionaries - storerooms with infrequently visited and dusty corners.
Richard W. Bailey
big egos - big shields for lots of empty space.
Dianne Black
biggest bore - the person who is bored by everyone and everything.
Frank Tyger

Big Mac - burger named after a big raincoat whose taste it so closely resembles.
Jo Brand
big machines - the awe-inspiring cathedrals of the 20th century.
Daniel Kleppner
big man - one who makes us feel bigger when we are with him.
John C. Maxwell
bigot - one who is obstinately and zealously attached to an opinion that you do not entertain.
Ambrose Bierce
bigotry - the anger of people who have no opinions.
G.K. Chesterton
big shots - only little shots that keep on shooting.
Christopher Morley
big sisters - the crabgrass in the lawn of life.
Charles M. Schulz
bikini - the last beautiful shield before the naked truth.
Pablo Picasso
bilious - in debt.
David R. Scott
billiards - a cue-rious game.
Raghu Srinivasan
billiard table - the paradise of the ball.
Alfred E. Crawley
bimbo - a young woman who's not pretty enough to be a model, not smart enough to be an actress, and not nice enough to be a poisonous snake.
P.J. O'Rourke
binoculars - the artillery of indiscretion.
Georges Pompidou
biographer - an artist upon oath.
Desmond MacCarthy
biography - voyeurism embellished with footnotes.
Robert Skidelsky
(see also: literary biography, writing biography)
biology - the search for the chemistry that works.
R.J.P. Williams
biophone - a person with a mighty voice, thus not needing a phone.
Christoph Bouthillier
birdwatcher - a person who likes to watch fowl play.
Gail S. Angel

birth - the search for a larger apartment.
Rita Mae Brown
(see also: giving birth, prepared childbirth)
birth of twins - an infant replay.
Linda Williams
birth control - a way of avoiding the issue.
Louis A. Safian
birth control pill - the other thing a woman can put in her mouth to keep from getting pregnant.
Jack Kolb
birthday - an annual reminder that the more you slow down, the more time accelerates.
Edmund H. Volkart
bisexual - a guy who likes girls just as well as the next guy.
Milton Berle
bisexuality - what doubles your chances for a date on Saturday night.
Woody Allen
bishop - merely a clergyman with political interests.
St. John Hankin
bitch - underdog.
Piet Grijs
bitterness - indigestion of the heart.
Colin Bowles
black hole - a celestial vacuum cleaner.
Rick Bayan
black panthers - simply leopards that happen to have very dark brown hair.
Michael Boorer
blandscape artist - an uninspired painter.
Vera Colyer
blank page - the beginning of a new book.
Bert Schierbeek
blank verse - poetry written without rhyme, often without reason.
Edmund H. Volkart
blasphemy - the comic verse of belief.
Brendan Behan
blatteroon - a person who won't shut up.
Kris Brand
bleeding ponytail - an elderly sold-out baby boomer who pines for hippie or pre-sellout days.
Douglas Coupland

blennophobia - fear of slime.
Matt Groening
blind date - love without a face.
Lejo van Kuijeren
blind man - someone who cannot believe his own eyes.
Gerd de Ley
blindness - point of view.
Michel Laclos
block grant - a solid mass of money surrounded on all sides by governors.
Ross K. Baker
blogger - someone with nothing to say writing for someone with nothing to do.
Guy Kawasaki
(see also: weblog)
blood - a red liquid material often found in the alcohol streams of certain individuals.
Leonard Rossiter
blood transfusion - the most boring way to get Aids.
Guy Mortier
blow-job - the cure for starvation in India and the cure for overpopulation - both in one big swallow.
Erica Jong
blows - sarcasms turned stupid.
George Eliot
Bluebeard - a husband with the neatest solution to the alimony problem.
Leonard L. Levinson
blue jeans - trousers that should be worn by farm girls milking cows.
Yves Saint-Laurent
(the) blues - an autobiographical chronicle of catastrophe, expressed lyrically.
Ralph Waldo Ellison
blunderbuss - a pram.
Michael Desky
blunderer - a man who starts a meat market during Lent.
James Montgomery Bailey
bluntness - a clumsy attempt to make a fine point.
Dr. Mardy
blush - a weakness of youth and an accomplishment of experience.
Oliver Herford

boast - always a cry of despair, except in the young it is a cry of hope.
Bernard Berenson
body - a remarkable factory, with many industrial secrets.
Herman Brusselmans
body bag - a snake bite emergency kit.
Mitch Hedberg
bodybuilding - making oneself seem larger than life.
Mariah Burton Nelson
body odor - the window to the soul.
David Byrne
body of a woman - an erotic museum, of which man is the night watchman.
Johan Anthierens
body piercing - a powerful, compelling visual statement that says, 'Gee, in today's competitive job market, what can I do to make myself less employable?'
Dennis Miller
Bohemia - nothing more than the little country in which you do not live.
O. Henry
boldness - a mask for fear, however great.
John Dryden
Bolivians - barely metamorphosed llamas, who have learned to talk but not to think.
Jose Merino
Bolshephobia - fear of Bolshevism.
Matt Groening
Bolshevism - Czarism in overalls.
George Jean Nathan
Bombi - terrorist deer.
Bill Sadgarden
bombs - firework to the sleepy.
Norman Mailer
bombshell - the exclusion of a cricketer from a team.
J.B. Morton
bon mots - the words other people wish they had said.
Jean Cocteau
bonus - one of the great give-aways in business enterprise. It is the annual salve applied to the conscience of the rich and the wounds of the poor.
E.B. White

booby trap - a bra that is too small and too tight.
Kevin Goldstein-Jackson
book - a riverbank for the river of language.
Cynthia Ozick
(see also: best book, bestseller, obscene book, real book, well-composed book)
book-collector - someone who combines the worst characteristics of a dope fiend with those of a miser.
Robertson Davies
bookie - a pickpocket who lets you use your own hands.
Henry Morgan
book review - a brief but informative essay that spares readers the ordeal of digesting an actual book.
Rick Bayan
book reviewer - a barker before the door of a publisher's circus.
Austin O'Malley
bookselling - a trade in which the amateurs think they are better than the professionals.
Roger Page
booksellers - the most agreeable servants of civilization.
Rebecca West
bookstore - one of the only pieces of evidence we have that people are still thinking.
Jerry Seinfeld
boo-merang - a ghost that keeps coming back.
Doug Packer
boomerang - a piece of wood that is homesick.
Patrick de Witte
borders - the scars of history.
Emmanuel Berl
bore - a person whose life is an open book... that you don't want to read.
Joey Adams
(see also: biggest bore, real bores)
boredom - the sense of one's faculties slowly dying.
John Berger
boretender - a cocktail party waiter.
Bess Beavers
boring - the right thought at the wrong time.
Jack Gardner
born executive - a guy whose father owns the business.
Harvey Kurtzman

born leader - someone who's afraid to go anywhere by himself.
Clifford Hanley
borrower - a man who tries to live within your means.
O.A. Battista
borrowers of books - mutilators of collections, spoilers of the symmetry of shelves, and creators of odd volumes.
Charles Lamb
boss - someone who is always on time only to see who isn't.
Hans Söhnker
(see also: tactful boss)
boss' son - the young man who is willing to start at the bottom for a few days.
Robert Myers
Boston - a city with champagne tastes and beer pocketbooks.
Alan Friedberg
Bostonian - an American, broadly speaking.
George E. Woodberry
Boston man - the east wind made flesh.
Thomas Gold Appleton
botany -the art of insulting flowers in Latin and Greek.
Alphonse Karr
boundary - in political geography, an imaginary line between two nations, separating the imaginary rights of one from the imaginary rights of another.
Ambrose Bierce
bourbon - the tasty ingredient which, along with scotch, makes polluted water potable.
Edmund H. Volkart
bourgeois - someone who only is what he owns.
Pierre Daninos
bourgeoisie - the washed un-great.
Dan Wick
bourgeois morality - largely a system of making cheap virtues a cloak for expensive vices.
George Bernard Shaw
bowling - marbles for grown-ups.
L.L. Levinson
bowling ball - the natural enemy of the egg.
Michael Davis
boxing – show business with blood.
Frank Bruno
(see also: championship boxing)

boy - the most unmanageable of all animals.
Plato
boycott - a male's bed.
Doug Aiken
boyfriend - the hoodlum your daughter is going to marry someday over your dead body.
Joyce Armor
boyhood - the natural state of rascality.
Herman Melville
BP - a good name for a gas company but a bad name for a honey company.
Elden Carnahan
braggart - a guy who enters a conversation first.
Tom O'Connor
brain - a wonderful organs that starts working the moment you get up in the morning, and does not stop until you get into the office.
Robert Frost
Brainiac - the show that does for science what five pints of lager does for ugly women.
Richard Hammond
brainstorming - the privilege of people who cannot afford to think properly.
Gerrit Komrij
brassière - a bust stop.
John S. Crosbie
brave - afraid without quick legs.
Gerd de Ley
bravery - being the only one who knows you're afraid.
Franklin P. Jones
bravest politician - generally the one who isn't afraid of the ridiculous.
Wincenty Rzymowski
bravo - a word with an exclamation mark included.
Piet Grijs
break dancing - a recent, popular terpsichorean invitation to visit a chiropractor.
Edmund H. Volkart
breakdown - surprise car problem that enables tourists to see something of the landscape.
Jan Vercammen

breakfast - a meal without dessert, eaten without wine, and served on a table without a tablecloth. It is best slept through.
Henry Beard
(see also: horseracing breakfast, outback breakfast)
breakfast cereal - made of all those curly wooden shavings you find in pencil sharpeners.
Roald Dahl
breakfast-time - the critical period in matrimony.
A.P. Herbert
breath - air no one else wanted anymore.
Piet Grijs
brevity - the soul of lingerie.
Dorothy Parker
brick - the most efficient remote control.
Patrick de Witte
bridge - a sport of the mind.
Omar Sharif
bridegroom - a man who has spent a lot of money on a suit that no one notices.
Josh Billings
bridge - a game that separates the men from the boys. It also separates husbands and wives.
George Burns
briefly - summary of the short life of an insect.
Joseph Harris
brilliant conversationalist - one who talks to you about yourself.
Lisa Kirk
brilliant epigram - a solemn platitude gone to a masquerade ball.
Lionel Strachey
brilliant man - one who is shrewd enough to recognize you're a genius.
O.A. Battista
Britain - the society where the ruling class does not rule, the working class does not work and the middle class is not in the middle.
George Mikes
British - people with a Socialist mind and a Conservative heart.
Albert Finney
British cook - a foolish woman who should be turned for her iniquities into a pillar of salt which she never knows how to use.
Oscar Wilde

British Film Industry - a bunch of people in London who can't get green cards.
Alan Parker
Briton - someone who, walking into a department store, is capable of knocking and asking: 'no inconvenience?'
Herman de Coninck
broadband - an all girl musical group.
Gunjan Saraf
broad-mindedness - the result of flattening high-mindedness out.
George Santayana
Broadway - a branch of the narcotics world run by actors.
Bertolt Brecht
Broadway Musical - currently a circus without elephants of memorable tunes, aimed at impressionable out-of-towners who mistake garishness for entertainment, and grandiosity for talent.
Rick Bayan
Broadway openings - the 'first-knife' audience.
Alexander Woollcott
broccoli - something that's difficult to say anything nice about except that it has no bones.
Johnny Martin
broke - a word expressing the ultimate condition of one who is too much bent on speculating.
Gideon Wurdz
brokee - someone who buys stock on the advice of a broker.
Jim Fisk & Robert Barron
broken promises - crimes with words.
Johannes Rau
broker - the end-result of turning a large fortune into a small one.
Kurt Brouwer
broom - witch craft.
Lars Hanson
broommates - ridesharing witches.
Linda Williams
brothel - the only place where a man adjusts his tie while he looks into the mirror on the ceiling.
Charles Bernard
brother - a sister of the stronger sex.
Clem Schouwenaars
brotherhood - the very price and condition of man's survival.
Carlos Pena Romulo

brouhaha - the joy of cooking.
J.B. Hapgood
Brussels Sprouts - vegetables with a delayed smell.
Dirk Denoyelle
Buddhist nudist - one who practises yoga bare.
John S. Crosbie
budding astronaut - a young man who is determined to go far.
O.A. Battista
buddy - someone who measures his own strength against his buddy's lesser strength and increases his own lead.
Elfriede Jelinek
budget - a way of going broke methodically.
Groucho Marx
budgeting - a black art practised by bureaucratic magicians.
David Muchow
buffalo - greeting between two nudists.
Richard Lederer & James Ertner
buffet - a French term. It means "Get up and get it yourself."
Greg Ray
builder's bum - one of Britain's great institutions.
Frank Douglas
builder's estimate - a sum of money equal to half the final cost.
Neil Collins
building - a string of events belonging together.
Chris Fawcett
bullet - a contraceptive pill with retrospective force.
Gaby vanden Berghe
bullfight - an abattoir in fancy dress.
Colin Bowles
bullfighting - men in fancy dress tormenting cattle.
John Carey
bungee-jumping - suicide for indecisive people.
Jimmy Carr
bunker shot - the only shot in golf when you don't have to hit the ball.
Sandy Parr
bureaucracy - the art of making the possible impossible.
Javier Pascual Salcedo
bureaucrats - the only people in the world who can say absolutely nothing and mean it.
Hugh Sidey
(see also: perfect bureaucrat)

burglar - someone who will only show remorse if he is caught.
Marie-Cécile Moerdijk
burglesque - a poorly planned break-in.
Jennifer Hart
burqua - the cheapest form of plastic surgery.
Raf Coppens
business - the art of extracting money from another man's pocket without resorting to violence.
Max Amsterdam
(see also: big business)
business consultancy - an expensive way of hiring someone from outside to tell you exactly how you have been running your business for the past twenty years.
Michael Schiff
business ethics - never telling a lie unless you can get away with it.
Kenneth Cook
businessman - someone who sells under the price, pays more taxes than he earns and invests the credit balance in real estate.
Julien de Valckenaere
(see also: tired businessman)
business slump - when sales are down 10% and sales meetings are up 100%.
Robert Orben
bustard - a very rude Metrobus driver.
Christopher Hapner
busybody - a popular prostitute.
Edmund H. Volkart
butler - a solemn procession of one.
P.G. Wodehouse
butterfly - a flying flower.
Ponce-Denis Ecouchard Lebrun
buttress - a long strand of derrière hair.
Jennifer Hart
buying stock - exactly the same as going to a casino, only with no cocktail service.
Ted Allen
buzz words - the official language of insects.
Jacob Braude

C

cabbage - a familiar kitchen-garden vegetable about as large and wise as a man's head.
Ambrose Bierce
cable television - proof God is a man.
Cy DeBoer
cab drivers - the living proof that practice does not make perfect.
Howard Ogden
caddie - someone who accompanies the golfer and didn't see the ball either.
Joe Francis
café - a failed restaurant.
Colin Bowles
café au lait - a mulatto drink.
Ramon Gomez de la Serna
cafeteria - a women's coffeehouse, where the clients drink coffee and cry.
Michael A. Genz
calamity - the perfect glass wherein we truly see and know ourselves.
William Davenant
Calcutta - the definition of obscenity.
Geoffrey Moorhouse
(see also: O Calcutta)
calendar - memento morning.
Piet Grijs
California - a great place if you happen to be an orange.
Fred Allen
Californians - the biggest collection of losers who ever met on one piece of real estate.
David Karp
call girl - someone who hates poverty more than she hates sin.
Sydney Biddle Barrows
Call me Ishmael - archaic novel opening, now updated to 'E-mail me Ishmael'.
Mike Barfield
calm down - the worst thing you can say to someone who just lost his calm.
Yasmina Reza

calmness - the cradle of power.
Josiah Gilbert Holland
calumny - only the noise of madmen.
Diogenes
camel - animal made on the last day of Creation, with the leftovers.
Simon Carmiggelt
camera - an instrument that teaches people how to see without a camera.
Dorothea Lange
camera obscura - the one used in making most modern films.
Edmund H. Volkart
camp - a lie that tells the truth.
Philip Core
camping - nature's way of promoting the motel business.
Dave Barry
Canada - a country built on dead beavers.
Margaret Atwood
(see also: Montreal, Ottawa, Quebec, Toronto)
Canadian - a person who knows how to make love in a canoe.
Pierre Berton
canape - a small urinal.
Joseph Leff
canapes - dead things on toast.
Jack Segal
cancer - a word that sounds like shattering glass.
Wannes van de Velde
candy striper - a person who paints peppermints.
Michael K. Thompson
canned music - audible wallpaper.
Alistair Cooke
Cannes - the city where you lie on the beach and stare at the stars - or vice versa.
Rex Reed
cannibal - a guy who goes into a restaurant and orders the waiter.
Jack Benny
(see also: converted cannibal)
cannibalism - the ultimate form of recycling.
Chaz Bufe
canon - a law that is fired with religion.
Colin Bowles
canopy - the state of being unable to urinate.
David Elsensohn

canter - the cure for every evil.
Benjamin Disraeli
canticle - a modular office space so small and lightless that it saps an employee of all motivation.
Jacob Weinstein
capital - that part of wealth which is devoted to obtaining further wealth.
Alfred Marshall
capital formation - shifting from the entrepreneur who invests in the future to the pension trustee who invests in the past.
Peter F. Drucker
capitalism - government of the busy by the bossy for the bully.
Arthur Seldon
capitalist - a gymnast with many telephones.
Ramon Gomez de la Serna
capital punishment - killing people who kill people to prove that killing people is wrong.
Sister Helen Prejean
car - horsepower given to donkeys.
Karel Jonckheere
(see also: safe car)
carat cake - a diamond cutter's favourite dessert.
Kim Adams
caravan - vehicle in which you can do anything, but not at the same time.
Seth Gaaikema
cardiac - obsessed poker player.
Ray Hand
cardiologist - poker Champion.
Stan Kegel
career - a job that has gone on too long.
Jeff MacNelly
career girl - a female who gets a man's salary without having to marry one.
Lee Daniel Quinn
career woman - one who would rather go out and take orders than stay home and be boss.
Joey Adams
careful driver - one who is following a traffic cop.
O.A. Battista
carefulness - a euphemism for fear.
Jules Renard

carelessness - the unmarried mother of the china cabinet.
Toon Verhoeven
caricature - putting the face of a joke upon the body of a truth.
Joseph Conrad
caring - a powerful business advantage.
Scott Johnson
caring husband - a man who is so interested in his wife's happiness that he'll hire a detective to find out who's responsible for it.
Milton Berle
carnival - a decadent form of group sex, but with fancy dress and lots of booze.
Peter Andriesse
carnivore - one who only eats at drive-in restaurants.
Jasmine Birtles
carpet - a nodding dog found in the back of an automobile.
Willie Meikle
carress - a blow in the face of a masochist.
Myriam Thys
cartoon - a song sung in an automobile.
Lorraine A. Bellis
cartoonist - someone who does the same thing every day without repeating himself.
Charles Schulz
cash - the one gift everyone despises and no one turns down.
Mignon McLaughlin
cashflow - an oxymoron.
Bruce Boston
cashpoint - the sharp end of banking.
Keith Miles
cash purchases - debt defying acts.
Stan Kegel
casino - a place where you lose a hundred dollars in a slot machine and shrug your shoulders, then lose one dollar in a Coke machine and swear like crazy.
Jeff Shaw
castanet - what a fisherman does to catch fish.
Leopold Fechtner
casting - deciding which of two faces the public is least tired of.
Marcia Lynch
castration - a eunuch experience.
Paul Jennings

cat - a waste of fur.
Rita Rudner
(see also: perfect cat)
catatonic - your feline's favourite drink.
Richard Lederer & James Ertner
catch-frases - blank cheques of intellectual bankruptcy.
Oliver Wendell Holmes
caterpillar - the butterfly's disguise.
Marty Rubin
catnip - vodka and whisky to most cats.
Carl Van Vechten
Catholic clergy - God's storm troopers.
Dave Allen
catholicism - die now and pay later.
Woody Allen
cat owner - an amusing, though common, oxymoron.
Chaz Bufe
cauliflower - cabbage with a college education.
Mark Twain
caution - the mother of all vices.
Francis Blanche
caviar - a luxury for the general, but a necessity for a particular gourmet.
Ted Saucier
cavity - a tiny hole in your child's tooth that takes many, many dollars to fill.
Bill Dodds
C.B. - it may stand for Citizens' Band, but sometimes when you listen to it for a long time it stands for 'Constant Bore'.
Ron Rich
cease-fire - a mutually agreed upon time-out in the game of war, brief enough to prevent peace but long enough to permit reinforcements.
Edmund H. Volkart
ceiling - another man's floor.
Paul Simon
celebrity - a person who works hard all his life to become known, then wears dark glasses to avoid being recognized.
Fred Allen
(see also: professional celebrity, true celebrity)
celibacy - the brief period between any two acts of sexual intercourse.
Mike Barfield

cell phone - phone used by prisoners.
Tim Bruening
cemetery - a place where dead people live.
Dr. Mardy
censor - someone who chews our meat for us and decides what we should spit out.
Colin Bowles
censorship - publicity paid for by the government.
Federico Fellini
censure - the tax a man pays to the public for being eminent.
Jonathan Swift
centaur - a man with a horse where his pants ought to be.
Milton Berle
centimeter - a parking meter that takes pennies.
Leo Rosten
Central Park - a bunch of trees surrounded by noise.
Samuel Barber
centrifuge - a dreaming watchman.
Willie Meikle
CEO - the one who must conduct the corporate orchestra.
Tema Frank
cereal killer - someone who puts poison in a person's corn flakes.
Clynch Varnadore
ceremony - nothing more than middle-aged men dressing up like refugees from a pack of cards.
Philip Howard
cesarean section - a district in Rome.
Mike McKinley
chair - anti-gravity machine.
Richard Feynman
chaise longue - yawn furniture.
Daisy Brown
chamber music - a conversation between friends.
Catherine Drinker Bowen
champagne - ginger ale that knows somebody.
Alan Alda
champion - someone who gets up when he can't.
Jack Dempsey
(see also: true champion)
championship boxing - Tasteful Attire Prohibited.
Matt Groening

chance - the pseudonym of God when he does not wish to sign his work.
Anatole France
change - the true Gospel of consistency.
Mark Twain
Channel - a slipper bath of irony through which we pass these serious Continentals in order not to be infected by their gloom.
Alan Bennett
chaos - unperceived order.
Fred Hoyle
character - doing what is right when no one is looking.
J.C. Watts
character actress - an actress too ugly to be called a leading lady.
Kathy Burke
charisma - mysterious something that bald, dull billionaires have.
Sam Ewing
charity - giving someone the washing machine it wasn't worth having mended.
Faith Hines
(see also: true charity)
charity ball - a tax deductible dance.
P.J. O'Rourke
charm - a way of getting the answer yes without asking a clear question.
Albert Camus
charming woman - one who notices me.
John Erskine
chaste girl - one who hasn't been asked yet.
Pierre Perret
chastitute - the opposite of a prostitute.
John B. Keane
chastity - the facile ability to keep the legs crossed.
Colin Bowles
chastity belt - a labour-saving device.
Joyce Armor
chat-chat-chat - dance, performed by three French cats.
Guy Bernaert
chatterbox - someone with a good memory - and a tongue hung in the middle of it.
Louis A. Safian
chauvinism - what a prisoner feels for his cell.
Frans Kellendonk

cheating - two wrong people doing the right thing.
Milton Berle
check enclosed - the two most beautiful words in the English language.
Dorothy Parker
cheerfulness - the atmosphere under which all things thrive.
Jean Paul
cheese - milk's leap toward immortality.
Clifton Fadiman
chef - any cook who swears in French.
Henry Beard
chemistry - a trade for people without enough imagination to be physicists.
Arthur C. Clarke
cherish - description of a woman over fifty pretending to be twenty.
Willie Meikle
cherry cobbler - shortcake with a soul.
Edna Ferber
cherry tomato - a marvelous invention, producing as it does a satisfactorily explosive squish when bitten.
Judith Martin
chess - boredom made complicated.
Lesley Woolf Hedley
chess genius - a human being who focuses vast, little-understood mental gifts and labors on an ultimately trivial human enterprise.
George Steiner
chewing gum - television for the teeth.
Rick Bayan
chic - knowing which fingers to put in your mouth when you whistle for the waiter.
Milton Berle
chickens - the only creatures you can eat before they are born and after they are dead.
Alex King
chicken teriyaki - the name of the only living Japanese kamikaze pilot.
Isaac Asimov
chihuahua - a dog that looks like a dog that is still far away.
Billiam Coronel

childhood - the glorious time of life when all we had to do to lose weight was take a bath!
Alfredo La Mont
(see also: happy childhood)
childish game - one in which your wife beats you.
Don Epperson
child prodigy - grandchild.
Juul Kinnaer
(see also: prodigy)
children - nature's very own form of birth control.
Dave Barry
(see also: kid, raising kids, well-raised child)
child support - politically correct alimony.
Lenny Schafer
chimpanzee - God's first draft of a politician.
Colin Bowles
China - the country where a dog also is known by its pseudonym 'walking dinner'.
Patrick de Witte
Chinese - a language in which very wise things have been said, but that sounds to a Westerner like the sound of a moving bicycle wheel.
Simon Carmiggelt
Chinese Food - poetry in little cups.
Marc Callewaert
Chinese proverb - refined wisdom, packed in a banal one-liner.
Guido van Heulendonk
Chinese voyeur - a Peking Tom.
John S. Crosbie
chip - the English contribution to world cuisine.
John Cleese
chiropractor - a slipped disc jockey.
Milton Berle
chivalry - a man's inclination to protect a woman from every man but himself.
Brian Johnston
choice - the only thing you kill by making it.
Oleg Vishnepolsky
cholesterol - a substance in the blood that causes you to eat salad.
Richard Carleton

chopsticks - one of the reasons the Chinese never invented custard.
Spike Milligan
Christian - a man who feels repentance on Sunday for what he did on Saturday and is going to do on Monday.
Thomas R. Ybarra
Christianity - a great idea that's never been tried.
Alex Ayres
Christian theology - the grandmother of Bolshevism.
Oswald Spengler
Christmas - the time of year kids get toys their fathers can play with.
Milton Berle
(see also: early Christmas shopper)
Christmas cards - only junk mail from people you know.
Patricia Marx
Christmas eve - the day on which you decide to do the Christmas shopping for next year one week earlier.
Peter Darbo
Christmas expense - mistle dough.
Robert Myers
Christmas morning - toynado.
Robert Myers
Christmas presence - when the family is all together.
Jim Bryson
Christmas pudding - festering gobs of adamantine suet that the Brits think of as fun food.
Joe Queenan
Christmas shopping - when we go dashing through the dough.
Joseph Leff
Christmas surprises - cases of Claus and effect.
Linda Williams
Christmess - five minutes after the gifts are opened.
Robert Orben
chromatic scale - what you use to give the effect of drinking a quinine martini and having an enema simultaneously.
Philip Larkin
chronic - describing an entity that will not go away, despite the doctor's best efforts; sometimes a disease, often a patient.
George Thomas & Lee Schreiner
Chrysanthenum - a flower which, by any other name, would be much easier to spell.
William Johnson

church - a place in which gentlemen who have never been to heaven brag about it to people who will never get there.
H.L. Mencken
Church of England - the perfect church for those who don't go to church.
Gerald Priestland
chutzpa - a small boy peeing through someone's letter box, then ringing the doorbell to ask how far it went.
Maureen Lipman
cigar - a fire at one end and a fool at the other.
Horace Greeley
cigarette - the only legal product that, when used as directed, causes death.
Anna Quindlen
(see also: smoking)
cinema - an uncomfortable way of watching television.
Sheila Black
(see also: film, Hollywood)
cinema criticism - a total waste of everybody's time.
Glenda Jackson
cinemascope - movie mogul's mouthwash.
Dan Gillespie
cinemuck - the combination of popcorn, soda, and melted chocolate which covers the floors of movie theaters.
Rich Hall
cinephobe - a person who waits for a movie to be released on tape before seeing it in order to avoid paying too much to watch it at the cinema.
Ben Loewen
circle - the longest distance to the same point.
Tom Stoppard
circumstances - the rulers of the weak, the instruments of the wise.
Samuel Lover
circumvent - the opening in the front of boxer shorts.
Greg Arnold
circus - a place where horses, ponies and elephants are permitted to see men, women and children acting the fool.
Ambrose Bierce
citation - reputation by repetition.
Gerhard Uhlenbruck

city - a human zoo.
Desmond Morris
(see also: big city, great city)
city slicker - what follows an ice storm.
Joseph Leff
Civil Service - a difficulty for every solution.
Herbert Samuel
civilization - the evolution from being a dirty man in a clean world to a clean man in a dirty world.
Jacques Embrechts
civilized husband - a creature who has ceased to be a man.
Elizabeth von Arnim
civilized society - one which tolerates eccentricity to the point of doubtful sanity.
Robert Frost
clams - the castanets of the sea.
Ramon Gomez de La Serna
clarinets - the nursing bottles of music.
Ramon Gomez de La Serna
clarity - the politeness of the man of letters.
Jules Renard
clash - a Peking auto accident.
Joseph Leff
classical music - music written by famous dead foreigners.
Arlene Heath
classical quotation - the parole of the literati.
Samuel Johnson
classic authors - those for whom the royalty agreements have expired.
Gerrit Komrij
classic book - a book that makes you sick in class.
Karel Jonckheere
class reunion - a meeting where three hundred people hold in their stomachs for four hours while writing down the names and addresses of friends they'll never contact.
Brenda Davidson
claustropedic - to be terrified of being trapped in a folding bed.
Carolyn May
claustrophobia - fear of Father Christmas.
Andy Hamilton
clean desk - a sign of an empty mind.
Felix Frankfurter

clean house - the sign of a misspent life.
Emily Christensen
cleanliness - what is next to impossible.
Aubrey Austin
clear - those ideas which have the same degree of confusion as their own.
Marcel Proust
clear conscience - the sign of a bad memory.
Steven Wright
clemency - the noblest trait which can reveal a true monarch to the world.
Pierre Corneille
clergyman - a ticket speculator outside the gates of heaven.
H.L. Mencken
clerk - a salesman minus enthusiasm.
Harry F. Banks
(see also: ward clerk)
clever woman - one who knows how to give a man her own way.
Hal Roach
cliché - a metaphor that knew better times.
Jan Boerstoel
climate - the weather in a foreign country.
Colin Bowles
cloak - the mating call of a Chinese frog.
Tony Blackburn
clock - an instrument that enables us to measure how unpunctual we are.
Pedro F. Moret
clock-radio - the mechanical reincarnation of the rattlesnake.
Johan Anthierens
clone - a cell mate.
Angie Papadakis
cloning - the sincerest form of flattery.
Janet Jacobsen
closet - a place for hanging things after you run out of doorknobs.
Doug Larson
clothes - nudity in its most refined form.
Jan Schepens
cloud - a sheep with no legs.
Bill Sadgarden
clown - a poet in action.
Henry Miller

clubs - places where men spend all their time thinking angrily about nothing.
Viscount Castlerosse
clue - what the police find when they fail to arrest a criminal.
J.B. Morton
CNN - one of the participants in the war.
Arthur C. Clarke
coagulation - the only proof that blood is thicker than water.
Kathy Lette
coal - portable climate.
Ralph Waldo Emerson
coalition - an alliance in which one party loses its power and all parties lose face.
Helmar Nahr
coarse actor - one who can remember his lines but not the order in which they come.
Michael Green
coarse drinker - a man who blames his hangover on the tonic water and not the gin.
Michael Green
coarse golfer - one who has to shout "fore" before he putts.
Michael Green
coarse sailor - one who in a crisis forgets nautical language and shouts, 'For God's sake turn left.'
Michael Green
co-author - the one who did most of the writing, receives the least praise and most of the criticism.
Edmund H. Volkart
cobra - a shared undergarment.
Willie Meikle
cocaine - God's way of saying you're making too much money.
Robin Williams
(see also: taking cocaine)
cockiness - the feeling you have just before you know better.
Milton Berle
cockroaches - the unstable birthmarks of the night.
Ramon Gomez de La Serna
cocktail party - a device for paying off obligations to people you don't want to invite to dinner.
Charles Merrill Smith
cocktail party hostess - a din mother.
Raymond J. Cvikota

cocktails - all the disagreeability of a disinfectant without the utility.
Shane Leslie
co-dependence - taking someone else's temperature to see how you feel.
Linda Ellerbee
co-destruction - the only alternative to co-existence.
Jawaharlal Nehru
coercion - the least efficient means of obtaining order.
Ursula K. Le Guin
coexistence - what the farmer does with the turkey - until Thanksgiving.
Mike Connolly
coffee - a beverage that puts to sleep when not drunk.
Alphonse Allais
(see also: coppoccino, instant coffee)
coffee break - America's biggest advance yet in the area of communications.
Herbert V. Prochnow
coin - something that's useful for getting the wrong number in a telephone box.
Jack Cruise
coincide - what you do when it starts raining.
Peter Darbo
coincidence - God's way of remaining anonymous.
Bernie Siegel
coition - a slight attack of apoplexy.
Democritus of Abdera
coitus - occasion to call on the gods of the clan. It is a sacred act, pure, absolute, bringing invisible forces into action.
Frantz Fanon
colic - a sheep dog.
Mike McKinley
Colin - the sort of name you give your goldfish for a joke.
Colin Firth
collaboration - the process whereby two people create something each thinks is his own.
Frank A. Clark
college - a place where you have to go in order to find out that there's nothing in it.
Kin Hubbard

college professor - someone smart enough to get a Ph.D., but too crazy to make a living.
Ralph Noble
collision - what happens when two motorists go after the same pedestrian.
Bob Newhart
colonel - someone who could never be a general.
Theo Mestrum
Colonel Sanders - the only man who can satisfy a woman in two minutes.
Fran Drescher
Columbus - another man who wouldn't ask the way.
Michael Moore
colonoscopy - nature's way of telling you to eat a low fat diet.
Ryan James
colorado beetle - insect that is still angry at us because we ate his potato.
Piet Grijs
colours - the deeds and sufferings of light.
Johann Wolfgang von Goethe
comb - the musical staff for dead ideas.
Ramon Gomez de La Serna
comedian - someone who knows a good joke when he steals one.
Joey Adams
(see also: real comedian)
comedy - tragedy plus time.
Woody Allen
(see also: stand-up comedy, tragedy)
comedy script-writing - one of the few trades that doesn't have to fear competition from the Japanese.
Denis Norden
comfort - a reproach to sorrow.
Luc Delafortrie
comic - the antithesis of the mob mentality.
Bill Hicks
comics - famously tragic people.
Marlon Brando
command - in computer science, a statement presented by a human and accepted by a computer in such a manner as to make the human feel as if he is in control.
Peter Darbo

commerce - the selling of goods for more money than they are worth.
Geerten Meijsing
commercials - God's way of punishing you for watching TV.
Neil Steinberg
commercialism - doing well that which should not be done at all.
Gore Vidal
commercial television - the only sedative you take with your eyes.
Vittorio de Sica
commitment - what every woman wants; men can't even spell it.
Laura Zigman
committee - a group of the unwilling, picked from the unfit, to do the unnecessary.
Richard Harkness
commonplaces - the tramways of intellectual transportation.
José Ortega Y Gasset
common sense - the measure of the possible.
Henri-Fréderic Amiel
common weaknesses - the strongest binding agents.
Sigmund Graff
communication - something so simple and difficult that we can never put it in simple words.
T.S. Matthews
communism - the opiate of the intellectuals.
Clare Boothe Luce
(see also: Russian communism)
communist - a person who publicly airs his dirty Lenin.
Jack Pomeroy
community - gathering around a fire and listening to someone tell a story.
Bill Moher
(see also: ideal community)
commuters - people who get there slowly but surly.
Martin Baker
comparison - a sophisticated judgement.
Richard Wilkins
compassion - a luxury of the affluent.
Tony Randall
competent person - someone who makes mistakes according the rules.
Paul Valéry

competition - the struggle for a cake of ice in hell.
Kin Hubbard
(see also: unfair competition)
competitor - the other one.
Juul Kinnaer
complacency - the enemy of progress.
Dave Stutman
complaining - a way of killing time.
August Willemsen
complaints department at the parachute packing plant - the quietest place in the world.
Jackie Martling
complete arrogance - the result of incomplete data.
Beston Jack Abrams
complex - a quiet theatre.
Victoria Tarrani
compliance - the path of least persistence.
Gordon Baker
compliment - a friendly truth with a little make-up.
Hannelore Schroth
composer - someone who connects heaven with earth by threads of music.
Alan Hovhaness
(see also: modern composer)
composing - remembering a little melody that no one has come up with before.
Robert Schumann
compost - e-mail.
Willie Meikle
compound - a comical combination of two or more elements.
John S. Crosbie
comprehension - something that one has to get in order to get it.
Dave Peters
compromise - the art of dividing a cake so that everybody believes he or she got the biggest piece.
Ludwig Erhard
compulsion - a highbrow term for a temptation we're not trying too hard to resist.
Hugh Allen

computer - apparatus to relieve you of all the work which you wouldn't have had without it.
Joachim Graf
(see also: command, digital computer, hardware, Internet, PC, printer, programmer, reliable computer, software, user)
computer dating - a terrific experience if you're a computer.
Rita Mae Brown
computer error - human error in operating computer.
Russell Ash
computer expert - grandson.
Peter Darbo
computer hacker - office worker with a cold.
Mark States
computerization - part of a long-term historical process in which work has become increasingly abstract.
Soshana Zuboff
computer literacy - ability to move words on a screen without ever appreciating their capacity to move minds.
Rick Bayan
computer literate - synonym for between 2 and 18 years of age.
Mike Barfield
computer programmer - a creator of universes for which he alone is responsible. Universes of virtually unlimited complexity can be created in the form of computer programs.
Joseph Weizenbaum
computer science - a study akin to numerology and astrology, but lacking the precision of the former and the success of the latter.
Stan Kelly-Bootle
computer scientist - someone who, when told to "Go to Hell," sees the "go to," rather than the destination, as harmful.
Roger M. Firestone
computer terminal - an interface where the mind and body can connect with the universe and move bits of it about.
Douglas Adams
computer user - a stressed, usually female, being who has to work with useless programs, incomprehensible manuals and incompatible peripherals at a screen that hurts the eyes, knowing that all these things could be done in half the time without a computer.
Joachim Graf

computer viruses - the modern equivalent of nasty little boys ringing doorbells and running away.
Libby Purves
conceit - the ability to think about absolutely nothing when it is absolutely necessary.
Ray Knight
concentration camps - the attempt of mankind to achieve complete equality.
Karel van Isacker
concern - the first time you can't do it the second time.
Isaac Asimov
concert - on-stage talent playing to a chorus of coughs.
Rick Bayan
conclusion - the place where you got tired of thinking.
Robert Matz
(see also: in conclusion)
condominium - just an apartment with a down payment.
Robert D. Specht
condoms - devices that should be marketed in three sizes, jumbo, colossal and super-colossal so that men do not have to go in and ask for the small.
Barbara Seaman
condos - apartments with nice doors.
Silver Rose
Coney Island - where the surf is one third water and two thirds people.
John Steinbeck
conference - an admission that you want somebody to join you in your troubles.
Will Rogers
confession - telling tales on yourself.
Fons Jansen
confidence - that quiet assured feeling you have before you fall flat on your face.
Leonard Binder
conformist - someone who is too lazy to think and too tired to get up.
Colin Bowles
confusion - a word we have invented for an order which is not understood.
Henry Miller
Congress - the antonym of progress.
Jonny Groves

congressman - a man who doesn't know where he's going, and he wants us to follow him.
Milton Berle
conjugal bedroom - the coexistence of brutality and martyrdom.
Karl Kraus
connoisseur - someone who can sip a glass of wine and tell you not only what year it was bottled, but who jumped on the grapes.
Stanley Davis
conscience - that quiet voice which whispers that someone is watching.
Julian Tuwim
(see also: bad conscience, clear conscience, uneasy conscience)
consciousness - annoying time in between naps.
Michael Powell
consensus - when everyone agrees to say collectively what no one believes individually.
Abba Eban
consensus politician - someone who does something that he doesn't believe is right because it keeps people quiet when he does.
John Major
consequence - the line-up at the jail.
John Fenn
conservation - the application of common sense to the common problems for the common good.
Gifford Pinchot
conservation area - a place where you can't build a garage but you can build a motorway.
James Gladstone
conservationists - people who pour trouble on oiled waters.
Joel Rothman
conservatism - the worship of dead revolutions.
Clinton Rossiter
conservative - someone who believes that nothing should be done for the first time.
Alfred Wiggam
consistency - the last refuge of the imaginative.
Oscar Wilde
(see also: foolish consistency)
conspiracy - the plural of conscience.
Arthur Henderson
constancy - a saint without a worshipper.
Stanislas Jean de Boufflers

constipation - nature's way of making pregnant women practice pushing.
Joyce Armor
constitutional law - a ship with a great deal of sail but a very shallow keel.
Robert H. Bork
constitutional statesman - a man of common opinions and uncommon abilities.
Walter Bagehot
constitutions - the self-imposed restraints of a whole people upon a majority of them to secure sober action and a respect for the rights of the majority.
William Howard Taft
consultancy - the last refuge of rascals.
Barry Devlin
consultant - a jobless person who shows executives how to work.
Rick Bayan
consultant's client - someone with a very expensive watch who doesn't know what time it is.
Robert J. Lewis
consultation - a meeting doctors have to pass the time while the patient dies.
Colin Bowles
consumer - a shopper who is sore about something.
Harold Coffin
consumerism - our national religion.
Jennifer Stone
(see also: under-consumption)
contemplation - the fornication of the mind.
Gary Benson
content - a word unknown to life; it is also a word unknown to man.
Loren Eiseley
contentment - the smother of invention.
Ethel Watts Mumford
continence - a melancholy sexual perversion.
Aldous Huxley
contortionist - a fellow who pawned his skeleton.
Ramon Gomez de La Serna
contraceptive - a pill or gadget that enables a couple to savour the mirth without the birth.
Rick Bayan

contracrostipunctus - a study in levels of meaning.
Doug Hofstadter
contract - an agreement to do something if nothing happens to prevent it.
L.L. Levinson
contradiction - the essence of all physical theorems.
Ron Koolman
control - a short, ugly inmate.
Paul Benoit
control freak - any man who behaves like a woman and a nymphomaniac is any woman who behaves like a man.
Patrick Murray
conundrum - a jailbird on a percussion instrument.
Joseph Leff
convenience - the basis of mercantile law.
William Murray Mansfield
convent - supreme egotism resulting in supreme self-denial.
Victor Hugo
conventional intercourse - something like squeezing jam into a doughnut.
Germaine Greer
conventionality - the adoration which both vice and virtue offer up to worldliness.
Arthur Helps
converted cannibal - one who, on Friday, eats only fishermen.
Emily Lotney
(to) convince - to conquer without conception.
Walter Benjamin
cookbook - a volume that is full of stirring passages.
Connie Lund
cooking - the only premarital thing girls don't do these days.
Omar Sharif
coolie - a quickie in the snow.
Milton Berle
cooperation - wasting time explaining to the other person that his ideas are stupid.
Wolinski
co-opt - baby talk for corrupt.
John Leonard
coppoccino - police officer's espresso.
Paul Woodward

coquette - a woman without any heart, who makes a fool out of a man that hasn't got any head.
Dorothée de Luzy
coriander - a giant hoax perpetrated by a perverted society.
Stephen Fry
corkscrew - a useful key to unlock the storehouse of wit, the treasury of laughter, the front door of fellowship, and the gate of pleasant folly.
W.E.P. French
corn - bacon after it has been processed by a pig.
William D. Hickman
corporal - a barking soldier.
Bernard Seulsten
corporation - an ingenious device for obtaining individual profit without individual responsibility.
Ambrose Bierce
corpulence - the curse of the eating class.
Gaby vanden Berghe
corpus delicti - a delicious body.
Julian Tuwim
correct English - the slang of prigs.
George Eliot
corruption - nature's way of restoring our faith in democracy.
Peter Ustinov
(see also: political corruption)
cosigner - a damn fool with a ballpoint pen.
Milton Berle
cosmetics - the best way of falsifying your birth certificate.
Olga Tschechowa
cosmopolitan critics - men who are the friends of every country save their own.
Benjamin Disraeli
cosmos - the smallest hole a man can hide his head in.
G.K. Chesterton
costliest women - the ones who cost nothing.
Alfred de Musset
costs - amount required to bankrupt the acquitted.
Miles Kington
cost-of-living index - a list of numbers which proves that high prices are not expensive.
Richard Weiss
cotton balls - the final stage of beer nuts.
Georges Carlin

cough - something that you yourself can't help, but everybody else does on purpose just to torment you.
Ogden Nash
coughing - the music provided by the throat when all is quiet.
Arno Breekveld
counsel - advice with a price tag.
L.L. Levinson
counterfeiter - a man who gets into trouble by following a good example.
Joey Adams
counter tenor - anyone who can count to ten.
Denis Norden
country - a piece of land surrounded on all sides by boundaries, usually unnatural.
Joseph Heller
(see also: neutral country)
country music - three chords and the truth.
Harlan Howard
countryside - the space between two cities.
Marnix Gijsen
coup de grace - lawnmower.
Vicky Satter
courage - grace under pressure.
Ernest Hemingway
(see also: great courage)
court - a place where they dispense with justice.
Arthur Train
courtesy - the most polite form of despair.
G.M. van der Wal
courtiers - poor men who have become rich by begging.
Nicolas de Chamfort
courtroom - a place where Jesus Christ and Judas Iscariot would be equals, with the betting odds in favour of Judas.
H.L. Mencken
courtship - a period when a man pursues a girl who is running toward him.
Joey Adams
couturier - an architect for design, a sculptor for shape, a painter for color, a musician for harmony and a philosopher for temperance.
Cristobal Balenciaga
cow - a machine that makes it possible for people to eat grass.
John McNulty

coward - a man in whom the instinct of self-preservation acts normally.
Soraya Esfandiari
cowardice - the surest protection against temptations.
Mark Twain
cowboy - a farm boy in leather britches and a comical hat.
Edward Abbey
cramberries - student's snack.
Raymond D. Love
crank - someone with a new idea - until it catches on.
Mark Twain
craziness - doing the same thing and expecting a different result.
Tom DeMarco
(to) create - to think more efficiently.
Pierre Reverdy
creation - the opposite of war.
Jonathan Larson
creative urge - the demon that will not accept anything second-rate.
Agnes De Mille
creative work - one of life's greatest pleasures, and the only one we will gladly interrupt.
Mignon McLaughlin
creativity - postponed death.
Gerd de Ley
creativity in science - the act of putting two and two together to make five.
Arthur Koestler
creator - a comedian whose audience is afraid to laugh.
H.L. Mencken
credibility gap - what happens to the same news between the morning telecast and the evening paper.
O.A. Battista
credit - a person who can't pay, gets another person who can't pay, to guarantee that he can pay.
Charles Dickens
credit card - plastic passport to the valley of the shadow of debt.
Rick Bayan
credit card holder - member of the debt set.
Bill Sadgarden
creditor - something with nothing.
Gideon Wurdz

credulity - the man's weakness, but the child's strength.
Charles Lamb
creed - an ossified metaphor.
Elbert Hubbard
cremation - a waste of energy.
J.O. Stigter
crick - the noise made by a Japanese camera.
John S. Crosbie
cricket - a game which the English, not being a spiritual people, have invented in order to give themselves some conception of Eternity.
Lord Mancroft
cricketer - a creature very nearly as stupid as a dog.
Bernard Levin
crime - something that is committed by the lower class and punished by the upper class.
David Frost & Anthony Jay
criminal - a person with predatory instincts who has not sufficient capital to form a corporation.
Howard Scott
criminal law - one of the few professions where the client buys someone else's luck.
William Burroughs
crisis - a productive situation - you only have remove the aftertaste of catastrophe.
Max Frisch
(see also: times of crisis)
crisis management - the ability to make anything sound much worse than it really is.
Robert Myers
critic - a legless man who teaches running.
Channing Pollock
(see also: bad critic, cosmopolitan critics, drama critic, good critic, true critic)
criticism - insults permitted by law.
Jean-Louis Barrault
(see also: art criticism, cinema criticism)
critic's job - to walk on live bodies and make them bleed.
Eric Bentley
crocodiles - suitcases that travel on their own.
Ramon Gomez de la Serna
crook - a businessman without an office.
Brendan Behan

croquet - polo for people who are too fat to get on a horse.
Frankie Boyle
croquette - hash that has come to a head.
Irvin S. Cobb
cross - the true shape of a tortured woman.
Patti Smith
crossword puzzle - the abacus of boredom.
Johan Anthierens
crown - merely a hat that lets the rain in.
Frederick the Great
crucifixion - one of those parties which got out of hand.
Lenny Bruce
cruise - prison with the possibility of drowning.
Billy Connolly
crying baby - the best form of birth control.
Carole Tabbron
cubism - a cathedral of shit.
Francis Picabia
cuckoldry - an essential appendage of wedlock.
François Rabelais
cuddling - pleasant act of affection always requested at the wrong time.
Jeff Green
culinary art - undoubtedly the one that feeds us best.
Pierre Dac
cult - a religion with no political power.
Tom Wolfe
cult figure - a guy who hasn't got the musical ability to make it to the charts.
John Cale
cult film - a movie seen about fifty times by about that many people.
Rick Bayan
cultural philosopher - someone who discovers the obvious.
Gerrit Komrij
culture - what your butcher would have if he were a surgeon.
Mary Pettibone Poole
cultured people - the glittering scum which floats upon the deep river of production.
Winston Churchill
cultured person - one who can entertain himself, entertain guests, and entertain ideas.
Laurence J. Peter

cunning - the dark sanctuary of incapacity.
Lord Chesterfield
cupboard - a place for hanging things after you run out of doorknobs.
Doug Larson
Cupid - blind gunner.
George Farquhar
curiosity - the vulgar stare and the refined peek through a crack.
Josh Billings
curling - the only sport where they have to speed up the action replays.
A.A. Gill
curse (noun) - a prayer of an agnostic.
Georges Elgozy
(to) curse - praying for bitterness.
Hendrik Carette
cursing Frenchman - a scenario that God prefers to a praying Englishman.
Heinrich Heine
curve - a straight line, but more human.
Eric van der Steen
custard powder - one of our minor national tragedies.
Jane Grigson
customer - the most important part of the production line.
W. Edwards Deming
customer service - what you get when your tip is big enough.
Jacob Braude
cyberpunk - the futuristic bandit of the information highway: a black-hatted gunslinger with a microchip on his shoulder and a modem in his holster.
Rick Bayan
cyberspace - a consensual hallucination experienced daily by billions of legitimate operators, in every nation, by children being taught mathematical concepts...
William Gibson
cycology - the science of propelling one's self through the environment to enhance well-being.
Bill Sadgarden
cynic - a man who, when he smells flowers, looks around for a coffin.
H.L. Mencken
cynicism - an unpleasant way of saying the truth.
Lillian Hellman

D

dachshund - a German draught-excluder.
Billy Connolly
dadaism - an exotic movement in modern art and literature, the nature of which is best conveyed by the infantile name it adopted.
Edmund H. Volkart
daily column - a grave two inches wide and twenty inches deep.
Don Marquis
daily routine - the woodworm of happiness.
Jules de Corte
dainty - where residents of Copenhagen begin a golf game.
Joseph Leff
dance - a poem of which each movement is a word.
Mata Hari
(see also: tango)
dance school - disco tech.
Jacob Braude
dancing - the perpendicular expression of a horizontal desire.
George Bernard Shaw
 (see also: disco dancing, lap dancing)
dandruff - hair pollution.
Joel Rothman
dandyism - the last flicker of heroism in decadent ages.
Charles Baudelaire
danger - sauce for prayers.
Benjamin Franklin
Daniel - the only man who wasn't spoiled by being lionized.
Herbert Beerbohm Tree
daring - one of the most conspicuous qualities of a man in security.
Ambrose Bierce
dark - the sound of a dyslexic dog.
Chris Cox
dark ages - knight Time.
Stan Kegel
darling - the popular form of address used in speaking to a member of the opposite sex whose name you cannot at the moment recall.
Oliver Herford

data - what distinguishes the dilettante from the artist.
George V. Higgins

data superhighway - the most important marketplace of the 21st century.
Al Gore

date - a job interview that lasts all night. The only difference is that in not many job interviews is there a chance you'll wind up naked at the end of it.
Jerry Seinfeld

dating - a social engagement with the threat of sex at its conclusion.
P.J. O'Rourke

datum - what young men like to do with pretty young women.
Joseph Leff

daughter - a mother's gender partner, her closest ally in the family confederacy.
Victoria Secunda

dawn - the moment when intelligent people go to bed.
Jack de Graef

day - a miniature eternity.
Ralph Waldo Emerson

daydreaming - a sigh of fancy.
Ramon Gomez de La Serna

Day-Lewis, Daniel - the child of former Poet Laureate Cecil Day-Lewis and not, as some Americans assume, Doris Day's son by Jerry Lewis.
Mark Steyn

daylight - harsh overhead lighting that is so unflattering to the heavy smoker.
Fran Lebowitz

daytime sleep - a cursed slumber from which one wakes in despair.
Iris Murdoch

daytime TV - a plot by corporations to punish workers for staying home.
Linda Rae Stowell

daze - constituent parts of weekz and yeerz.
Willie Meikle

dead atheist - someone all dressed up and nowhere to go.
Woody Woodbury

dead end - just a good place to turn around.
Naomi Judd

deadline - the ultimate inspiration.
Nolan Bushnell
deadwood - anyone in your office who is more senior than you are.
Jim Fisk & Robert Barron
deaf Trappist - the only decent diplomat.
John Le Carré
death - the first condition of immortality.
Stanislaw Jerzy Lec
(see also: die, dying, natural death)
debate - the death of conversation.
Emil Ludwig
debauchery - an act of despair in the face of infinity.
Edmond & Jules de Goncourt
debentures - false teeth bought on credit.
John Allen
debts - the only way to be recognized by businessmen.
Jean Carmet
debugged program - one for which you have not yet found the conditions that make it fail.
Jerry Ogdin
debut - the first time a young girl is seen drunk in public.
F. Scott Fitzgerald
decathlon - nine Mickey Mouse events and the 1500 metres.
Steve Ovett
decency - an even more exhausting state to maintain than its opposite.
Quentin Crisp
decent man - someone who is ashamed of the government he lives under.
H.L. Mencken
decent woman - a woman that gives what others sell.
Comtesse Diane
deceptionist - office worker who fibs about the boss's whereabouts.
Michael Fitzgerald
deceptions - the oil to the wheels of life.
Sidney Tremayne
decision - what a man makes when he can't find anybody to serve on a committee.
Fletcher Knebel
decisiveness - the art of timely cruelty.
Henry Becque

declaration of love - emotional variant of a bounced cheque.
Georges-Armand Masson
décolletage - the only place men want depth in a woman.
Zsa Zsa Gabor
decolonization - the replacing of a certain "species" of men by another "species" of men.
Frantz Fanon
decorum - just the delicacy of the indelicate.
Walter Raleigh
defeat - a school in which truth always grows strong.
Henry Ward Beecher
defecation - the natural coarse.
John S. Crosbie
deficit - what you have after paying your taxes.
Arnold H. Glasow
deflation - the easiest thing to avoid; you just print more money.
Milton Friedman
defrock - a group of Japanese sheep.
Joseph Leff
déjeuner - the breakfast of an American who has been in Paris. Variously pronounced.
Ambrose Bierce
Delaware - a state that has three counties when the tide is out, and two when it is in.
J.J. Inglis
delay - the deadliest form of denial.
C. Northcote Parkinson
Deli-ban - terrorist group trying to stop sales of all sliced pastrami.
Maurizio Mariotti
deliberated - what happens when a woman gets married.
Gary Hallock
delicatessen - shop selling the worst parts of animals more expensively than the nice bits.
Mike Barfield
delusion - belief said to be false by someone who does not share it.
Thomas Szasz
demagogue - a person with whom we disagree as to which gang should mismanage the country.
Don Marquis

democracy - system in which you say what you like and do what you are told.
Dave Barry

democrat - someone who is against dictatorships under which he cannot earn money.
C. Buddingh'

democratic party - in American politics, the party of the people, as opposed to the Republican Party, which is also the party of the people, but the wrong kind.
Edmund H. Volkart

democratic society - one in which the majority is always prepared to put down a revolutionary minority.
Walter Lippmann

demonstrate - monster who isn't gay.
Phil Hudson

demonstration - a riot by people you agree with.
Thomas Sowell
(see also: mob violence)

denial - a river in Egypt.
Mark Twain

dentist - someone who noses around in your mouth.
Huguette de Backer

dentist's waiting room - a smartly furnished chamber of horrors.
Shelley Berman

dentopedology - the science of opening your mouth and putting your foot in it.
Duke of Edinburgh

deodorants - commercial products that can't conceal the malodorousness of the programs they sponsor.
Edmund H. Volkart

dependency - slavery by mutual agreement.
Robert Anthony

depression - rage turned inwards.
Robin Green

deprivation - frugality without creativity.
Amy Dacyczyn

deputy - the second-in-command who frequently has to lead.
Jan Schepens

derange - de place where de cowboys ride home to.
Kevin Goldstein-Jackson

dermatologists - people who make rash judgments.
Patricia Makewski

descriptive passage - the dull part in a novel, thankfully lost in the TV adaptation.
Mike Barfield
desert - an ocean of sand.
Dr. Mardy
desertion - the poor man's method of divorce.
Arthur Hays
design - what the designer has when time and money run out.
James Poole
(see also: good design)
designer - someone who is only as good as the star who wears her clothes.
Edith Head
desire - a renewable commodity.
Christine Brückner
desk - a wastebasket with drawers.
Bruce W. van Roy
despair – the dark little sister of happiness.
Simon Carmiggelt
desperation - a man who shaves before weighing himself on the bathroom scales.
R.E. Dorsey
despondency - the most unprofitable feeling a man can indulge in.
DeWitt Talmadge
destiny - an invention of the cowardly and the resigned.
Ignazio Silone
detached garage - one of the few remaining reasons that forces some people to take a walk.
O.A. Battista
detectives - only policemen with smaller feet.
Selwyn Jepson
detective stories - the modern fairy tales.
Graham Greene
determination - the wake-up call to the human will.
Anthony Robbins
detour - a straight road which turns on the charm.
Albert Brie
Detroit - Motor Town.
Linda Lewis
Deus-ex-machina - God falling out of a plane.
Guy Commerman

developing countries - countries that are inhabited by people that have learned to eat with their mouths shut in expectation of food to be sent to them by civilized nations.
Ward Ruyslinck
devil - God when He's drunk.
Tom Waits
dew - Mother Nature's goodnight kiss for the flowers.
Hugo Olaerts
diagnosis - the most current disease.
Karl Kraus
diagnosis by intuition - a rapid method of reaching a wrong conclusion.
J. Chalmers Da Costa
diagnostic program - a program to tell you what you already know - your file is fried.
Guy Kawasaki
dialectics - the longest way from one chatterbox to another.
Pierre-Robert Leclercq
dialect words - those terrible marks of the beast to the truly genteel.
Thomas Hardy
dialogue - a good monologue spoiled by somebody else talking.
Peter Ustinov
diamond - a lump of coal with a migraine.
L.P. Whitney
diamond necklace - a kind of platonic strangulation.
Albrecht Vergheynst
diaper rash - a boo-boo you'd rather not fix with a kiss.
Joyce Armor
diary - photography with a pencil.
Wim Kan
.diatribe - a statement made by someone else with which you disagree. If you agreed with it, it would be an eloquent masterpiece.
Walter H. Schramm
DiCaprio, Leonardo - patently the result of an unnatural act of passion between William Hague and the piglet from *Babe*.
A.A. Gill
dichotomy - operation performed on lesbians to make them normal.
Kenneth Tynan

Dickensian - adjective used to describe (a) snow at Christmas, (b) very long novels.
J.B. Morton
dictator - the alpha male in a tribe of baboons.
Rick Bayan
dictatorship - a ship that needs to be torpedoed.
Gerd de Ley
dictionary - the only place where success comes before work.
Vidal Sassoon
(see also: big dictionaries)
(to) die - to go in another direction.
Ursula K. Le Guin
diet - the temporary triumph of will over metabolism.
Rick Bayan
(see also: balanced diet, ideal diet, infallible diet, liquid diet, successful dieting)
diet book - a word to the wides.
Jasmine Birtles
dieter - one who whishes others wouldn't laugh at his expanse.
Al Bernstein
dieting - eating sensibly.
Leonard Rossiter
difficulty - the honour of the problem.
Robert Sabatier
diffidence - the better part of knowledge.
Charles Caleb Colton
digestion - the great secret of life.
Sydney Smith
digital computer - a third-grader counting on her fingers.
Robert Myers
digital watches - death's dominoes.
Heathcote Williams
dignity - a mask we wear to hide our ignorance.
Elbert Hubbard
dilate - to live long.
Mike McKinley
dilated pupils - lamaze class graduates.
Diane Briody
dilemma - a politician trying to save both of his faces at once.
John A. Lincoln
dilettante - a philanderer who seduces the several arts and deserts each in turn for another.
Oliver Herford

diligence - the virtue of the untalented.
Sigmund Graff
dimmer switch - the greatest sex and beauty aid known to womankind.
Kathy Lette
(going out to) dinner - an expensive kind of foreplay.
Theo Mestrum
(see also: family dinners)
dinner theatre - a way of positively guaranteeing that both food and theater will be amateur and mediocre, which means unthreatening and therefore desirable.
Paul Fussell
Dior's New Look - clothes worn by a man who doesn't know women, never had one and dreams of being one.
Coco Chanel
diploma - just a confirmation that you finished something.
Piet Sterckx
diplomacy - to do and say the nastiest thing in the nicest way.
Isaac Goldberg
(see also: American diplomacy)
diplomat - a person who can tell you to go to hell in such a way that you actually look forward to the trip.
Caskie Stinnett
direct action - the most drastic and usually the most effective remedy for fear.
William Burnham
director - the most overrated artist in the world. He is the only artist who, with no talent whatsoever, can be a success for fifty years without his lack of talent ever being discovered.
Orson Welles
(see also: best director)
director's wife - the female of 'director'.
Philippe Destouches
dirt - only matter out of place.
John Chipman Gray
dirty laugh - a fart with ambition.
Rudy Vandendaele
dirty mind - a joy forever.
Lew Epstein
dirty old man - a guy who has three daughters and only one bathroom.
Joey Adams

dirty woman - one that does everything I want from her.
Wolinski
disagreement - the shortest cut between two minds.
Kahlil Gibran
disappointment - simply a dream that doesn't want to become a reality.
Richard Wilkins
disasters - the rule of an exception.
Piet Theys
disaster tourism - the most successful sector of the tourist industry.
Raf Coppens
disbelief - the most enduring religion.
Bertus Aafjes
discipline - the bridge between goals and accomplishment.
Jim Rohn
disc-jockeys - electronic lice.
Anthony Burgess
disco - a period of McDonald's music.
Melba Moore
discobar - entertainment opportunity for the hard-of-hearing.
Juul Kinnaer
disco dancing - dancing for people who hate dancing... There is no syncopation, just the steady thump of a giant moron knocking in an endless nail.
Clive James
discomfort - always a necessary part of the process of enlightenment.
Pearl Cleage
discontent - the beginning of intent.
Mack Reynolds
discovery - an accident meeting a prepared mind.
Albert Szent-Györgi
(see also: great discovery)
discretion - the better part of getting your ass kicked.
Dave Henry
discussion - the sieve of the truth.
Stefano Guazzo
diseases - the tax on pleasures.
John Ray
(see also: illness)
disgruntled - a castrated pig.
David Elsensohn

dishonesty - the second-best policy.
George Carlin
disillusionment - what takes place when a youngster asks his dad for help with his algebra.
Herbert V. Prochnow
Disneyland - purgatory, with better parking space.
Herman le Compte
(see also: Euro Disneyland, ideal world, Venice)
Disneyworld - Mauschwitz.
Douglas Coupland
disobedience - the true foundation of liberty. The obedient must be slaves.
Henry David Thoreau
dispatch - the soul of business.
Philip Dormer Stanhope
dissatisfaction - the wheel pushing progress.
Lu Xun
dissatisfied man - a poor man who thinks.
Jean-Claude Brisville
dissent - the highest form of patriotism.
Thomas Jefferson
distance - the soul of reality.
Louis-Ferdinand Céline
distinction - the consequence, never the object, of a great mind.
Washington Allston
distributed system - one in which the failure of a computer you didn't even know existed can render your own computer unusable.
Leslie Lamport
distrust - a necessary qualification of a student of history.
Samuel Johnson
divas - singers who demand the earth and then complain when it's muddy.
Daisy Donovan
diversity - the most basic principle of creation. No two snowflakes, blades of grass or people are alike.
Lynn Maria Laitala
dividends - hush money to shareholders.
Jim Fisk & Robert Barron
divorce - from the Latin word meaning to rip out a man's genitals through his wallet.
Robin Williams

divorced person - one who, when angry, takes it out on whoever's nearest.
Mignon McLaughlin
divorcée - a woman who gets richer by decrees.
John S. Crosbie
divorce-lawyers - God's way to tell you to stay single.
I.C. Rapoport
divorce papers - rift certificates.
Robert Myers
DIY - Damage-It-Yourself.
Mike Allen
doctor - a person who acts like a humanitarian and charges like a plumber.
Joey Adams
(see also: best doctor, physician, smart doctor, successful doctor)
doctorship - the art of getting one up on the patient without actually killing him.
Stephen Potter
doctor's bill - the bitterest pill of all.
Gust Gils
doctor's prescription - a passport to a pharmacist's smile.
Ramon Gomez de la Serna
doctrine - nothing but the skin of truth set up and stuffed.
Henry Ward Beecher
dog - the only friend you can buy for money.
Joey Adams
(see also: guard dog, lap dog)
dogma - the attempt to create a one-ended stick.
Gabriël Laub
dogmatism - puppyism come to its full growth.
Douglas W. Jerrold
dogmatist - someone who is always right as a matter of principle.
J.V. Teunissen
doing nothing - the hardest work of all.
Malcolm S. Forbes
doltergeist - a spirit that decides to haunt someplace stupid, such as your sceptic tank.
David Genser
domestic hearth - the real theatre of the sex war.
Germaine Greer
domestic violence - the front line of the war against women.
Pearl Cleage

domestic work - the most elementary form of labour. It is suitable for those with the intelligence of rabbits.
Rebecca West
(see also: housework)
Domino's - a good name for a pizza place but a bad name for a construction company.
Tiffany Getz
donation - a confession of guilt.
Jan Greshoff
Don Juan - a tourist in a hurry.
Maurice Donnay
donkey - a horse translated into Dutch.
Georg Christoph Lichtenberg
donkey's bray - the most candid cry in all creation.
Ramon Gomez de la Serna
donsmanship - the art of criticising without actually listening.
Stephen Potter
doodling - the brooding of the hand.
Saul Steinberg
door - what a dog is perpetually on the wrong side of.
Ogden Nash
doorman - a genius who can open the door of your car with one hand, help you in with the other, and still have one left for the tip.
Dorothy Kilgallen
Dorian Graying - the unwillingness to gracefully allow one's body to show signs of aging.
Douglas Coupland
dot - simply a bribe designed to overcome the disinclination of the male.
H.L. Mencken
double feature - a show that enables you to sit through a picture you don't care to see, so you can see one you don't like.
Henry Morgan
double rape - when neither party is willing.
Raf Coppens
doublethink - the power of holding two contradictory beliefs in one's mind simultaneously, and accepting both of them.
George Orwell
doubt - a necessary precondition to meaningful action.
Donald Barthelme
douche - a female duke.
George Carlin

doughnut - the circle of life.
Steven Schwartz
downscale - instrument used by feather merchants.
Lars Hanson
downsizing - corporate euphemism for 'Let's save a little money by firing half our staff and making the other suckers work twice as hard.'
Rick Bayan
draft - white people sending black people to fight yellow people to protect the country they stole from red people.
James Rado
dragoon - a soldier who combines dash and steadiness in so equal measure that he makes his advances on foot and his retreats on horseback.
Ambrose Bierce
drama - life with the dull bits cut out.
Alfred Hitchcock
drama critic - a person who surprises the playwright by informing him what he meant.
Wilson Mizner
drama criticism - venom from contented rattlesnakes.
Percy Hammond
dramatic art - an exact science about which we have no facts.
Tristan Bernard
dramatic measures - Latin for a whopping.
F. Anstey
dramatist - ventriloquist of the soul.
Stanislaw Jerzy Lec
drastic - tic which takes desperate actions.
Tim Bruening
drawer - a mess with a knob on the end.
Henry Beard
drawing - a way of reasoning on paper.
Saul Steinberg
dread - a remote infinity of possibility.
Howard P. Kainz, Jr.
(to) dream - to live with closed eyes.
Jean Cocteau
dream (noun) - a serious psychic disease.
Yevgeni Zamyatin
(see also: daydream, nightmares)

dreamer - one who can only find his way by moonlight, and his punishment is that he sees the dawn before the rest of the world.
Oscar Wilde
dreaming - the poor retreat of the lazy, hopeless and imperfect lover.
William Congreve
dream research - a wonderful field. All you do is sleep for a living.
Stephen LaBerge
dress - a vase which the body follows.
Pierre Cardin
dress code - the unwritten law that teenagers must dress alike to assert their independence.
Joyce Armor
dressing - the one art the unqualified must practice.
Elizabeth Bowen
dried fish - a staple food in Iceland: it varies in toughness. The tougher kind tastes like toenails, and the softer kind like the skin of the soles of one's feet.
W.H. Auden
drink - what prevents you seeing yourself as others see you.
Desmond MacCarthy
drinking - the only thing you don't get better at the more you do.
J.R. Moehringer
drinks party - a room packed full of people, all rapidly talking to each other while eagerly looking for someone else.
Cindy Blake
drive-in movie - wall to wall car petting.
M. Rose Pierce
drive-in theater - a place where a guy gets to shut off his engine so he can try out his clutch.
Robert Myers
driver - the most dangerous part of a car.
Léo Campion
driving - America's last surviving form of guerrilla warfare.
Gene Perret
drug - that substance which, when injected into a rat, will produce a scientific report.
Robert Matz
 (see also: marijuana, morphine, narcotics, opium)
drunk - an alcoholic who doesn't have to go to all those boring old meetings.
Jackie Gleason
(see also: alcoholic, occasional drinker)

drunkenness - a device people employ to avoid having to think of having anything to say.
Alan Simpson
Dubai - Debbie from Birmingham.
Graeme Garden
Dublin - a city with the great advantage that it's easy to get out of.
Oliver St. John Gogarty
(see also: true Dubliner)
duchy - the wife of a duke.
Leo Rosten
duck - a bird that walks like it has been on horseback all day.
Hans Ferrée
duct tape - a babysitters best friend.
Mark Morfey
dullness - the first requisite of a good husband.
W. Somerset Maugham
dumbwaiter - one who asks if the kids would care to order dessert.
Joyce Armor
dummy teat - silencer.
Pelicano
dumpling - a very small, very rundown apartment.
P.C. Swanson
dungeon - laundry room in the basement.
Cy DeBoer
dust - a protective coating for fine furniture.
Mario Buatta
Dutch - not so much a language as a disease of the throat.
Mark Twain
Dutchmen - Germans who thinks they are not Germans because they drink milk.
Gerard Reve
Dutch treat - the major achievement of the women's movement in the nineteen-seventies.
Nora Ephron
duty - what you ask from other people.
Alexandre Dumas the younger
duty-free liquor - flying blind.
Colin Bowles
duty free shopping - Government-sponsored smuggling.
Ross Benson

dying - one of the few things that can be done just as easily lying down.
Woody Allen
dysfunctional family - any family with more than one person in it.
Mary Karr
dyspeptic - a man that can eat his cake and have it too.
Austin O'Malley

E

ear - the way to the heart.
Madeleine de Scudéry
early Christmas shopper - the only thing worse than a reformed cigarette smoker.
Liz Scott
early retirement - option now available to school-leavers.
Mike Barfield
earnestness - stupidity sent to college.
P.J. O'Rourke
Earth - the lunatic asylum of the solar system.
Samuel Parks Cadman
Earth Day - the only day of the year where being able to hacky-sack will get you laid.
Jon Stewart
earthquake - God grabbing the earth and saying, "Cough."
Richard Belzer
ease - the desire of all men.
Dorothy Parker
Easter - a national celebration of chocolate.
Mike Barfield
easy - an adjective used to describe a woman who has the sexual morals of a man.
Nancy Linn-Desmond
eating - just foreplay before having a shit.
Nigel Williams
eccentric - a man too rich to be called crazy.
Leo Rosten
eclectic - putting anything together as long as it's expensive.
Chauncey Howe
eclipse - what a cockney barber does for a living.
Edward Thompson
ecologist - someone who writes a 1,000 page book asking where have all the trees gone.
Joel Rothman
ecology - the belief that a bird in the bush is worth two in the hand.
Stanley Gibbons

economic development - development of more intensive ways of exploiting the natural environment.
Richard Wilkinson
economic independence - the foundation of the only sort of freedom worth a damn.
H.L. Mencken
economics - the science of telling you things you've known all your life, but in a language you can't understand.
Dick Armey
economic growth - a tiger from which we fear to dismount.
Richard Greene
economic theory - a systematic application and critical evaluation of the basic analytic concepts of economic theory, with an emphasis on money and why it's good.
Woody Allen
economist - someone who doesn't have the personality to be an accountant.
Robert Reich
economy - going without something you do want in case you should, some day, want something which you probably won't want.
Anthony H. Hawkins
(see also: mixed economy, planned economy)
ecotourism - a contradictio in terminis.
M.P.J.G. Claessens
ecstasy - the feeling you feel when you feel you are going to feel a feeling you never felt before.
Larry Wilde
Edinburgh - the loft extension of England.
Al Murray
editing - quarreling with writers.
Harold Ross
edition - the art of defiling expensive paper with ink just to make it unsaleable.
René Julliard
editor - one who separates the wheat from the chaff and prints the chaff.
Elbert Hubbard
(see also: good editor, great editor)
editorial - what keeps the ads apart.
Roy Herbert Thomson

Edmonton - not exactly the end of the world... but you can see it from there.
Ralph Klein
E-dophile - a word for a chat-room *nonce*.
Viz
(to) educate - to try to fill a new generation with your own prejudices.
Simon Carmiggelt
educated man - one who knows a lot and says nothing about it.
Gracie Fields
education - learning what you didn't even know you didn't know.
Daniel J. Boorstin
(see also: formal education, good education)
educational television - the bright gray blackboard.
Henri Dieuzaide
eel - a slimy, cold-blooded, snake-like creature which has provided inspiration to entire generations of district attorneys.
Chaz Bufe
effective communication - 20% what you know and 80% how you feel about what you know.
Jim Rohn
efficiency - intelligent laziness.
David Dunham
efficiency expert - a guy who puts unbreakable glass on all the fire alarms.
Milton Berle
efficient organization - one in which the accounting department knows the exact cost of every useless administrative procedure which they themselves have initiated.
E.W.R. Steacie
effort - the mode by which the inevitable comes to pass.
Sri da Avabhas
egghead - one who stands firmly on both feet in mid air on both sides of an issue.
Homer Ferguson
ego - the illusion of being only one person.
Tim Daly
egocentricity - one of the hallmarks of strong characters and original minds.
Andrew Garve
ego trip - a journey to nowhere.
Robert Half

egoism - the essence of a noble soul.
Friedrich Nietzsche
egoist - someone who cares more for himself than me.
Julian Tuwim
egomaniac - a guy who thinks he's always right and he's wrong.
Gene Perret
egotism - the anesthetic that dulls the pain of stupidity.
Frank Leahy
egotist - a person of low taste, more interested in himself than in me.
Ambrose Bierce
(see also: true egotist)
Egypt - where the Israelites would still be if Moses had been a bureaucrat.
Laurence J. Peter
Eiffel Tower - a tragic waste of meccano.
Al Murray
eighty - the time of your life when even your birthday suit needs pressing.
Bob Hope
elected official - one who gets 51 percent of the vote cast by 40 percent of the 60 percent of voters who registered.
Dan Bennett
elections - things that are held to see if the polls were right.
Joey Adams
time - when the air is full of speeches... and vice versa.
Peter Eldin
election year - the time politicians want to help us out of all the trouble they got us into in the first place.
Gil Stern
electrician - a man who wires for money.
Stan Kegel
electricity - organised lightning.
George Carlin
elegance - controlled extravagance.
Walter von Rathenau
elegy - a posthumous ode.
C. Buddingh'
elephant - the only mammal that can masturbate and keep his hands free.
François Cavanna

elevator operator - someone who never hears the end of a good story.
Les Dawson
elitist - someone who corrects your spelling.
Michael Brooke Symons
eloquence - saying the proper thing and stopping.
Stanley Link
eloquent man - he who is no beautiful speaker, but who is inwardly and desperately drunk with a certain belief.
Ralph Waldo Emerson
(to) e-mail - to play ping-pong in the universe.
Jos Ghysen
e-mail - the gateway drug of the Internet.
Clay Shirky
emancipated - a woman who behaves as badly as a man.
Mike Barfield
emancipation - the progression of women from a position of privilege to equal rights.
Marcello Mastroianni
embrace - the most common vicious circle.
Elsie Attenhofer
emergency tomato soup - hot water and ketchup.
P.J. O'Rourke
emerging intellectual - one who periodically examines himself for signs of nits.
Archie Pratt
emotion - breathing with the heart.
Pierre Reverdy
emotional health - facing reality at any cost.
Morgan Scott Peck
emotional sickness - avoiding reality at any cost.
Morgan Scott Peck
empathy - the least comfortable of human emotions.
Frances Gray Patton
employee of the month - a good example of how somebody can be both a winner and a loser at the same time.
Demetri Martin
empowered organization - one in which individuals have the knowledge, skill, desire, and opportunity to personally succeed in a way that leads to collective organizational success.
Stephen R. Covey

empty fridge - something you come to expect when you live through the locust phase of adolescence.
Ellen Goodman
encryption - a powerful defensive weapon for free people. It offers a technical guarantee of privacy, regardless of who is running the government... It's hard to think of a more powerful, less dangerous tool for liberty.
Esther Dyson
encyclopedia - a system for collecting dust in alphabetical order.
Mike Barfield
endless loop - see loop, endless.
Isaac Asimov
endurance - patience concentrated.
Thomas Carlyle
enema - an object used to brainwash men.
Nancy Grey
enemies - friends who are a little confused.
Gerrit Komrij
energy - the driving power of the nation.
Zona Gale
engagement - the first step to divorce.
Pierre Doris
engineer - someone who can build for a dollar what any damn fool can build for ten.
Robert A. Heinlein
(see also: good engineer)
engineering - the art of using imperfect solutions in search of perfect ones.
Andrej Krivda
England - the only country in the world where the food is more dangerous than sex.
Jackie Mason
(see also: Britain, London, Oxford)
English - a word in the dictionary between enema and entrails.
Tony Hancock
English (the language) - the perfect language to sell pigs in.
Michael Hartnett
(see also: bad English, correct English)
English Catholics - just Protestants, protesting against Protestantism.
D.H. Lawrence
English coffee - just toasted milk.
Christopher Fry

English countryside - scoops of mint ice cream with chips of chocolate cows.
Jim Bishop
English film - the only film that takes longer to see than to read the novel.
J.H. Goldfuss
English gentleman - a man with a passion for horses, playing with a ball, probably one broken bone in his body and in his pocket a letter to *The Times*.
René Gimpel
Englishmen - a race of cold-blooded queers with nasty complexions and terrible teeth who once conquered half the world, but still haven't figured out central heating.
P.J. O'Rourke
(see also: British, Briton)
English novel - a story in which two people fall in love and then complain to each other for 400 pages.
Colin Bowles
English Saturday - a cross between a Sunday and a Monday.
Ramon Gomez de la Serna
English spelling - an affair of memory, not of reason.
Georgina Goddard King
English winter - season ending in July, to recommence in August.
Lord Byron
engraving - the art of scratch.
John Ruskin
enjoyable - what Cain couldn't do.
Joseph Leff
(see also: favourable)
enjoyment - the way to reduce discomfort.
Theo Mestrum
ennui - the disease of hearts without feeling, and of minds without resources.
Jeanne Manon Roland
enough - better than too much.
Piet van Hoek
enough money - just a little more than you have.
Sam Ewing
enterprise - balancing risk with profit.
Pieter Klaas Jagersma
enterprising taxi driver - one who starts his meter running the instant you wave him down.
O.A. Battista

enterprising young man - one who becomes interested in a company because the owner would make a good father-in-law.
O.A. Battista
entertaining - a method of avoiding people.
Elisabeth Bibesco
enthusiasm - reason on fire.
Peter Marshall
entrepreneur - what you're called when you don't have a job.
Ted Turner
entrepreneurial profit - the expression of the value of what the entrepreneur contributes to production.
J.A. Schumpeter
entrepreneurship - the last refuge of the troublemaking individual.
Mason Cooley
environment - everything that isn't me.
Albert Einstein
environmentalist - someone concerned with the influence of affluence.
Joel Rothman
envy - hatred without a cure.
Bahya Ben Asher
enzymes - things invented by biologists that explain things which otherwise require harder thinking.
Jerome Lettvin
epic - any film so unnecessarily long that one has to go out and urinate during it.
Mike Barfield
epidural - a needle you put in a woman's back that makes her numb from the waist down... for years.
Chip Franklin
epigone - someone looking for his own identity and finds someone else's.
Sulamith Sparre
epigram - a platitude on its night out.
Philip Guedalla
(see also: brilliant epigram)
epiphany - a whim that sticks.
Brian Stanley
epitaph - a message challenging death to a duel.
Ramon Gomez de La Serna
equality - a slogan based on envy.
Alexis de Tocqueville

equator - an imaginary line that scientists draw around the world to see where the warm spots are.
Louis Verbeeck
equestrians - just pedestrians with a stable influence.
Linda Williams
equinox - a cross between a cow and a horse.
Willie Meikle
equitable tax - the one someone else pays.
Robert P. Crum
erection at will - the moral equivalent of a valid credit card.
Alex Comfort
erosion - shore leave.
Joel Rothman
erotic - word used to describe any material that's not quite pornographic enough.
Mike Barfield
erotica - the expensive, legal, respectable class of pornography.
Edmund H. Volkart
eroticism - the pornography of the liberals.
Gaston Bonheur
error - one of the sources of transformation.
Pierre Audouard
escargot - French for "fat crawling bag of phlegm".
Dave Barry
escort - a prostitute with knowledge of the theatre.
Mike Barfield
Eskimoses - the Chief Rabbi of the Eskimos.
Kevin Goldstein-Jackson
ESP - Essentially Silly People.
Cleveland Amory
esplanade - to attempt an explanation while drunk.
Kevin Mellema
esprit de corps - embalming fluid.
R.S. MacLeod
essay - a literary device for saying almost everything about almost anything.
Aldous Huxley
essayist - a lucky person who has found a way to discourse without being interrupted.
Charles Poore
estate agents - people who did not make it as second-hand car salesmen.
Billy Connolly

esteem - the basis of every friendship.
Joanna Russ
(see also: self esteem)
et cetera - the expression that makes people think you know more than you do.
Herbert V. Prochnow
eternal boredom - the price of constant vigilance.
Marion J. Levy
eternal grief - one of the pursuits of those who have nothing to do.
Madame Nerville d'Aubernon
eternal love - eternity in its most transitory form.
Hans Krailsheimer
eternity - just like now but without us.
Herman de Coninck
ethical man - a Christian holding four aces.
Mark Twain
ethics - the obligations of morality.
Lajos Kossuth
Ethiopia - a part of the world that the Creator must have fashioned when He was in a bad mood.
Ladislas Farago
ethnic cleansing – a crime justifying foreign intervention.
Paul Oestreicher
etiquette - the difference between stable manners and table manners.
Texas Bix Bender
(see also: manners)
eulogy - praise of a person who has either the advantages of wealth and power, or the consideration to be dead.
Ambrose Bierce
eunuch - a man who has had his works cut out for him.
Robert Byrne
(see also: unique)
euphemisms - unpleasant truths wearing diplomatic cologne.
Quentin Crisp
Euro Disneyland - a cultural Chernobyl.
Ariane Mnouchkine
Europe - an association of general interests, weakened by a multitude of personal interests.
Jean Amadou
European Parliament - a place that needs a laxative.
Bob Geldof

European technocrat - a gentleman who studied for a long time in order to make hens in Berry lay 27,04 eggs a month and those in Holland 28,93.
Pierre-Robert Leclercq
euthanasia - a way of putting old people out of their family's misery.
Mike Barfield
evangelism - selling a dream.
Guy Kawasaki
Eve - the better and revised edition of Adam.
Helen Vita
everything - a lot for him who doesn't expect anything.
J.C. Bloem
Eve's leaves - the first mini-skirts.
Hazel M. Beuchat
evil - that which one believes of others. It is a sin to believe evil of others, but it is seldom a mistake.
H.L. Mencken
evolution - means you're from a long line of winners.
Phil French
example - contagious behaviour.
Charles Reade
exams - sadistic lotteries.
Gerrit Komrij
(see also: final exam)
exaggeration - a truth that has lost its temper.
Kahlil Gibran
exasperation - the mind's way of spinning its wheels until patience restores traction.
George L. Griggs
Excalibur - a good name for a security company but a bad name for a tampon.
Jeff Brechlin
excellence - to do a common thing in an uncommon way.
Booker T. Washington
exceptions - rules without exceptions.
Zarko Petan
exchange - still the same.
Joseph Leff
excise - a hateful tax levied upon commodities.
Samuel Johnson
exclamation mark - a question mark with an erection.
Pierre Alechinsky

exclusiveness - a characteristic of recent riches, high society, and the skunk.
Austin O'Malley
excruciate - the ligament that attaches your ex-wife to your paycheck.
Kevin Cuddihy
excursion - detour to a restaurant.
Wim Kan
excuse - the mark of a moral coward.
Joseph Cimino
executive - an ulcer with authority.
Fred Allen
(see also: best executive, honest executive, modern executive, successful executive, valuable executive, well-adjusted executive)
executive ability - the art of getting the credit for all the hard work somebody else does.
Joey Adams
exercise - what cures all illnesses except those it causes.
Henry Root
Exeter - the second oldest college in Oxford - unless you count lodging houses, in which case it is the fourth.
Eric Arthur Barber
exhibition - a bazaar where mediocrity spreads itself out with impudence.
J.A.D. Ingres
exhibitionist - a naked man commonly arrested for standing in a window so that he might be glimpsed by a woman standing outside; when a naked *woman* is in the window and the man is standing outside, he is then arrested as a Peeping Tom.
Rick Bayan
exhilaration - that feeling you get just after a great idea hits you, and before you realize what's wrong with it.
Rex Harrison
exile - a tomb in which you can get mail.
Germaine de Staël
existence - plagiarism.
E.M. Cioran
existentialism - means that someone else can take a bath for you.
Delmore Schwartz
existentialist - someone who swims with the tide - but faster.
Quentin Crisp
exit - an entry somewhere else.
Tom Stoppard

exit door - the best part of a hospital.
Tom Brady
exodus - departure for the seaside.
J.B. Morton
expedients - the only real substitute for morals.
Holbrook Jackson
expense - equals salary plus forty bucks.
Jeffrey Jena
experience - something you don't get until after you need it.
Steven Wright
experimental psychologist - a scientist who pulls habits out of rats.
L.L. Levinson
expert - someone called in at the last minute to share the blame.
Sam Ewing
(see also: efficiency expert)
explain - simple breakfast, as opposed to with asparagus, ham, and hollandaise sauce.
Cynthia MacGregor
exploration - the essence of the human spirit.
Frank Borman
explosion - blow with which an anarchist proves his point.
Battus
extinct - a dead skunk.
Richard Lederer & James Ertner
extrajudical - an even higher degree of Kosher food.
Joseph Leff
extra money - that which you have in your possession just before the car breaks down.
Dick Armey
extravagance - the way the other fellow spends his money.
T. Harry Thompson
extravagant neighbour - one who lives beyond your means.
O.A. Battista
extremist - someone who does what he thinks God would do if He knew the facts.
Marijke Höweler
eye - the jewel of the body.
Henry David Thoreau
eye swatter - a tall, cool, natural drink.
Cynthia MacGregor

F

face - the soul of the body.
Ludwig Wittgenstein
Facebook - an internet site linking people with a shared interest: themselves.
Mike Barfield
face card - look at the comic.
Joseph Leff
face-lift - temporary restoration of the visage we wore in youth, but one size smaller.
Rick Bayan
fact - an internet rumour.
Mike Barfield
factorial - someone's attempt to make math look exciting.
Steven Wright
fag - a homosexual gentleman who has just left the room.
Truman Capote
failure - the quickest method known for making money.
Gideon Wurdz
fairies - nature's attempt to get rid of soft boys by sterilizing them.
F. Scott Fitzgerald
fairness - the opposite of passion.
Kathleen Betsko
fair play - even-handed cheating.
Mike Barfield
fair price for oil - whatever you can get plus ten per cent.
Ali Ahmed Attiga
fair tax structure - one that allows everybody to cheat evenly.
Milton Berle
fair woman - a paradise to the eye, a purgatory to the purse, and a hell to the soul.
Elizabeth Grymeston
fairway - a narrow strip of mown grass that separates two groups of golfers looking for lost balls in the rough.
Henry Beard
fairyland - nothing but the sunny country of common sense.
G.K. Chesterton

fairy stories - stories about one king going to another king to borrow a cup of sugar.
Angela Carter
faith - an illogical belief in the occurrence of the improbable.
H.L. Mencken
faithful woman - a woman who doesn't want two men suffer at the same time.
Jan Vercammen
faithless - he that says farewell when the road darkens.
J.R.R. Tolkien
Falkland Island - a small piece of land entirely surrounded by advice.
Penelope Gilliatt
(to) fall in love - to create a religion that has a fallible god.
Jorge Luis Borges
falling in love - uncorking the imagination and bottling the common sense.
Helen Rowland
false honesty - little more than a cunning deceit.
François de La Rochefoucauld
falsehood - the jockey of misfortune.
Jean Giraudoux
false modesty - a very refined form of vanity.
Jean de La Bruyère
false promise - feint hope.
Charles G. Waugh
falsies - the bust that money can buy.
Bob Levinson
fame - a happy combination of talent and timing.
Colin Bowles
(see also: literary fame)
familiarity - the opiate of the imagination.
Arnold Toynbee
family - a group of individuals united by blood and arguing about money.
Etienne Rey
(see also: dysfunctional family, happy family, very close family)
family budget - a process of checks and balances; the checks wipe out the balances.
Arthur Langer

family dinners - an ordeal of nervous indigestion, preceded by hidden resentment and ennui and accompanied by psychosomatic jitters.
Mary Frances Kennedy Fisher
family fireside - the best of schools.
Arnold H. Glasow
family jokes - the bond that keeps most families alive.
Stella Benson
family life - the normal context in which we can learn that a life filled with thinking about others instead of ourselves is the sure road to the most fulfilling joys and satisfactions.
Alan Keyes
family man - the greatest criminal of the century.
Hannah Arendt
family mealtimes - often little more than domestic abuse with a cherry on top.
Julie Burchill
family planning - working out how to keep the children occupied for the whole weekend.
Jasmine Birtles
family reunions - that time when you come face to face with your family tree and realize some branches need to be cut.
René Hicks
family room - what the bathroom becomes as soon as one wishes to use it.
Edmund H. Volkart
family vacation - one where you arrive with five bags, four kids and seven I-thought-you-packed-its.
Ivern Ball
famous - to be forgotten fifty years later than usual.
I. Boerema
fan - a compromise between storm and draught.
Tomi Ungerer
fanarchy - chaos around a celebrity.
John Hind
fanatic - someone who can't change his mind and who won't change the subject.
Winston Churchill
(see also: foolish fanatics)
fanaticism - spiritual chauvinism.
Hans Kudszus

fan club - a group of people who tell an actor he is not alone in the way he feels about himself.
Jack Carson
fantasy - the eye of the soul.
Joseph Joubert
FAQ - a company's attempt to answer commonly asked questions such as, "How do I get technical support?"
Guy Kawasaki
farce - a tragedy with the trousers down.
Brian Rix
farewell - the first step towards reunion.
Werner Lauber
farm - a hunk of land on which, if you get up early enough mornings and work late enough nights, you'll make a fortune - if you strike oil on it.
Fibber McGee
farmer - a handy man with a sense of humus.
E.B. White
farming - a pleasanter way of losing money than most.
Josephine W. Johnson
fart - a sigh in the wrong direction.
Gerd de Ley
(see also: brain fart, intestinal distress, phewy, rattler, tail-gunner)
farther - a woman breaking wind.
Willie Meikle
farticane - a humorous neologism based on 'hurricane', referring to a powerful blowing of wind.
Peter Furze
farting - a habit that is cute when babies do it and disgusting when their fathers do it.
William Sadgarden
fascism - capitalism plus murder.
Upton Sinclair
(see also: nazism)
fascist - anyone who disagrees with you.
John Koski
fashion – a substitute for taste.
R.G. Hawtrey
(see also: gut-featuring fashion, Haute Couture, women's fashion)
fashion designer - someone who does the second most beautiful thing in the world: to dress women.
Marcello Mastroianni

fashion editors - just advertising departments with legs and high heels
Richard Avedon
fast food - food delivered promptly because it isn't worth waiting for.
Mike Barfield
(see also: rabbit)
fast lane - the one you are never in.
Cy DeBoer
fat - the last preserve for unexamined bigotry.
Jennifer A. Coleman
fate - God's little nephew.
Herman Brusselmans
fathead - one person who cannot be helped by a diet.
O.A. Battista
father - a man with pictures in his wallet where his money used to be.
Milton Berle
(see also: a good father)
fatherhood - pretending that the present you love is soap-on-a-rope.
Bill Cosby
fatherly love - the ability to expect the best from your children, despite the facts.
Jasmine Birtles
father's day - mother's day with less expenses.
Hervin Hodas
fatigue - the best pillow.
Benjamin Franklin
fatness - the curse of the eating class.
Gaby vanden Berghe
fault - the name I give to my experiences.
J. Goudsblom
favourable - what Cain wanted Adam *not* to do.
Joseph Leff
(see also: enjoyable)
Fawkes, Guy - the only man who had a proper understanding of Parliament.
George Bernard Shaw

fax - a modern enhancement of the telephone, enabling us to send and receive illegible information in seconds; also ideal for communicating bad news without the inconvenience of having to talk to the person at the other end.
Rick Bayan
F.E.A.R. - False Evidence Appearing Real.
Anthony Robbins
fear - that little darkroom where negatives are developed.
Michael Pritchard
February - comes from the Latin word 'Februarius', which means 'fairly stretch of time during which one expects the professional ice-hockey season to come to an end but it does not.'
Dave Barry
February thaw - merely nature's way of warning us against overoptimism.
Bill Vaughan
Federal aid - a system of making money taken from the people look like a gift when handed back.
Carl Workman
feedback - the breakfast of champions.
Ken Blanchard
feet - incorrigible trouble makers.
Robert Morley
fellowship - the grave of learning.
Mark Pattison
felon - a person of greater enterprise than discretion.
Ambrose Bierce
female librarian - someone who completely conforms to her caricature.
Gerrit Komrij
female woman - one of the greatest institooshuns of which this land can boste.
Artemus Ward
feminine intuition - a quality perhaps even rarer in women than in men.
Ada Leverson
feminine virtue - nothing but a convenient masculine invention.
Ninon de Lenclos
femininity - one of those pivotal qualities that is so important no one can define it.
Caroline Bird

feminism - the result of a few ignorant and literal-minded women letting the cat out of the bag about which is the superior sex.
P.J. O'Rourke
feminist - a woman who intends to fulfil her destiny by aping the worst traits of her oppressors. Also a man who believes that siding with women will get him more dates.
Rick Bayan
(see also: male feminists)
feminist academics - are politically correct stupid bitches.
Camille Paglia
Feng Shui - Chinese for 'Move the sofa out a bit, that'll be £200 please'.
Jeremy Hardy
fertilizer shortage - the endangered faeces list.
Joel Rothman
fervour - the weapon of choice of the impotent.
Frantz Fanon
fetus - a benign tumor, a vampire who steals in order to live. The so-called miracle of birth is nature getting her own way.
Camille Paglia
fever - a change in body temperature that decreases a doctor's sleep, but increases his income.
Howard Bennett
fever spike - something that happens the night before a patient is scheduled for nursing home placement.
Rip Pfeiffer
fibroids - a breakfast cereal.
Victoria Wood
fiction - the truth inside the lie.
Stephen King
(see also: historical fiction)
fiddle - an instrument to tickle human ears by friction of a horse's tail on the entrails of a cat.
Ambrose Bierce
fidelity - not having more than one man in bed at the same time.
Frederic Raphael
field of flowers - a fairytale for the bees.
Marc van Halsendaele
fifties - a time of fevered fantasies - dreams of freedom and adulthood.
Colette Dowling

fifty - the age where you stop fooling yourself that if you just eat granola nobody will notice.
Stephen King
51st state - the state of denial.
Kurt Vonnegut
fight - an angry embrace.
Jan Decleir
fighting - a game where everybody is the loser.
Zora Neale Hurston
fig Newton - the force required to accelerate a fig 39.37 inches sec.
J. Hart
filing cabinet - a place where you can lose things systematically.
T. Harry Thompson
filing system - an orderly manner in which to classify important papers in such a way that you'll never find them again.
Hans Ferrée
film - fairy tales for grown-ups.
Sergio Leone
(see also: cinema, English film, Hollywood, making a film)
film directors - people too short to become actors.
Josh Greenfield
film-making - a kind of hysterical pregnancy.
Richard Lester
final decision - the one you make when you've checked with your wife.
Alfredo La Mont
final delusion - the belief that one has lost all delusions.
Maurice Chapelan
final exam - a legal form of mental child abuse.
Fons Jansen
finance - the art of passing currency from hand to hand until it finally disappears.
Robert W. Sarnoff
(see also: high finance)
finance director - someone who likes playing with number, but lacks the charisma to be an accountant.
Paul Miller
financier - a pawnbroker with imagination.
Arthur Wing Pinero
fin de siècle - tail light of a bicycle.
Russell Lucas

fine art - that in which the hand, the head, and the heart of man go together.
John Ruskin
fine artist - one who makes familiar things new and new things familiar.
Louis B. Nizer
fine soft day - a day of incessant rain accompanied by a force nine gale.
Donal Foley
fine wine - one that merely stained my teeth without stripping the enamel.
Clive James
finger painting - handscape.
Robert Myers
finish line - only the beginning of a whole new race.
Susan Saint James
Finland - a nation of drunken Captain Birds eyes.
A.A. Gill
fir - tree which keeps its leaves all year round except during Christmas.
Mike Barfield
fire - the burning of objects not intended for burning.
Tatyana Tolstaya
fireplace - an office used for discharging people.
Helen Hoke
fireproof - what you are when you marry the boss's daughter.
Joey Adams
first humans - short, hairy, tree-dwelling creatures that strongly resembled Danny DeVito.
Dave Barry
First Impressions - a good name for a dating service but not for a bungee jumping centre.
Russell Beland
First Lady - an unpaid public servant elected by one person: her husband.
Lady Bird Johnson
first love - a kind of vaccination which saves a man from catching the complaint a second time.
Honoré de Balzac
first-rate laboratory - one in which mediocre scientists can produce outstanding work.
Patrick M.S. Blackett

first-time parents - people who are anxious for their child to start talking.
Jasmine Birtles
fiscal fraud - a tax-payer who stubbornly tries to keep a little money for his own use.
Philippe Bouvard
fish - the only food that is considered spoiled once it smells like what it is.
P.J. O'Rourke
(see also: dried fish)
fish bone - posthumous revenge of the fish.
Tristan Bernard
fishing - an excuse to drink in the daytime.
Jimmy Cannon
(see also: fly-fishing, good fishing)
fish net - nothing but a lot of little holes tied together.
J.R. Miller
fitness - the first requisite to happiness.
Joseph H. Pilates
Fjord - a Norwegian automobile.
Norm Gilbert
flabbergasted - appalled over how much weight you have gained.
Michelle Feeley
flashlight - a great gadget for storing dead batteries.
Milton Berle
flat - a place where you switch off your radio and realise that it was your neighbour making the noise.
Piet Knobbeldam
flatterer - someone who feeds you with an empty spoon.
Cosino Degregorio
flattery - the art of telling someone exactly what he thinks of himself.
Paul H. Gilbert
flatulence - effect of sitting on your eyeglasses.
Stan Kegel
flea - an insect which has gone to the dogs.
Julian Tuwim
flesh - the reason why oil painting was invented.
Willem de Kooning
flextime - the essence of respect for and trust in people.
David Packard
flies - the price we pay for summer.
Ann Zwinger

flippancy - the most hopeless form of intellectual vice.
George Gissing
(to) flirt - the art of sinking into a woman's arms without falling into her hands.
Sacha Guitry
flirtation - to be intimate from a distance.
Hellmut Walters
flirting - the gentle art of making a man feel pleased with himself.
Helen Rowland
floor - the one thing you will never find in a teenager's bedroom.
Bruce Lansky
floppy disc - serious curvature of the spine.
Kris Brand
Florence - the city of tranquillity made manifest.
Katherine Cecil Thurston
Florida - God's waiting room.
Glenn Le Grice
flower - the smile of a plant.
Peter Hille
(see also: field of flowers, fuchsia, rose)
fluent tongue - the only thing a mother doesn't like her daughter to resemble her in.
Richard Brinsley Sheridan
fluorescent jacket - the true costume of Official Britain, where the standard keywords are 'health and safety'.
Jonas Andersson
flush toilet - the basis of Western civilisation.
Alan Coult
fly-fishing - the most fun you can have standing up.
Arnold Gingrich
flying - hours and hours of boredom sprinkled with a few seconds of sheer terror.
Gregory "Pappy" Boyington
flying saucers - just an optical conclusion.
Leo Rosten
flying squad - a special contingent of police whose business is to arrive at the scene of a crime shortly after all those connected with it.
J.B. Morton
focused mind - one of the most powerful forces in the Universe.
Swami Vivekananda
focus group - the plural of moron.
James A. Wolf

folk dance - originally, a way to kill wasps.
Toon Verhoeven
folklore - a collection of ridiculous notions held by other people, but not by you and me.
Margaret Halsey
folksinger - someone who sings through his nose by ear.
Bill Sadgarden
folk singing - just a bunch of fat people.
Bob Dylan
folk song - a song that nobody ever wrote.
Vicky Satter
fondu party - a huge bowl full of bubbling lava smelling of sulphur in which you dip pieces of bread and the idea is that you eat them.
Max Arab
food - an important part of a balanced diet.
Fran Lebowitz
fool - an idiot who made a career.
Gabriël Laub
(see also: learned fool)
foolish consistency - the hobglobin of little minds, adored by little statesmen and philosophers and divines.
Ralph Waldo Emerson
foolish fanatics - the men who form the lunatic fringe in all reform movements.
Theodore Roosevelt
foolproof - evidence of stupidity.
Joseph Leff
football - a game designed to keep coalminers off the streets.
Jimmy Breslin
(see also: Premier League football, soccer)
football coach - a person who is willing to lay down your life for the good of the team.
Bill Sadgarden
footballers - miry gladiators whose sole purpose in life is to position a surrogate human head between two poles.
Elizabeth Hogg
football hooligans - a compliment to the English martial spirit.
Alan Clark
football memoir - a literary form that ranks at least two grades below the trashiest airport novel.
Alan English

footnotes - the chamberpots under the bed of a book.
Francisco Gomez de Quevedo Y Villegas
forecast - a pretence of knowing what would have happened if what does happen hadn't.
Ralph Harris
forecasting - an important sense *backward*-looking, vividly compared to steering a ship by its wake.
Ralph Harris
foreign aid - taxing poor people in rich countries for the benefit of rich people in poor countries.
Bernard Rosenberg
foreign correspondent - someone who flies around from hotel to hotel and thinks that the most interesting thing about any story is the fact that he has arrived to cover it.
Tom Stoppard
foreigner - someone who doesn't understand cricket.
Anthony Couch
foreign policy - an imitation of war by other means.
Jean-François Revel
forensics - eloquence and reduction.
Gertrude Stein
foresight - the spending of fifty years of adult life in comparative drudgery in order to be able to spend the remaining ten in a nursing home.
Lambert Jeffries
forestall - to delay a golf game.
Joseph Leff
forever - a long time, but not as long as it was yesterday.
Dennis H'Ornies
forfeit - what most animals stand on.
Leopold Fechtner
forger - a person who writes things you can't bank on.
Lee Daniel Quinn
forgetfulness - an indispensable condition of the memory.
Alfred Jarry
forgetting - a poor excuse for not remembering.
J.R. DeBleyker
forgiveness - the sweetest revenge.
Isaac Friedman
forgiving - the only way to survive.
Molly Ringwald
form - the balance between tension and relaxation.
Ernest Toch

formal education - an organised attempt at preventing the birth of knowledge.
Cornelis Verhoeven
fortitude - that quality of mind which does not care what happens so long as it does not happen to us.
Elbert Hubbard
fortune - an evil chain to the body, and vice to the soul.
Epictetus
fortune-teller - someone who earns more money than someone who tells the truth.
Georg Christoph Lichtenberg
forty - the age at which we become what we are.
Charles Péguy
forum - two um plus two um.
Audrey Cowper
foundation - a large body of money completely surrounded by people who want some.
Dwight MacDonald
fountain of youth - a mixture of gin and vermouth.
Cole Porter
fox - a wolf who sends flowers.
Ruth Weston
foxhunting - the unspeakable chasing the uneatable.
Oscar Wilde
fragrance - a flower's intelligence.
Henry de Montherlant
(see also: smell)
frame - a country where the money falls apart and you can't tear the toilet paper.
Billy Wilder
(see also: Paris)
Benjamin Frankenstein - monster that flies his kite in a rain storm.
Clynch Varnadore
Frankenstein - a book about what happens when a man tries to have a baby without a woman.
Anne Mellor
frankness - usually a euphemism for rudeness.
Muriel Spark
fraud - the homage that force pays to reason.
Charles P. Curtis
freedom - the right to tell people what they do not want to hear.
George Orwell

freedom of the press - freedom to print such of the proprietor's prejudices as the advertisers don't object to.
Hannen Swaffer
free enterprise - getting other people to do your work.
Lewis Grizzard
freelance writer - a man who is paid per piece or per word or perhaps.
Robert Benchley
freeloader - the man who is always willing to come to dinner.
Damon Runyon
free love - sometimes love, but never freedom.
Elizabeth Bibesco
free press - one that prints a dictator's speech but doesn't have to.
Laurence J. Peter
free society - a society where it's safe to be unpopular.
Adlai Stevenson
free speech - making long distance calls on other people's phones.
Lee Daniel Quinn
freeway - a training ground for the sharpening of survival skills.
Sheila Ballantyne
free will - the choice between breathing and choking.
Karlheinz Deschner
French (language) - the language that turns dirt into romance.
Stephen King
Frenchman - a German with good food.
Fran Lebowitz
(see also: cursing Frenchman)
frequently - the best way to hold your tongue.
O.A. Battista
Freud, Sigmund - the father of psychoanalysis. It has no mother.
Germaine Greer
Freudian slip - when you say one thing but mean your mother.
- garment designed to be worn under a see-through blouse.
John S. Crosbie
friend - someone who sees through you and still enjoys the view.
Wilma Askinas
(see also: good friend, real friend)
friend in need - an acquaintance.
Mariella Frostrup

friendliness - to listen with a smile to things you already know, told by someone who doesn't.
Maurice Donnay
friendly word - costs nothing and is the best of all gifts.
Daphne du Maurier
friendship - tenderness without sex.
Jeanne Moreau
 (see also: esteem, old friendship, true friendship)
frienemy - a friend who acts like an enemy; a fair-weather or untrustworthy friend.
John Hind
frisbeetarianism - the belief that when you die, your soul goes up on the roof and gets stuck there.
George Carlin
frivolity - the privilege of the secure, or the refuge of the desperate.
Matthew d'Ancona
frost bite - what you get if you cross a snowman and a vampire.
Gail S. Angel
frostitute - an Eskimo hooker.
Joey Adams
(see also: hooker, prostitute)
frugality - being mean to yourself.
L.L. Levinson
fruit - a vegetable with looks and money.
P.J. O'Rourke
frustration - the wet nurse of violence.
David Abrahamsen
fuchsia - the world's most carefully spelled flower.
Jimmy Barnes
(to) fuck - to have a labial blow job.
Herman Brusselmans
fuck you - the right answer to the wrong question.
Gerd de Ley
full maturity - achieved by realizing that you have no choices to make.
Angela McBride
fundamentalist - anyone who takes the Word of God too seriously.
Rick Bayan
funeral - the best live entertainment in Ireland.
Des MacHale

funeral eulogy - a belated plea for the defense delivered after the evidence is all in.
Irvin S. Cobb
funeral insurance - the only insurance of which you are certain never to see a penny.
Fons Jansen
fur - a skin that changes from animal to animal.
Aurélien Scholl
furbling - having to wander through a maze of ropes at an airport or bank even when you are the only person in line.
Rich Hall
furious activity - no substitute for understanding.
H.H. Williams
furniture dealer - one who will offer to buy your best Edwardian chest for the price you had hoped to get for the kitchen table.
Mignon McLaughlin
fusillade - the only way to silence Parisians.
Gustave Flaubert
future - the past in preparation.
Pierre Dac
future shock - the shattering stress and disorientation that we induce in individuals by subjecting them to too much change in too short a time.
Alvin Toffler
future tense - a reason to relax now.
Joseph Leff
Futurism - spliced cinematography in paintings and diarrhoea in writing.
Ezra Pound
futurologist - someone who looks back to the year 2500.
Helmut Qualtinger

G

gaffe - when a politician tells the truth.
Michael Kinsley
gala nights - events organised by people who do nothing for people who have nothing.
Wolinski
Galaxy - five or six actresses.
J.B. Morton
gambit - a part of a leg.
Cynthia MacGregor
gambler - every man who ever created anything.
Kerry Packer
gambling - a way of getting nothing for something.
Wilson Mizner
games - the last resort of those who do not know how to idle.
Robert Lynd
game show - how television send us the message that greed is cute.
Rick Bayan
gamesmanship - the act of winning games without actually cheating.
Stephen Potter
gaming - a disease of barbarians superficially civilized.
William R. Inge
gangs - nontraditional organised crime.
George Carlin
garage sale - selling odds to meet ends.
Jacob Braude
garbage - the waste that civilization finds easy to produce, difficult to collect, and all but impossible to dispose of.
Edmund H. Volkart
garden - a thing of beauty and a job forever.
Joey Adams
 gardening - more or less a warfare against nature.
James Shirley Hibberd
gargoyle - an olive-flavoured mouthwash.
Jennifer Hart
garlic sandwich - two pieces of bread travelling in bad company.
Denison Flamingo

gasoline - the incense of civilization.
Ramon Gomez de La Serna
gay people - a people at war inside a society at peace.
Scott Thompson
gays - the epitome of capitalism.
Steven Shifflett
gelatine - a pain in the aspic.
Henry Beard
genderplex - the predicament of a person in a restaurant who is unable to determine his or her designated restroom (e.g., turtles and tortoises).
Rich Hall
genealogy - the silly idea that there is no such thing as a bastard.
Nicholas Martin
general - someone who risks *your* life for *his* country.
Gerrit Komrij
generalist - someone who generally knows nothing about everything.
Kevin Goldstein-Jackson
general manager – someone who fires personnel all the time; that way there is always a job for him.
Leo de Haes
general opinion - the opinion of one or a few for which the public is held responsible.
Muhammad Hijazi
generation gap - the difference between a ukulele and an electric guitar.
Joey Adams
generosity - the most efficient form of revenge.
Emanuel Wertheimer
genes - the hand we are dealt in the poker game of life.
Rick Bayan
genitals - a great distraction to scholarship.
Malcolm Bradbury
genius (person) - someone who understands the obvious first.
Hermann Bahr
(see also: real genius, true genius)
genius (noun) - the talent of a man who is dead.
Edmond & Jules de Goncourt
genocide - ethnic cleansing.
George Carlin

genteel - a mighty catafalque of service-with-a-smile and flattering solicitude smothering every spontaneous movement of thought or feeling.
Marshall McLuhan
gentiles - people who eat mayonnaise for no reason.
Robin Williams
gentility - what is left over from rich ancestors after the money is gone.
John Ciardi
gentle - a lovely word used to describe the action of a laxative.
William Feather
gentleman - someone who removes his hat when he's hitting a woman.
Marcel Achard
 (see also: real gentleman, southern gentleman, true gentleman)
gentleman farmer - a man who raises nothing but his hat.
Don Bale
gentleman's wash - a hurried washing of the male genitals (usually in a pub toilet sink) in anticipation of forthcoming sex.
Viz
geriatric - a German footballer scoring three goals.
Bob Monkhouse
Germans - a cruel race. Their operas last for six hours and they have no word for fluffy.
Ben Elton
German (the language) - the most extravagantly ugly language, like someone using a sick-bag on a 747.
William Rushton
Germany - the only country where pop-singers look just like their songs.
André Heller
gesticulation - any movement made by a foreigner.
J.B. Morton
getting caught - the mother of invention.
Robert Byrne
getting fired - nature's way of telling you that you had the wrong job in the first place.
Hal Lancaster
getting revenge - something you do to the other fellow to make yourself feel worse.
O.A. Battista
gibberish - creativity that nobody else understands.
Jack Gardner

Gibraltar - a little piece of Aldershot in Andalucia.
Nick Cohen
gift - a charming form of bribery.
Juul Kinnaer
gifted - a word used by critics to describe an author or performer they find too promising to disparage, and too disappointing to promote.
Edmund H. Volkart
gift shop - a place where you can see all the things you hope your friends won't send you for Christmas.
Jack Woolsey
gigolo - a fee-male.
Isaac Goldberg
gimme - an agreement between two golfers... neither of whom can putt very well.
Jim Bishop
gin - intoxication reduced to its simplest essence.
Ralph Bates
giraffe - an animal in which a little food goes a long way.
Leopold Fechtner
girdle - an accessory after the fat.
Jasmine Birtles
girl - a Jewish baby who isn't circumcised.
Henny Youngman
(see also: intelligent girl, nice girl, pretty girl, smart girl, teenage girl, well educated girl)
giving - letting someone have something you didn't want anyway.
Jan Schepens
giving advice - showing our wisdom at the expense of others.
Anthony Shaftesbury
giving birth - something like pushing a piano through a transom.
Fanny Brice
giving up - the ultimate tragedy.
Robert J. Donovan
gladiator - how a cannibal feels after a good meal.
Ian Barker
glamour - what makes a man ask for your telephone number and a woman for the name of your dressmaker.
Lilly Daché
glamour girl - a thing of beauty and an expense forever.
Lee Daniel Quinn

Glasgow - the sort of industrial city where most people live nowadays but nobody imagines living.
Alasdair Gray
glass - a well-dressed matchmaker between wine and tongue.
Julien Vandiest
Glaswegian atheist - a bloke who goes to a Rangers-Celtic match to watch the football.
Sandy Strang
globalization - Europe provides the money, Asia manufactures the goods, the U.S. provides the soldiers.
Noam Chomsky
glory - one of the forms of human indifference.
Valéry-Larbaud
glossary - shoeshine stand.
Ray Hand
glutton - an abonimable stow man.
Shelly Friedman
gluttony - an emotional escape, a sign something is eating us.
Peter de Vries
gnu - an animal of South Africa, which in its domesticated state resembles a horse, a buffalo and a stag. In its wild condition it is something like a thunderbolt, an earthquake and a cyclone.
Ambrose Bierce
goal - a dream with a deadline.
Diana Scharp Hunt
(see also: short-term goals)
God - the Celebrity-Author of the World's Best-Seller.
Daniel J. Boorstin
go home - the way to cure homesickness.
Edna Ferber
going bald - nature's way of stopping men having any more crap hairstyles.
Joe Becker
going to the opera - a sin that carries its own punishment with it.
Hannah More
gold - the king of kings.
Antoine de Rivarol
gold-digger - a girl without a heart who takes over a man without a head.
O.A. Battista
golden age - an age in which there was no governing.
Claude-F.A. Lezay-Marnesia

golden wedding - the most impressive evidence of tolerance.
Lode Marley
goldfish - flowers that move.
Han Suyin
gold rush - what happens when a line of chorus girls spot a man with a bank roll.
Mae West
golf - a game in which a ball one and a half inches in diameter is placed on a ball 8,000 miles in diameter. The object is to hit the small ball but not the larger.
John Cunningham
(see also: caddie, gimme, good golfer, professional golf)
golf cart - a vehicle with a fore cylinder engine.
Daryl Stout
golf club - a stick with a head on one end and a fool at the other.
Damien Muldoon
golf course - a poolroom moved outdoors.
Leo McCarey
golfer - a person who yells "fore," takes six,
and puts down five.
Geechy Guy
(see also: good golfer, handicapped golfer)
good - the greatest rival of the best.
Nellie L. McClung
good advice - something a man gives when he is too old to set a bad example.
François de La Rochefoucauld
good answer - what you think of later.
Sam Ewing
good apple pies - a considerable part of our domestic happiness.
Jane Austen
good art - art that allows you to enter it from a variety of angles and to emerge with a variety of views.
Mary Schmich
good behaviour - the last refuge of mediocrity.
Henry S. Haskins
good book - a friend that turns its back on you and remains a friend.
Laurence J. Peter
(The) Good Book - one of the most remarkable euphemisms ever coined.
Ashley Montagu

good bookshop - just a genteel black hole that's learnt to read.
Terry Pratchett
good breeding - an expedient to make fools and wise men equals.
Richard Steele
good cheekbones - the brassière of old age.
Barbara de Portago
good coach - someone who will make his players see what they can be rather than what they are.
Ara Parseghian
good conscience - the best make-up.
Arletty
good conversation - a poor substitute for good food.
Robert Lynd
good conversationalist - not one who remembers what was said, but says what someone wants to remember.
John Mason Brown
good cook - a sorceress who dispenses happiness.
Elsa Schiaparelli
good critic - the sorcerer who makes some hidden spring gush fort unexpectedly under our feet.
François Mauriac
good design - clear thinking made visual.
Edward Tufte
good editor - a charming man, who sends me large checks, praises my work, my physical beauty, and my sexual prowess, and who has a stranglehold on the publisher and the bank.
John Cheever
good education - the next best thing to a pushy mother.
Charles M. Schulz
good engineer - a person who makes a design that works with as few original ideas as possible. There are no prima donnas in engineering.
Freeman Dyson
good example - the most boring form of generosity.
Gerd de Ley
good executive - a man who isn't afraid to correct a mistake made by his secretary - no matter how pretty she is.
O.A. Battista
good family - one that used to be better.
Cleveland Amory
good father - a little bit of a mother.
Lee Salk

good fishing - just a matter if timing. You have to get there yesterday.
Milton Berle
good friend - one who tells you your faults in private.
Ken Alstad
good golfer - someone who has the determination to win and the patience to wait for the breaks.
Gary Player
good government - a bad one in a hell of a fright.
Joyce Carey
good guest - someone who knows when to leave.
Prince Philip
good hairdresser - someone who can express every mood and every passion of the human heart.
W. Somerset Maugham
good holiday - one spent among people whose notions of time are vaguer than yours.
J.B. Priestley
good humour - one of the best articles of dress one can wear in society.
William Makepeace Thackeray
good husband - one who is never the first to go to sleep at night or the last to awake in the morning.
Honoré de Balzac
good intentions - the source of more folly than all other causes put together.
Robert A. Heinlein
good joke - a tautology, because a bad joke isn't a joke.
Herman Brusselmans
good journalist - a kind of cross between Galahad and William Randolph Hearst.
I.F. Stone
good laugh - the best pesticide.
Vladimir Nabokov
good leader - a person who solves more problems than he creates.
Al Schock
good life - one inspired by love and guided by knowledge.
Bertrand Russell
good listener - a good talker with a sore throat.
Katharine Whitehorn
good loser - a person who can stick to a diet.
O.A. Battista

good lover - someone who can read a woman's body.
Goedele Liekens
good luck - another name for tenacity of purpose.
Ralph Waldo Emerson
good man - a failed villain.
Adriaan Morriën
good management - the art of making problems so interesting and their solutions so constructive that everyone wants to get to work and deal with them.
Paul Hawken
good manager - a man who isn't worried about his own career but rather the careers of those who work for him.
H.S.M. Burns
good manners - traffic rules for society.
Michael Levine
good marriage - the union of two forgivers.
Ruth Graham
good memory - one trained to forget the trivial.
Clifton Fadiman
good morning - a contradiction of terms.
Jim Davis
good music - wine turned to sound.
Ella Wheeler Wilcox
goodness - easier to recognize than to define.
W.H. Auden
good neighbour - a fellow who smiles at you over the back fence, but doesn't climb over it.
Arthur Baer
good newspaper - a nation talking to itself.
Arthur Miller
good old days - period when our ancestors had a very difficult time.
C. Buddingh'
good order - the foundation of all good things.
Edmund Burke
good painting - a postage stamp which a century ago sticks on itself in order to certify its delivery in the future.
Ramon Gomez de La Serna
good patient - one who, having found a good doctor, sticks to him until he dies.
Oliver Wendell Holmes

good person - somebody who does good, but usually not very well.
Alex Ayres
good philosopher - one who does not take ideas seriously.
Edward Abbey
good poem - the capturing of a specific emotional moment.
Philip Larkin
good politician - a breed quite as unthinkable as an honest burglar.
H.L. Mencken
good poster - a visual telegram.
A.M. Cassandre
good president - someone who exerts control and leadership over a meeting that is, in any event, superfluous because of his expert planning.
Cornelis Verhoeven
good programmer - someone who looks both ways before crossing a one-way street.
Doug Linder
good pun - its own reword.
Stephanie Maxey
good salesman - one who can convince his wife that polyester us the generic name for mink.
Milton Berle
good referee - the one you don't see.
Henry Root
good review - just another stay of execution.
Dustin Hoffman
Good Scout - the sort of man who if a woman trusts him with one-hundredth of her heart will take the whole heart and twist and batter it and read the paper and smoke his pipe and pay the bills: serenely unaware.
Mary MacLane
good sense - a thing all need, few have, and none think they want.
Benjamin Franklin
good speaker - one who gets more applause when he is finished than when he is introduced.
O.A. Battista
good storyteller - a person who has a good memory and hopes the other people haven't.
Irvin S. Cobb
good taste - the modesty of the mind.
Emile de Girardin

good teacher - one who protects his pupils from his own influence.
Bruce Lee
good teaching - one-fourth preparation and three-fourths theater.
Gail Godwin
good title - the title of a successful book.
Raymond Chandler
good wife - someone who lets you keep your fishing maggots in the fridge during warm weather.
Paul Carman
goodwill - the one and only asset that competition cannot undersell or destroy.
Marshall Field
good wine - what starts and ends with a smile.
William Sokolin
good women - hidden treasures who are only safe because nobody looks for them.
Dorothy Parker
good writer - a writer who allows himself plenty of carelessness.
Renate Rubinstein
good writing - to say an old thing a new way or to say a new thing and old way.
Richard Harding Davis
gorgonzola - the corpse of a dead cheese.
Colin Bowles
(to) gossip - to hear something you like about someone you don't.
Earl Wilson
gossip (noun) - the only thing that travels faster than e-mail.
Angie Papadakis
(see also: malicious gossip)
(to) gossip about yourself - the only way you can talk about yourself without boring the others.
Eugène Marbeau
gossip columnist - Judas with a notebook.
Colin Bowles
goths - mimes with long hair and trenchcoats.
Adam Rixey
goto - a programming tool that exists to allow structured programmers to complain about unstructured programmers.
Ray Simard

gourmand - serious eater whose culinary opinions carry at least as much weight as he does.
Henry Beard
gourmet - a glutton who reads French.
Colin Bowles
gout - a physician's name for the rheumatism of a rich patient.
Ambrose Bierce
(to) govern - to choose how the revenue raised from taxes is spent.
Gore Vidal
governor - the most anxious man in the prison.
George Bernard Shaw
government - the only vessel known to leak from the top.
James Reston
(see also: art of government, best government, good government, over-government)
government bureau - the nearest thing to eternal life that we'll ever see on this earth.
Ronald Reagan
government regulation - a sledgehammer which misses the nut.
John Blundell
government subsidy - getting just some of your own money back.
Daniel J. Metzger
grace - the outward expression of the inward harmony of the soul.
William Hazlitt
grade school - the snooze button on the clock-radio of life.
John Rogers
grad student - a device for converting a mixture of pizza and caffeine into publications, etc.
Unca Ullu
graduation ceremony - an event where the commencement speaker tells thousands of students dressed in identical caps and gowns that individuality is the key to success.
Robert Orben
grammar - the grave of letters.
Elbert Hubbard
grammar schools - public schools without the sodomy.
Tony Parsons
Grand Canyon - a marvellous place to drop one's mother-in-law.
Ferdinand Foch
grandchildren - the flash backs of your children.
Kris Jan Jacobs

grandmother - an old lady who keeps your mother from spanking you.
Robert Myers
Grand Old Man - anyone with snow-white hair who has kept out of jail till eighty.
Stephen Leacock
grand opera - a form of musical entertainment for people who hate music.
Edward Abbey
grandparents - people who come to the house, spoil the children, and then go home.
Steve Allen
graphic design - making vehicles for thoughts.
Jurriaan Schrofer
grass widow - the wife of a vegetarian.
John S. Crosbie
gratitude - the rosemary of the heart.
Minna Antrim
(see also: true gratitude)
gravity - a contributing factor in 73 percent of all accidents involving falling objects.
Dave Barry
Grease - a movie of such grubbiness that after seeing it I felt like washing my skull out with soap.
Clive James
great art - an instant arrested in eternity.
James Gibbons Huneker
great artist - one who conquers the romantic in himself.
Henry Miller
great city - one that handles art and garbage equally well.
Bob Talbert
great courage - the daughter of great fear.
Francisco Gomez de Quevedo Y Villegas
great dame - a soldier in high heels.
Marie Brenner
great discovery - a fact whose appearance in science gives rise to shining ideas, whose light dispels many obscurities and shows us new paths.
Claude Bernard
great editor - a man of outstanding talent who owns 51 per cent of his newspaper's stock.
Henry Watterson

greatest happiness - knowing that you do not necessarily require happiness.
William Saroyan
greatest hero - the one who is master of his desires.
Bhartrihari
greatest intelligence - precisely the one that suffers from its own limitations.
André Gide
greatest warrior - the one who fights for peace.
Holly Near
great events - frequently the result of little coincidences.
Boris Jeltsin
great journalist - someone who sells the candle while he burns his fingers.
Pierre Nora
great lawyer - someone who succeeds in telling his barber how his hair should be cut.
Maurice Garçon
great literature - simply language charged with meaning to the utmost possible degree.
George Orwell
great man - one who can have power and not abuse it.
Henry L. Doherty
great mind - one that can forget or look beyond itself.
William Hazlitt
greatness - a zigzag streak of lightning in the brain.
Herbert H. Asquith
great philosophers - poets who believe in the reality of their own poems.
Antonio Machado
great photograph - one that fully expresses what one feels, in the deepest sense, about what is being photographed.
Ansel Adams
great restaurants - mouth-brothels.
Frederic Raphael
great roe - a mythological beast with the head of a lion and the body of a lion, though not the same lion.
Woody Allen
great scandal - the public version of a great secret.
Sidney Tremayne
great society - a place where men are more concerned with the quality of their goals than the quantity of their goods.
Lyndon B. Johnson

great truth - a truth whose opposite is also a great truth.
Thomas Mann
great virtues - bank notes you cannot exchange.
Guy de Maupassant
great wealth - the immediate cause of poverty.
Jean de La Bruyère
great work - a landscape painted so well that the artist disappears in it.
Pierre Boulez
great writers - the saints for the godless.
Anita Brookner
Greece - a vineyard with no fence, squeezed by just a few people.
Vassilis Vassilikos
greed - envy with its sleeves rolled up.
George F. Will
(see also: private greed)
Greeks - dirty and impoverished descendants of a bunch of la-de-da fruit salads who invented democracy and then forgot to use it while walking around like girls.
P.J. O'Rourke
Greek tragedy - the sort of drama where one character says to another, "If you don't kill mother, I will."
Spyros Skouras
green fingers - the extension of a verdant heart.
Russell Page
grey - a colour that always seems on the eve of changing to some other colour.
G.K. Chesterton
grey hairs - God's graffiti.
Bill Cosby
grief - a mute sense of panic.
Marian Roach
(see also: eternal grief)
grin - the strip-tease of the smile.
Paul Rodenko
gripe - a ripe grape.
Bill Sadgarden
grocery store - the great equalizer where mankind comes to grips with the facts of life like toilet tissue.
Joseph Goldberg
gross ignorance - 144 times worse than ordinary ignorance.
Bennett A. Cerf

gross incompetence - 144 computer programmers.
James Crick
gross stupidity - 144 politicians.
Joseph Leff
growing old - being increasingly penalized for a crime you haven't committed.
Anthony Powell
grown-up - a child with layers on.
Woody Harrelson
growth - barely controlled damage.
James Richardson
(to) grow up - something for which you need a whole lifetime.
Lea Couzin
grumbling - the death of love.
Marlène Dietrich
grunge - lesbian feminist clothing and fashion in the 1970s.
Urvashi Vaid
guard dog - someone who is not hypocritical towards visitors.
Battus
guests - the delight of leisure, and the solace of ennui.
Agnes Repplier
(see also: good guest)
guide - a guy who knows where to find whiskey in the jungle.
John Wayne
guillotine - a French chopping centre.
John S. Crosbie
guilt - the Mafia of the mind.
Bob Mandel
guilty conscience - the mother of invention.
Carolyn Wells
guitar - a hole filled with wind instead of water.
Gerardo Diego
gullible - isn't in the dictionary and you can confirm that by looking it up.
Steven Wright
gun - the ambience of our society.
Mark Medoff
gun stripping - the tea ceremony of America.
Steve Aylett
gut-featuring fashion - the sartorial equivalent of talking loudly, and intimately, on a mobile phone in a crowded train.
Isabel Fonseca

gynaecologist - a man who will look in your vagina but never in your eyes.
Jennifer Saunders
gyrate - what a gigolo usually charges.
Stan Kegel

habit - the easiest way to be wrong again.
Laurence J. Peter
hacker - any person who derives joy from discovering ways to circumvent limitations.
Bob Bickford
haiku - an open door that looks shut.
Reginald H. Blyth
hair - the only one real cure for baldness.
Gene Perret
(see also: grey hairs)
haircut - a metaphysical operation.
Julio Cortazar
hairdresser's - a place where some women go to dye.
Geoff Tibballs
(see also: good hairdresser)
Hairy Krishna - a religious sect for baldies.
Milton Berle
halo - only one more thing to keep clean.
Christopher Fry
hamburger - a word which translates as health risk.
Jonathan Meades
Hamlet - a great play, but there are far too many quotations in it.
Hugh Leonard
hammer - a French screwdriver.
Reinhold Aman
hand - the cutting edge of the mind.
Jacob Bronowski
handicapped golfer - anybody who plays with his boss.
Milton Berle
handwriting - civilization's casual encephalogram.
Lance Morrow
hang-gliding - a novel enough way to commit suicide.
Viv Stanshall
hanging - the worst use man can be put to.
Henry Wotton
hangover - the wrath of the grapes.
Dorothy Parker

Hansard - history's ear, already listening.
Herbert Samuel
happily married man - husband with mistress as yet unknown to wife.
Mike Barfield
happily married woman - one who can enjoy a good cry without having a good reason for it.
O.A. Battista
happiness - nothing more than good health and a bad memory.
Albert Schweitzer
(see also: greatest happiness, perfect happiness, real happiness)
happy childhood - the best horseshoe nail.
Mignon McLaughlin
happy ending - our national belief.
Mary McCarthy
happy family - an earlier heaven.
John Bowring
happy home - one in which each spouse grants the possibility that the other may be right, though neither believes it.
Don Fraser
Happy Hour - a depressing comment on the rest of the day and a victory for the most limited Dionysian view of human nature.
John Ralston Saul
happy life - one spent in learning, earning and yearning.
Lillian Gish
happy marriage - usually an unearned miracle.
Sloan Wilson
happy slaves - the most bitter enemies of freedom.
Marie von Ebner-Eschenbach
happy youth - an invention of the old man.
Paul Guimard
hara-kiri - Caesarean for men.
Wim Kan
hard SF - a form of alternate universe fiction, set in a world where the world-view of American engineers in the late twentieth century is a precise reflection of The Way Things Are.
Soren F. Petersen
hardware - the part of the computer that can be kicked.
Jeff Pesis
(see also: software)
hard work - a series of easy jobs that you failed to do well.
O.A. Battista

harem - a floor show with a husband.
Milton Berle
harp - a nude piano.
Tom O'Horgan
harpist - a person who pulls strings to get ahead.
Leopold Fechtner
harpsicord - musical instrument that sounds like two skeletons copulating on a corrugated tin roof.
Thomas Beecham
haste - a Western form of laziness.
Albrecht Vergheynst
hat - the difference between wearing clothes and wearing a costume; the difference between dressed - and being dressed up; the difference between looking adequate and looking your best.
Martha Sliter
hatchet - what a hen does to an egg.
Leopold Fechtner
hate - recycled love.
Jeffrey Bernard
Haute Couture - what should be fun, foolish and almost unwearable.
Christan Lacroix
having a baby - one of the hardest and most strenuous things known to man.
Anna Raeburn
Hawaii - a great place to be lei'd.
M. Rose Pierce
hay fever - the real Flower Power.
L.L. Levinson
headache - an underestimated means of birth control.
Rogier van de Ree
head of department - someone who doesn't have to make his own tea.
Michael Schiff
head over heels in love - advanced intercourse position.
Mike Barfield
headscarf - a trademark; a Star of David for women.
Chahdortt Djavann
headstone - death's bookmark.
Les Coleman
health - having the same diseases as one's neighbours.
Quentin Crisp

health club patrons - men with breasts the size of lobby furniture.
Richard Jeni
health food - any food whose flavor is indistinguishable from that of the package in which it is sold.
Henry Beard
healthy person - someone who isn't examined for long enough by the doctors.
Walter van den Broeck
hearse - just Death's taxi.
Jeroen Brouwers
heart - something we are always losing but never get rid of.
Paul Rodenko
(see also: loving heart)
heart surgeon - highly qualified plumber.
A.G. Brom
heaven - an American salary, a Chinese cook, an English house, and a Japanese wife. Hell is defined as having a Chinese salary, an English cook, a Japanese house, and an American wife.
James H. Kabler, III
heavy metal - the idiot-bastard spawn of rock.
Tim Holmes
Hebrew - a male Jew, as distinguished from the Shebrew, an altogether superior creation.
Ambrose Bierce
heckler - a good example of why some animals eat their young.
Jim Samuels
heirlooms - all the things your grandmother wanted more than money.
Milton Berle
helicopter - a flying corkscrew.
Ramon Gomez de la Serna
hell - four men in a car talking about football.
David Bailey
hemorrhoids - nature's revenge for the American diet.
Chaz Bufe
hen - only an egg's way of making another egg.
Samuel Butler
herd - the result of love in bloom.
Texas Bix Bender
hereditary wealth - a premium paid to idleness.
William Godwin

heredity - what a man believes in until his son begins to behave like a delinquent.
Mort Sahl
heresy - another word for freedom of thought.
Graham Greene
heretic - a fellow who disagrees with you regarding something neither of you knows anything about.
William Brann
hero - the shortest-lived profession on earth.
Will Rogers
(see also: greatest hero, real heroes)
heroin - girl who is perfectly charming to live with, in a book.
Mark Twain
heroism - endurance for one moment more.
George Kennan
hero-worship - pooled self-esteem.
William R. Inge
(to) hesitate - to give fate time to be ahead of our decisions.
Julien de Valckenaere
heterodoxy - another man's doxy.
William Warburton
hibernation - a covert preparation for a more overt action.
Ralph Waldo Ellison
hick town - one in which there is no place to go where you shouldn't be.
Alexander Woollcott
hi-fi - Cuban greeting.
Toon Verhoeven
highbrow - person who reads a novel before it is adapted for television.
Mike Barfield
high finance - knowing the difference between one and ten, multiplying, subtracting and adding. You just add noughts. It is no more than that.
John Bentley
high-heeled shoe - a marvellously contradictory item; it brings a woman to a man's height but makes sure she cannot keep up with him.
Germaine Greer
high heels - shoes invented by a woman that was kissed on the forehead.
Jacques Fath

high official - a person who can stay away from his office without being missed.
Marc Callewaert
high salary - the slender thread that many a neurotic ego hangs by.
Mignon McLaughlin
high school - the only thing that ever kept me from going to college.
Edward Friedman
hijack - a tool for changing airline tires.
Leopold Fechtner
hills - the earth's gesture of despair for the unreachable.
Rabindranâth Tagore
hindsight - foresight without a future.
Mark Andrus
hip - the sophistication of the wise primitive in a giant jungle.
Norman Mailer
hippie - someone who looks like Tarzan, walks like Jane and smells like Cheeta.
Ronald Reagan
hippogriff - an animal (now extinct) which was half horse and half griffin. The griffin was a compound creature, half lion and half eagle. The hippogriff was, therefore, only one quarter eagle, which is $2.50 in gold. Zoology is full of surprises.
Ambrose Bierce
Hirst, Damien - the artist who can transform a pickled bovine into a cash cow.
Rachel Campbell-Johnston
historian - someone who wasn't there either.
Frithiof Brandt
historical analogy - the last refuge of people who can't grasp the current situation.
Kim Stanley Robinson
historical fiction - a standing reminder of the fact that history is about human beings.
Helen M. Cam
historical romance - the only kind of book where chastity really counts.
Barbara Cartland
historical words - words spoken by the great after their death.
André Prévot

history - the short trudge from Adam to atom.
L.L. Levinson
(see also: human history)
history-book - criminal record of humanity.
Wolfram Weidner
hits - texts that must be sung because they are too stupid to be recited.
Gisela Uhlen
hobby - dummy for grown-ups.
Julien de Valckenaere
hockey - football with crutches.
Piet Grijs
(see also: ice hockey)
holding - the plural of building.
Steven de Batselier
holding company - a thing where you hand an accomplice the goods while the policeman searches you.
Will Rogers
hole - nothing at all, but you can break your neck in it.
Austin O'Malley
hole-in-one - the difference between a male and female golfer.
Jim Davidson
holiday - short period between plans and memories.
Lea Couzin
(see also: perpetual holiday, summer holidays, vacation)
holiday resort - a place where they charge you enough for the eleven months you're not there.
Herbert V. Prochnow
holiness - an infinite compassion for others.
Ralph Iron
holistic medicine - not taking any notice of one's doctor.
Malcolm Burgess
Hollywood - a place where you spend more than you make, on things you don't need, to impress people you don't like.
Ken Murray
(see also: Beverly Hills, Los Angeles, movie star, Oscar statuette)
Hollywood aristocrat - anyone who can trace his ancestry back to his father.
Jay Leno
Hollywood Boulevard - the imitation of a Dream.
John Rechy
Hollywood contact man - mostly all con with no tact.
Rex Reed

Hollywood marriage - a good way to spend a weekend.
Leopold Fechtner
home - the place where the husband runs the show, but the wife still writes the script.
Cybill Shepherd
(see also: happy home)
home cooking - where many a man thinks his wife is.
Jimmy Durante
homeless musician - one without a girlfriend.
Dave Barry
home-made dishes - the ones that drive one from home.
Thomas Hood
homeopathist - the humorist of the medical profession.
Ambrose Bierce
homeopathy - a mingled mass of perverse ingenuity, of tinsel erudition, f imbecile credulity, and artful misrepresentation.
Oliver Wendell Holmes
homeowner - a person who is always on his way to a hardware store.
Herbert V. Prochnow Jr.
home pregnancy test - a chance to panic sooner.
Joyce Armor
home-sickness - to want something back that was never there.
Renate Rubinstein
homework - work that kids leave at home.
Jasmine Birtles
'homo' - the legitimate child of the 'suffragette'.
Wyndham Lewis
homogenous - a brilliant gay.
Stan Kegel
homophobia - the irrational fear that three fags will break into your house and redecorate it against your will.
Tom Ammiano
homo sapiens - a race that is dying out.
Gerd de Ley
homosexual - somebody who doesn't believe in mixed marriages.
Milton Berle
homosexuality - God's way of insuring that the truly gifted aren't burdened with children.
Sam Austin
honest executive - one who shares the credit with the person who did all the work.
E.C. McKenzie

honest man - someone who gets a little shy when he is told that he is honest.
Max Frisch
honest psychiatrist - one who will admit how much some of his patients help him.
O.A. Battista
honest politician - one who, when he is bought, will stay bought.
Simon Cameron
honest poverty - a gem that even a king might be proud to call his own, but I wish to sell out.
Mark Twain
honest statesmanship - the wise employment of individual meanness for the public good.
Abraham Lincoln
honesty - the best policy unless you are a crook.
Winston Groom
honeymoon - a short period of doting between dating and debting.
Roy Bandy
honeymooning - a very overrated occupation.
Noël Coward
honeymoon sandwich - lettuce alone without dressing.
Susan Richman
Hong Kong - a place where you went broke saving money.
Shirley MacLaine
Honolulu - a place that's got everything. Sand for the children, sun for the wife, sharks for the wife's mother.
Ken Dodd
honor - a badge that you cannot pin on yourself.
O.A. Battista
hoo - he or she (when gender is unknown).
Julia Kest
hooker - a working woman commonly despised by people who sell themselves for even less.
Rick Bayan
(see also: frostitute, prostitute)
hooliganism - not a British disease - we simply perfected it.
Laurie Graham
(to) hope - to give the lie to the future.
E.M. Cioran
hope (noun) - what keeps all suffering in place.
Robert Anthony

hormones - the little critters that make pregnant women act demented.
Joyce Armor
horn - modern day death bell.
Fernand Lambrecht
hors d'oeuvre - a ham sandwich cut into forty pieces.
Jack Benny
horse - an animal dangerous at both ends and uncomfortable in the middle.
Ian Fleming
(see also: racehorse)
horseracing breakfast - a cough and a copy of the *Sporting Life*.
Simon Barnes
horse sense - what keeps horses from betting on what people will do.
Ray Nash
horse show - a lot of horses showing their asses to a lot of horse's asses showing their horses.
Denis Leary
horse's turd - the status symbol of a sparrow.
Gerd de Ley
hospit - Equine Saliva.
M. Rose Pierce
hospital - a building that ought to have the recovery room adjoining the cashier's office.
Francis Walsh
hospital bed - a parked taxi with the meter running.
Frank Scully
hospitality - the virtue which induces us to feed and lodge certain persons who are not in need of food and lodging.
Ambrose Bierce
hotel - a place you give good dollars for bad quarters.
Marsha Coleman
hotel tea - to mix together a plastic envelope containing too much sugar, a small plastic pot of something which is not milk but has curdled anyway, and a thin brown packet seemingly containing the ashes of a cremated mole.
Frank Muir
hot lunch - sounds better than it tastes.
Cynthia Copeland Lewis
hot pants - breeches of promise.
M. Rose Pierce

hour record - 61 minutes.
Guy Mortier
house - a machine for living in.
Le Corbusier
household - a choreography of large and small mammals, pursuing their own cross-purposes.
Mary Catherine Bateson
household tasks - easier and quicker when they are done by somebody else.
James Thorpe
housekeeping - the acid test for women.
André Maurois
House of Commons - a Palace of Illogicalities.
Lord George Brown
House of Lords - a model of how to care for the elderly.
Frank Field
housewives -sleep-in maids.
Neil Simon
housework - something you do that nobody notices until you don't do it.
Mary Mannion
(see also: domestic work)
howl - the darkest cry in the landscape.
Ramon Gomez de La Serna
hug - the perfect gift - one size fits all, and nobody minds if you exchange it.
Ivern Ball
hula - welcome waggin'.
Frank Tyger
human being - an ingenious assembly of portable plumbing.
Christopher Morley
(see also: first humans, man)
human body - the only machine for which there are no spare parts.
Herman M. Biggs
human brain - something like a TV set. When it goes blank, it's time to turn off the sound.
Pat Elphinstone
human ego - the only thing that can keep growing without nourishment.
Marshall Lumsden

human history - the story of an ape playing with a box of matches on a petrol dump.
David Ormsby-Gore
humanism - progressivist optimism modified by fashionable despair.
Bernard Williams
humanitarianism - never sacrificing a human being to a purpose.
Albert Schweitzer
humanity - an unbearable family.
Tomi Ungerer
human leg - the best stocking stuffer.
Norm MacDonald
human life - a short period of helplessness.
Juul Kinnaer
human nature - something that has to be overcome.
Rita Rudner
human race - the chief obstacle to the progress of the human race.
Don Marquis
human service - the highest form of self-interest for the person who serves.
Elbert Hubbard
humiliation - a vast country of imprecise boundaries.
Mignon McLaughlin
humility - the virtue of a doormat at the foot of the stairs.
Antoon Vloemans
hummingbird - something between a butterfly and a bird.
Ramon Gomez de la Serna
humour - merely tragedy standing on its head with its pants torn.
Irvin S. Cobb
(see also: good humour, sense of humour)
humorist - a man who feels bad but who feels good about it.
Don Herold
hunch - creativity trying to tell you something.
Frank Capra
100 Year War - the event of that century.
Herman Brusselmans
Hungarian - a man who is behind you in a revolving door but gets out in front of you.
George Mikes
hunger - the handmaid of genius.
Mark Twain
(see also: real hunger)

hunter - the only animal in the forest that deserves to be hunted.
Kevin Langdon
hunting - ninety per cent of the fun of war for ten per cent of the risk.
Philip Warburton Lee
(see also: foxhunting)
hurry - the weakness of fools.
Baltasar Graciàn Y Morales
hurtful act - the transference to others of the degradation which we bear in ourselves.
Simone Weil
husband - a man who lost his liberty in the pursuit of happiness.
Milton Berle
 (see also: civilized husband, good husband, ideal husband, model husband)
hustler - a man who will talk you into giving him a free ride and make it seem as if he is doing you a great favour.
Bill Veeck
hydrogen - a light, odorless gas, which, given enough time, turns into people.
John P. Wiley Jr.
hygiene - the corruption of medicine by morality.
H.L. Mencken
hymen - a greeting to male companions.
Mike Leiwig
hymenopteran - a gynecologist specializing in examination of virgins.
Bob Dvorak
hypertonic - Turkish coffee.
Stan Kegel
hypochondria - the imaginary complaints of indestructible old ladies.
E.B. White
hypochondriac - someone who remembers how many measles he had.
Colin Bowles
(see also: real hypochondriac)
hypocrisy - the Vaseline of social intercourse.
J.R. Newman
hypocrite - a person who - but who isn't?
Don Marquis
(see also: true hypocrite)

hysteria - a snake whose scales are tiny mirrors in which the dead world takes on a semblance of life.
Nathanael West

I

i - the little finger of the alphabet.
Ramón Gómez de la Serna
I - the most popular letter in the alphabet.
Oliver Herford
ice hockey - a form of disorderly conduct in which the score is kept.
Doug Larson
ice skating - a sport where you talk about sequins, earrings and plunging necklines - and you are talking about men.
Christine Brennan
icicle - a stiff piece of water.
Fred Allen
icon - just another word for a washed-up has-been.
Bob Dylan
idea - salvation by imagination.
Frank Lloyd Wright
(see also: better ideas, simple ideas)
ideal - a wall with nothing behind it.
Adrien Vély
ideal community - one that has a place for every human gift.
Margaret Mead
ideal diet - one that takes off five pounds for good intentions.
Jacob Braude
ideal government - despotism tempered by assassination.
John C.W. Reith
ideal - one who treats his wife like a new car.
Dan Bennett
ideal income - a thousand dollars a day - and expenses.
Pierre Lorillard
idealism - the noble toga that political gentlemen drape over their will to power.
Aldous Huxley
idealist - a man with both feet planted firmly in the air.
Franklin D. Roosevelt
ideal job - one for which you are paid large sums for doing absolutely nothing at all.
Alan Coren

ideal love - a lie spread by the poets.
Alphonse Daudet
ideal man - the one who can conceal his true nature.
Jan Leyers
ideal marriage - marriage that consists of a deaf husband and a blind wife.
Pàdraic Colum
ideal mystery - one you would read if the end was missing.
Raymond Chandler
ideal place - the one in which it is most natural to live as a foreigner.
Italo Calvino
ideal school - one without pupils.
Paul Kiks
ideal society - a drama enacted exclusively in the imagination.
George Santayana
ideal stenographer - one who can type as fast as she can talk.
O.A. Battista
ideal wife - the one who left you.
Olivier de Kersauson
ideal woman - the one who, although faithful, is as nice to you as the one who cheats on you.
Hervé Bazin
ideal world - Disneyland without entrance fees.
Mike Barfield
identification - owning up to being the one who put that ding in the other car.
Cynthia MacGregor
identity - just a catalogue of our impotence. We are what we cannot be.
Arnon Grunberg
ieologies - ideas with weapons.
Ignazio Silone
idiophone - the work of the man who designed telephone boxes in such a way that however you approach them the door is always on the other side.
Denis Norden
idiot - a member of a large and powerful tribe whose influence in human affairs has always been dominant and controlling.
Ambrose Bierce
idiot box - the part of the envelope that tells a person where to place the stamp when they can't quite figure it out for themselves.
Rich Hall

idleness - an appendix to nobility.
Robert Burton
idlers - people who rust on their laurels.
Louis A. Safian
I do - the longest sentence you can form with two words.
H.L. Mencken
idol - the measure of the worshipper.
James Russell Lowell
if - a two letter word for 'futility'.
Louis Phillips
igloo - an icicle built for two.
John S. Crosbie
ignoramus - a person who is both stupid and an arsehole.
Victor Lewis-Smith
ignorance - the mother of research.
Laurence J. Peter
ignorant person - one who doesn't know what you have just found out.
Will Rogers
illness - a luxury only doctors can afford.
Wolfram Weidner
(see also: being ill, health)
illusion - the dust the devil throws in the eyes of the foolish.
Minna Antrim
(see also: lost illusions)
image - a stop the mind makes between uncertainties.
Djuna Barnes
imagination - something some people cannot imagine.
Gabriël Laub
imbecility - a more or less advanced feebleness of the intellectual faculties.
Henry Campbell Black
imitation - the sincerest form of television.
Fred Allen
imitator - a man who succeeds in being an imitation.
Elbert Hubbard
immigrant - an unenlightened person who thinks one country better than another.
Ambrose Bierce
imigration – the only problem communism ever solved.
Doug Newman
immobile - mobile phone after receipt of first call-bill.
Mike Barfield

immorality - the morality of those who are having a better time.
H.L. Mencken
immortal - someone who hasn't died yet.
Tom Holt
immortality - the only cause you can't die for.
Heathcote Williams
impale - to put in a bucket.
Kevin Goldstein-Jackson
impartiality - a pompous name for indifference, which is an elegant name for ignorance.
G.K. Chesterton
impatience - waiting in a hurry.
Evan Esar
impeccable - unable to be eaten by a chicken.
Ray Hand
imperfection - something which most of us accept as a condition of being human.
Mary Hocking
imperialism - the monopoly stage of capitalism.
Vladimir Lenin
impersonation - the sincerest form of plagiarism.
Jim Carrey
implementation - the sincerest form of flattery.
L. Peter Deutsch
important person - someone who will not allow himself not to allow himself something.
Liselotte Pulver
impossibilities - merely things of which we have not learned, or which we do not wish to happen.
Charles W. Chesnutt
impossible - a word only to be found in the dictionary of fools.
Napoleon Bonaparte
impotence - the only quality of a man that is not hereditary.
Georges Elgozy
impresario - a promoter with a cape.
L.L. Levinson
impressionism - the newspaper of the soul.
Henri Matisse
improbable - a distant cousin of the coincidence.
Frans Strijards
impropriety - the soul of wit.
W. Somerset Maugham

improvisation - a desperate attempt to remember the tune.
Leonid S. Sukhorukov
incense - Holy Shit!
Bert Kruismans
incentive - the possibility of getting more money than you can earn.
L.L. Levinson
incest - relations with one's relations.
Leonard Rossiter
incident - annoying word which your mother-in-law uses in reference to your wedding.
Cy DeBoer
incinerator - a writer's best friend.
Thornton Wilder
income - something you can't live without - or within.
Tom Wilson
income tax -the hardest thing in the world to understand.
Albert Einstein
income tax assessor - a person who follows you into a revolving door but comes out ahead of you.
Colin Bowles
income tax returns - the most imaginative fiction being written today.
Herman Wouk
income tax-time - when you test your powers of deduction.
Shelly Friedman
incompatiblity - any situation involving humans and computers.
D.J. Fleming
incompetence - a double-edged banana.
John Perry Barlow
(see also: gross incompetence)
incomprehensible jargon - the hallmark of a profession.
Kingman Brewster Jr.
in conclusion - the phrase that wakes up the audience.
Herbert V. Prochnow
incongruity - the mainspring of laughter.
Max Beerbohm
incongruous - sitting in the Senate or House.
Cynthia MacGregor
inconsistency - the only thing in which men are consistent.
Horace Smith

inconvenience - only an adventure wrongly considered; an adventure is an inconvenience rightly considered.
G.K. Chesterton
incorruptible - independently wealthy.
Mike Barfield
indecision - the basis for flexibility.
Andrew Filonov
indenture - the contents of false teeth.
Stan Kegel
independent - the guy who wants to take the politics out of politics.
Adlai Stevenson
index - a great leveller.
George Bernard Shaw
Indian - someone who wishes Columbus had been a farmer.
Robert Orben
Indian summer - a spell of beautiful weather brought on by putting away warm-weather clothing.
Doug Larson
indifference - the mildest form of intolerance.
Karl Jaspers
indigestion - post-burger trauma.
Mike Barfield
indignation - the seducer of thought. No man can think clearly when his fists are clenched.
George Jean Nathan
(see also: righteous indignation)
indiscreet person - something like an open letter that everybody can read.
Baltasar Graciàn Y Morales
indiscretion - the guilt of woman.
Ambrose Bierce
individual - a multitude of one million divided by one million.
Arthur Koestler
individualism - the cradle of vulgarity.
Nicolas Gómez Davila
individualist - someone who only feels lonely in company.
Wolfram Weidner
individuation - the source and primal cause of all suffering.
Friedrich Nietzsche
indolence - a word that makes my laziness seem classy.
Bern Williams

indulgence - an aristocratic form of contempt.
Rémy de Gourmont
industrial action - the continuation of negotiations by other means.
Denis McShane
industry - the root of all ugliness.
Oscar Wilde
inebriate - a man who thinks the whole world revolves around him.
O.A. Battista
ineffable - describes someone you absolutely cannot swear in front of, such as the Queen Mum.
Jessica Henig
inexperience - what makes a young man do what an older man says is impossible.
Herbert V. Prochnow
infallible diet - never eating while your wife is talking.
Barbra Streisand
infant prodigy - a small child with highly imaginative parents.
R.H. Creese
infant replay - the birth of twins.
Linda Williams
infantilism - probably the hallmark of our generation.
John Wells
infatuation - a love that is inconvenient to go on with.
Celia Fremlin
infidelity - reason enough for gun control.
Barbara Lazear Ascher
infinity - the quickest shortcut to the unknown.
Alan Harris
inflation -when you have money to burn but can't afford the match to light it.
Mitch Murray
inflexibility - the hallmark of the Tiny Mind.
John Sanborn
information - the seed for an idea that will only grows when it's watered.
Heinz von Bergen
information highway - where the telephone, television and computer merge onto a single high-tech turnpike, with tollbooths stationed at regular intervals.
Rick Bayan

initiative - doing the right thing without being told.
Irving Mack
injections - the best thing ever invented for feeding doctors.
Gabriel Garcia Marquez
injury - where many court cases are decided.
Cynthia MacGregor
inkling - a small bottle of ink.
Kevin Goldstein-Jackson
in-laws - Trojan Horses.
Theo Mestrum
inmate - a husband or wife that stays home.
Leopold Fechtner
innocence - the best aphrodisiac.
Jean Baudrillard
innocent - the person who explains nothing.
Albert Camus
innovation - the difference between a leader and a follower.
Steve Jobs
innumeracy - an ineptitude for mathematics which results in the fear of all sums.
Simon Stacey
in principle - another way of saying, "Yes, but..."
Juul Kinnaer
insanity - just imagination that hasn't found its way back to reality.
Wayne Coyne
(see also: mental illness, temporary insanity)
insect repellent - one of a number of joke items available in any chemist shop.
Henry Beard
insecurity - a weakness in normal people, the basic tool of the actor's trade.
Miranda Richardson
insider - where the cinnamon stick is found relevant to an alcoholic apple drink.
Cynthia MacGregor
insider trading - stealing too fast.
Calvin Trillin
insight - the best vision.
Malcolm S. Forbes
insincerity - merely a method whereby we can multiply our personalities.
Oscar Wilde

insinuate - Adam and Eve's least favourite word.
Johnny Hart
insomnia - the result of worry over sleeping-pill side effects.
Mike Barfield
inspiration - to remember the future.
Eric van der Steen
(see also: deadline)
instant coffee - just old beans that have cremated.
Jennifer Saunders
instinct - the nose of the mind.
Delphine de Girardin
institution - the lengthened shadow of one man.
Ralph Waldo Emerson
instruction manual - an explanation of how to use something written in a way that is easily understood only by the author.
Phil Smith
instrument flying - an unnatural act probably punishable by God.
Gordon Baxter
insurances - trade in fear.
Lévi Weemoedt
(see also: funeral insurance)
insurance policy - an agreement made up of words that are too big to understand, and type that is too small to read.
Joey Adams
integrity - to look as stupid as you really are.
Toon Verhoeven
(see also: real integrity)
intellect - a poor instrument for discovering what goes on in the heart.
Henry Root
intellectual - someone who goes into a library, even when it is not raining.
André Roussin
(see also: emerging intellectual)
intellectual brilliance - no guaranty against being dead wrong.
David Fasold
intellectualism - often the sole piety of the skeptic.
Richard Hofstadter
intellectual property - a figment of the imagination.
Crosbie Fitch
intellectual snob - someone who can listen to the William Tell Overture and not think of The Lone Ranger.
Dan Rather

intelligence - only an instinct that is mistaken.
Eugène Ionesco
(see also: artificial intelligence, greatest intelligence, unused intelligence)
intelligent agent - a query program with a user interface that is so obscure that you must anthropomorphize it in order to account for its behavior.
Jaron Lanier
intelligent girl - someone who knows that she will have more lovers after she is married than before.
Emmanuelle Arsan
intelligent human being - a large-scale manufacturer of misunderstanding.
Philip Roth
intelligent man - one who has successfully fulfilled many accomplishments, and is yet willing to learn more.
Ed Parker
intelligent woman - a woman with whom we can be as stupid as we like.
Paul Valéry
intemperance - the only vulgarity.
Ralph Waldo Emerson
intercessory prayer - loving our neighbour on our knees.
Charles Brent
intercourse - a hot pole in a pothole.
Richard Lederer
(see also: conventional intercourse)
interesting - a word a man uses to describe a woman who lets him do all the talking.
Peter Darbo
Internal Revenue Service - the world's most successful mail-order business.
Bob Goddard
International Rock Star - Gravy Maker Extraordinaire.
Ozzy Osbourne
internesia - the growing tendency to forget exactly where in Cyberspace you saw a particular bit of information.
Dave Birch
Internet - the most intellectually stimulating waste of time you can find.
Jeff Goslin
(see also: data superhighway, personal web pages, personal website, Usenet, Web)

Internet "browser" - the piece of software that puts a message on your computer screen informing you that the Internet is currently busy and you should try again later.
Dave Barry
Internet scams - dot cons.
Joseph Leff
Internet time - hours wasted surfing for bogus data.
Stephen Manes
interpretation - nothing but the possibility of error.
Paul de Man
interpreter - someone who lies in two languages.
Piet Grijs
interpretation - the great destroyer of beauty.
Arnon Grunberg
interview - the more polite version of a judicial interrogation.
J.M. Coetzee
interviewer - someone expecting intelligent answers to stupid questions.
Gerd de Ley
intestinal distress - a polite reference to an attack of flatulence.
Peter Furze
intestines - the home of tempests: in them is formed gas, as in the clouds.
Anthelme Brillat-Savarin
intimacy - a relation into which fools are providentially drawn for their mutual destruction.
Ambrose Bierce
intolerance - the besetting sin of moral fervour.
Alfred North Whitehead
(see also: tolerance)
introduce - to say hello to Mussolini.
Willie Meikle
intuition - woman's radar.
Milton Berle
inventing - a combination of brains and materials. The more brains you use, the less materials you need.
Charles F. Kettering
invention - the mother of necessity.
Thorsten Veblen
inventor - simply a fellow who doesn't take his education too seriously.
Charles F. Kettering

investigating journalist - one who can think up plausible scandals.
Lambert Jeffries
investment - how I explained the wearing of a waistcoat for formal dress to my American friends.
Joseph Harris
inveterate smoker - one who can shave without getting lather on his cigarette.
Robert Myers
invisible chains - those which weigh the most heavily.
John Norman
invitation - the sincerest flattery.
Carolyn Wells
Iran - an awful country. Women get stoned when they commit adultery. Unlike Britain, where women commit adultery when they get stoned.
Anthony Jay & Jonathan Lynn
Iranian moderate - one who has run out of ammunition.
Henry Kissinger
irascibility - muse of middle age.
Derek Walcott
Ireland - America's 52nd state.
Noel Browne
(see also: Dublin, funeral)
Irish (the language) - English set to music.
Mary Michael Malloy
Irish (the people) - a fair people; - they never speak well of one another.
Samuel Johnson
(see also: Irishman)
Irish atheist - one who wishes to God he could believe in God.
John P. Mahaffy
Irish coffee - a drink providing in a single glass all four essential food groups: alcohol, caffeine, sugar and fat.
Alex Levine
Irish literary movement - two writers on speaking terms with one another.
ugh Leonard
Irishman - just a machine for turning Guinness into urine.
Niall Toibin
(see also: true Irishman)
Irish politician - a man of few words but he uses them often.
Éamon Nally

Irish queer - a fellow who prefers women to drink.
Sean O'Faolain
Irish whisky - a drink that makes you see double and feel single.
Peter Cagney
iron age - the historical period preceding the Era of Permanent Press.
Sandra Zorn
ironing - the perpetuum mobile of the household.
Simon Carmiggelt
irony - a marvellous spice of life, but a paralysing way of life.
Simon May
 (see also: knee-jerk irony)
irrationality - the square root of all evil.
Doug Hofstadter
irreverence - the champion of liberty and its one sure defense.
Mark Twain
(see also: true irreverence)
irritation - raising your children under the eyes of your parents.
Jasmine Birtles
Islam - the youngest of the major religions and it has the arrogance of youth.
James Mark Cameron
island - what I do after a successful plane trip.
Gary Hallock
Islington - about as far as you can get from London without needing yellow-fever jabs.
A.A. Gill
Israel - the only country where one can say of someone that he is a Jew without being an anti-semite.
Jean-Paul Sartre
Istanbul - answer to the question "What is the light brown horned animal?"
Jack Meov
Italian (the language) - the only language in which the word *vago* (vague) also means 'lovely, attractive'.
Italo Calvino
Italian - a cowardly baritone who consumes 78.3 kilometres of carbohydrates a month and drives about in a car slightly smaller than he is, looking for a divorce.
Alan Coren
Italian singing - bestial howling and entirely frantic vomiting up of damned souls through their still carnal throats.
John Ruskin

Italy - a poor country full of rich people.
Richard Gardner
(see also: Naples, Rome, Venice, Vesuvius)

J

Jacket Fallacy - the deluded belief that the photograph on a book jacket resembles the writer of the book, or indeed that the blurb resembles the contents.
Miles Kington
jade - a semi-precious stone or a semi-precious woman.
Oliver Herford
jail - place where they keep the litter of the law.
L.L. Levinson
jailer - man with a confining job.
Robert Meyers
jam - a commodity found on bread, children and door-handles.
Jasmine Birtles
James, Henry - one of the nicest old ladies I ever met.
William Faulkner
janitor - a paid housewife.
Cy DeBoer
January - month of empty pockets.
Colette
January sales - fever on high heels.
Hugo Camps
Japan - the land where they don't have time to let the trees grow tall.
Jennifer Saunders
Japanese - a people with a genius for doing anything they set out to do as a matter of national decision.
George Ball
jargon - the opiate of the sociologists.
Leo Rosten
jaundice - the disease that your friends diagnose.
William Osler
Javascript - the duct tape of the Internet.
Charlie Campbell
jazz - five guys playing different songs.
Steve McGrew
jazz musician - a juggler who uses harmonies instead of oranges.
Benny Green

jealous man - a man who will always find more than he is looking for.
Madeleine de Scudéry
jealousy - the religion of the moderates.
Carlos Ruiz Zafón
Jehova - a God with many witnesses but never an alibi.
Piet Grijs
Jehova's Witnesses - people with very strong feet.
Mark Uytterhoeven
jester's cape - the most effective flak jacket.
Matthew Parris
jet travel - what lets us see less and less of more and more faster and faster.
Leopold Fechtner
Jew - neither a race or a religion but a complaint.
Irving Layton
jewelry - a woman's best friend.
Edna Ferber
Jewish Alzheimer - when you forget everything except a grudge.
Jackie Mason
Jewish novel - a story in which boy meets girl, boy gets girl and then worries what his mother will say.
Colin Bowles
Jewish nymphomaniac - a woman who will make love with a man the same day she has her hair done.
Maureen Lipman
Jewish porno film - one minute of sex and nine minutes of guilt.
Joan Rivers
Jewish Princess - a girl who makes love with her eyes closed - because she can't bear to see another person's pleasure.
David Steinberg
job - an invasion of privacy.
Danny McGoorty
(see also: ideal job, part-time job)
job application - a game without rules.
Piet van Caldenborgh
job sharing - what your boss does.
Jan Hyde
jockey - from jog, to move slowly, and key, something that makes fast. Hence, one who makes the pace fast or slow, according to instructions.
Gideon Wurdz

jogger - a pedestrian who's going down a dark street.
Milton Berle
jogging - something for people who aren't intelligent enough to watch Breakfast Television.
Victoria Wood
John Paul II - one of the few Polish guys who could find a job in Italy.
José Artur
Johnson, Boris - the sort of person who, 200 years ago, would have died aged 30 leading a cavalry charge into a volcano.
Frankie Boyle
joke - a kind of *coitus interruptus* between reason and emotion.
Arthur Koestler
(see also: good joke)
journalism - the second oldest profession.
Robert Sylvester
(see also: junk journalism, modern journalism)
journalist - an author that is certain of being published.
Sigmund Graff
 (see also: great journalist)
journal writing - a voyage to the interior.
Christina Baldwin
joy - one of the only emotions you can't contrive.
Bono
Joyce, James - a true artist from his head to his crotch.
Alec Guinness
jubilee - a milestone along the way to the grave.
Havank
Judas Iscariot - nothing but a low, mean, premature congressman.
Mark Twain
judge - a jurist who has to decide which party had the best lawyer.
Fons Jansen
Judgement Day - God's audit.
Hal Roach
juice of the grape - the liquid quintessence of concentrated sunbeams.
Thomas Love Peacock
July - that's not the truth.
Stan Kegel
June - the traditional month for weddings. The other eleven are for divorce.
Joe Hickman

junk - the ultimate commodity, the merchandise is not sold to the consumer - the consumer is sold to the merchandise.
William Burroughs
junk journalism - the evidence of a society that has got at least one thing right, that there should be nobody with the power to dictate where responsible journalism begins.
Tom Stoppard
junk mail - direct marketing.
George Carlin
junkyard - final rusting place.
Tanya Pongracz
jury - a group of twelve people of average ignorance.
Herbert Spencer
justice - a decision in your favour.
Harry Kaufman
just peace - when our side gets what it wants.
Bill Mauldin
juvenile behaviour - term used to describe everything you do after you've upset her.
Jeff Green
juvenile delinquents - people who have been given a free hand - but not in the proper place.
Hal Roach

Kama Sutra - the Mrs. Beeton of sex.
Aldous Huxley
kangaroo - pogo stick with a pouch.
Robert Myers
karaoke bars - bars that combine two of nation's greatest evils: people who shouldn't drink with people who shouldn't sing.
Tom Dreesen
karate - a form of martial arts in which people who have had years and years of training can, using only their hands and feet, make some of the worst movies in the history of the world.
Dave Barry
karate school - chopping center.
Stan Kegel
keyhole - a low-tech personal surveillance device.
Mike Barfield
key ring - a handy little gadget that allows you to lose all your keys at once.
kick - momentary freedom from the chains of the aging, cautious, nagging, frightened flesh.
William Burroughs
kid - pejorative term hated by children who want to be thought of as adults without actually behaving like them.
Mike Barfield
killing - an excellent way of dealing with a hostility problem.
Theodore J. Flicker
killing time - a kind of legal self-defence.
Paul Jacobs
kilohertz - mortal injuries.
Ray Hand
kilt - an unrivalled garment for fornication and diarrhoea.
John Masters
kindness - the beginning of cruelty.
Frank Herbert
(see also: unkindness)
king - the man who can.
Thomas Carlyle
(see also: monarchy, queen, virtuous king)

kiss - a lovely trick designed by nature to stop speech when words become superfluous.
Ingrid Bergman
kissing - just pressing your lips to the sweet end of 66 feet of intestines.
Drew Carey
kitchen - the laboratory of life.
Nora Seton
kitchenette - a narrow aisle that runs between a gas stove and a can of tomatoes.
Bob Burns
kitsch - the echo of art.
Kurt Tucholsky
kitten - a rosebud in the garden of the animal kingdom.
Robert Southey
kleptomaniac - a person who helps himself because he can't help himself.
Henry Morgan
Klopstokia - a far away country. Chief Exports: goats and nuts. Chief Imports: goats and nuts. Chief Inhabitants: goats and nuts.
Joseph L. Mankiewicz
knee-jerk irony - the tendency to make flippant ironic comments as a reflexive matter of course in everyday conversation.
Douglas Coupland
knicknack - a toy for those who no longer have toys.
Ramon Gomez de La Serna
knife - object that divides everything into left and right.
Battus
knower - part of the known.
Julian Jaynes
knowing - seeing inside oneself.
Joseph Joubert
knowledge - a polite word for dead but not buried imagination.
e.e. cummings
Krebs Cycle - a series of complicated biochemical reactions that show how everything we eat turns to fat.
Howard Bennett
krogt (chemical symbol: Kr) - the metallic silver coating found on fast-food game cards.
Rich Hall
Ku Klux Klan - they wear white sheets and their hats have a point - which is more than can be said for their beliefs.
David Frost & Michael Shea

L

lab - the kind of dog a mad scientist has.
Lars Hanson
Labour - Tory.
Jeremy Hardy
lack of education - an extraordinary handicap when one is being offensive.
Josephine Tey
lactomangulation - manhandling the "open here" spout on a milk carton so badly that one has to resort to using the "illegal" side.
Rich Hall
ladies' lingerie - the only concrete proof that God exists.
Roland Topor
ladle - the only thing that is edible in a pot of leek soup.
Henry Beard
lady - one who never shows her underwear unintentionally.
Lillian Day
lakes - the puddles left after the Freat Flood.
Ramon Gomez de la Serna
lambada - choreographed sex.
Joe Baltake
lancet - the magician's wand of the dark ages of medicine.
Oliver Wendell Holmes
land - the best cure for sea-sickness.
Ashleigh Brilliant
landscape - a passive creature which lends itself to an author's mood.
T.S. Eliot
language - all that separates us from the lower animals, and the bureaucrats.
Jerry Adler
language lab - a big name for a room and a tape recorder.
Eddie Izzard
lap dancing - the ultimate nightmare of man. It's porn that you can see.
Steven Moffat
lap dog - body-part of an old spinster.
Louis Verbeeck

laptop - what the dog did to the water in the bowl.
Keith Martin
large income - the best recipe for happiness.
Jane Austen
Las Vegas - the most religious city in the world: at any hour you can walk into a casino and hear someone say, "Oh, my God!"
Joey Adams
lateral coital position - having a bit on the side.
Liz Hughes
lateral thinking - a way of using information in order to bring about creativity.
Edward de Bono
(to) laugh - the most elegant way of showing our enemies our teeth.
Werner Finck
laugh (noun) - a smile that burst.
John E. Donovan
(see also: dirty laugh, good laugh)
laughing - the sensation of feeling good all over, and showing it principally in one spot.
Josh Billings
laughing gas - what does not work with on people who have no sense of humour.
François Cavanna
laughter - the closest distance between two people.
Victor Borge
laundromats - where patrons are taken to the cleaners.
Sandy Sibert
lava - the earth burning its mouth.
Hans-Horst Skupy
lavatory - volcano.
Ray Hand
lavatory seat - euphemism for an inner-city constituency.
Mike Barfield
law - a system that protects everybody who can afford to hire a good lawyer.
Joey Adams
lawful - compatible with the will of a judge having jurisdiction.
Ambrose Bierce
lawlessness - a self-perpetuating, ever-expanding habit.
Dorothy Thompson
lawn - nature under totalitarian rule.
Michael Pollan

lawnmower - weapon of grass destruction.
Sandy Sibert
law practice - the exact opposite of sex: even when it's good, it's bad.
Mortimer B. Zuckerman
law student - proof that evolution can reverse direction. An individual undergoing the difficult devolution from human being to primitive invertebrate. Put more succinctly, scum in training.
Chaz Bufe
lawsuit - worn by lawyers.
Jan Hyde
lawyer - a man who prevents somebody else from getting your money.
Milton Berle
(see also: divorce-lawyers, great lawyer, liar, perfect lawyer, trial lawyer)
laxative - the best remedy for coughing: then you dare not cough any more.
Coluche
(to) lay off - the best way to raise a child.
Shulamith Firestone
lazybones - a man who does not act like he is working.
Tristan Bernard
laziness - vice that protects you from many other vices.
Paul Jacobs
lazybones - a man who does not act like he is working.
Rodolphe Salis
lazy cow - a woman who does a man's work.
Jo Brand
leader - one who knows the way, goes the way and shows the way.
John C. Maxwell
(see also: good leader, real leaders)
leader of men - one who see which way the crowd is going and steps in ahead.
Milton Berle
leadership - the art of getting someone else to do something that you want done because he wants to do it.
Dwight D. Eisenhower
(see also: true leadership)
leading authority - anyone who has guessed right more than once.
Frank A. Clark

(to) learn - to add to one's ignorance by extending the knowledge we have of the things that we can never know.
Elbert Hubbard
learned fool - one who has read everything, and simply remembered it.
Josh Billings
learned man - an idler who kills time by study.
George Bernard Shaw
learned woman - the greatest of all calamities.
Marie von Ebner-Eschenbach
learning - finding out what you already know.
Richard Bach
lease-car - dummy for managers.
Pieter Klaas Jagersma
leasing - modern marriage.
Juul Kinnaer
leaves - the verbs that conjugate the seasons.
Gretel Ehrlich
lecture - a process by which the notes of the professor become the notes of the students without passing through the minds of either.
R.K. Rathbun
lecturer - a sound scholar, who is chosen to teach on the ground that he was once able to learn.
F.M. Cornford
lecturing - gymnastics, chest-expander, medicine, mind-healer, blues-destroyer, all in one.
Mark Twain
lecture theatre - the place where information passes from the notebook of the lecturer to the notebook of the student without necessarily passing through the mind of either.
Jim White
leek - a scallion
Hung like a stallion.
Caryl S. Avery
left - a group of people who will never be happy unless they can convince themselves that they are about to be betrayed by their leaders.
Richard Crossman
left hand - the hand that every married man in a singles bar keeps in his pocket.
Nancy Linn-Desmond

legend (person) - the consecration of fame.
Coco Chanel
legend (story) - a lie that has attained the dignity of age.
H.L. Mencken
leisure - the opiate of the masses.
Malcolm Muggeridge
leisure time - that five or six hours when you sleep at night.
George Allen
leniency - a friendly expression of indifference.
Georges Wolfromm
leopard - a form of dotted lion.
L.L. Levinson
leprosy - when there is more in your nose after picking it than there was before.
Kamagurka
lesbian - any woman who doesn't like me.
Jason Love
lesbianism - an extremely inventive response to the shortage of men.
Nora Ephron
Lesbos - no man's land.
Robert Scipion
letterbox - permission for a woman to fight.
Stan Kegel
letters - a good way to go somewhere without moving anything but your heart.
Phyllis Theroux
letter-writing - a most delightful way of wasting time.
John Morley
leverage - having something the other guy wants.
Donald Trump
Levis - biblical jeans.
Ivo de Wijs
Lewis, Sinclair - a writer who drank, not, as so many have believed, a drunk who wrote.
James Lundquist
lexicographer - a writer of dictionaries, a harmless drudge.
Samuel Johnson
liar - one who tells an unpleasant truth.
Oliver Herford
(see also: best liar)
libel letters - the Oscars of journalism.
Roisin Ingle

liberal - a conservative who's been arrested.
Thomas Wolfe
liberalism - the first refuge of political indifference and the last refuge of Leftists.
Harry Roskolenko
liberality - merely a form of timidity in the rich.
Friedrich Nietzsche
liberal Southerner - someone who wouldn't mind going to see *Green Pastures* provided it had an all-white cast.
Dick Gregory
liberated woman - one who has sex before marriage and a job after.
Gloria Steinem
liberation - an ever shifting horizon, a total ideology that can never fulfill its promises.
Arianna Stassinopoulos
liberation woman - a person who believes she is as human as a man.
Ghada al-Samman
libertarian - just an anarchist on the gold standard.
Alexis Gilliland
liberty - the right to tell people what they do not want to hear.
George Orwell
librarians - the secret rulers of the universe. They control information.
Spider Robinson
library - just a place where homeless people go to shave and go to the bathroom.
Seth MacFarlane
librettist - a mere drudge in the world of opera.
Robertson Davies
licorice - the liver of candy.
Michael O'Donoghue
(to) lie - another way of dealing with the truth.
Anita Witzier
lie (noun) - a truth that didn't make it.
Hans Kilian
lie detector - mouth trap.
Stan Kegel
life - an awkward gap between the cradle and the grave.
Alan Bennett
(see also: good life, happy life, human life, real life)

life after death - as improbable as sex after marriage.
Madeline Kahn
life insurance - death insurance.
Russell Ash
lifestyle - the art of discovering ways to live uniquely.
Jim Rohn
light - God's eldest daughter.
Thomas Fuller
light music - music whose seriousness remains unnoticed.
Hans Keller
light-year - a year that has 40 percent less calories than a regular year.
Milton Berle
limbo - place where arms and legs go when they die.
Ray Hand
litigation - a form of hell whereby money is transferred from the pockets of the proletariat to that of lawyers.
Kin Hubbard
limited nuclear war - belief that a nuclear war in which not quite everyone is annihilated is possible.
Russell Ash
Lindbergh, Charles - the first man to fly the Atlantic alone - and the last to arrive at the same time as his luggage.
Bob Barker
line - a dot that went for a walk.
Paul Klee
lion - the only animal with a knowledge of history.
Ramon Gomez de la Serna
liposuction - how teenagers kiss.
Willie Meikle
lips - the curtains of the heart.
Kees van Kooten
lipstick - a device to make every kiss tell.
L.L. Levinson
liquid diet - the powder is mixed with water and tastes exactly like powder mixed with water.
Art Buchwald
liquor - a nice subsitute for facing adult life.
Dorothy B. Hughes
(to) lisp - to call a spade a thspade.
Oliver Herford

listening - the sincerest form of flattery.
Joyce Brothers
(see also: skillful listening)
listless - what men become when their wives don't give them a list.
Johnny Hart
lite - the new way to spell "light", but with twenty per cent fewer letters.
Jerry Seinfeld
literary agent - somebody whom you pay to make bad blood between yourself and your publisher.
Angela Thirkell
literary biography - the Meals-on-Wheels service of the book world.
Sheridan Morley
literary fame - the only fame of which a wise man ought to be ambitious, because it is the only lasting and living fame.
Robert Southey
literary men - a perpetual priesthood.
Thomas Carlyle
literary movement - five or six people who live in the same town and hate each other.
George William Russell
literature - news that *stays* news.
Ezra Pound
(see also: great literature, Roman literature)
litigation - a machine which you go into as a pig and come out of as a sausage.
Ambrose Bierce
litter - any object left lying about which is too small to be offensive.
J.B. Morton
little problems - big problems for little minds.
Tom Zimmerman
(to) live - the only known way to die.
H. Drion
Liverpool - a kind of collision caused by the English trying to get out while the Irish are trying to get in.
Nancy Banks-Smith
living (noun) - the dead on holiday.
Maurice Maeterlinck

living at risk - jumping off a cliff and building your wings on the way down.
Ray Bradbury
living hell - the best revenge.
Adrienne E. Gusoff
llama - a woolly sort of fleecy hairy goat,
With an indolent expression and an undulating throat.
Hilaire Belloc
loafer - someone who always has the correct time.
Kin Hubbard
loafing - the Science of living without trouble.
Barry Pain
loan - in modern banking, the lending of money at interest to those who have no need to borrow it.
Chaz Bufe
lobbyists - people who go to Washington to mix business with pressure.
Lane Olinghouse
local delicacy - usually code for something revolting.
Lillian Marsano
locksmiths - key personnel.
Sandy Sibert
locomotive - an insane reason to commit a crime.
Johnny Hart
logarithm - music in the forest.
Tim Bruening
logic - the art of going wrong with confidence.
Morris Kline
logical consequences - the scarecrows of fools and the beacons of wise men.
Henrietta A. Huxley
logical person - anyone who can prove that you are right.
O.A. Battista
loiter - not now.
Leopold Fechtner
loitering - the crime of doing nothing in particular, particularly in public.
Rick Bayan
London - a splendid place to live for those who can get out of it.
George John Gordon Bruce
(see also: Paddington Station)
Londoner - one who has never been to Madame Tussaud's.
Craig Willis

London Zoo - an animal microcosm of London, and even the lions, as a rule, behave as if they had been born in South Kennington.
Leonard Woolf
loneliness - something you can't walk away from.
William Feather
lonely person - a tragedy that luckily comes alone.
Nils-Fredrik Nielsen
longevity - the revenge of talent upon genius.
Cyril Connolly
Long Island - American's idea of what God would have done with Nature if he'd had the money.
Peter Fleming
long marriage - two people trying to dance a duet and two solos at the same time.
Anne Taylor Fleming
long walk - the best remedy for a short temper.
Jacqui Lee Schiff
loop, endless - see endless loop.
Isaac Asimov
loquacity - a disorder which renders the sufferer unable to curb his tongue when you wish to talk.
Ambrose Bierce
Los Angeles - a city with all the personality of a paper cup.
Raymond Chandler
(see also: Hollywood)
loser - a stowaway on a kamikaze plane.
Charlie Manna
(see also: true loser)
lost illusions - discovered truths.
Multatuli
lost luggage - just an opportunity to start afresh.
Chris Evans
lottery - a tax upon imbeciles.
Camillo Benso di Cavour
(see also: state run lotteries)
loudness - impotence.
Johann Kaspar Lavater
louse - a cow in the eyes of a microbe.
Nico Scheepmaker
(to) love - to look together in the same direction.
Antoine de Saint-Exupéry

love (noun) - more easily made than defined.
Eric van der Steen
(see also: art of love, being in love, first love, free love, ideal love, pain of love, pure love, ordinary love, parental love, perfect love, richest love, romantic love, real love, true love, unhappy love)
love affairs - simply servings of self-pity for two.
Alan Brien
love at first sight - that magic moment when you realise that you both have the same neurosis.
Kees van Kooten & Wim de Bie
love letters - the campaign promises of the heart.
Robert Friedman
lovely face -the solace of wounded hearts and the key of locked-up gates.
Sa'di
love of parents - the only love for which you are not responsible.
Bernhard Schlink
lover - someone who loves me instead of me.
Fernand Auwera
(see also: good lover)
love song - a caress set to music.
Sigmund Romberg
loving heart - the beginning of all knowledge.
Thomas Carlyle
loving wife - one who will do anything for her husband except stop criticizing and trying to improve him.
J.B. Priestley
loyalty - the one thing a leader cannot do without.
A.P. Gouthey
LSD - an awfully overrated aspirin and very simular to old people's Disneyland.
Captain Beefheart
(see also: PC)
luck - a matter of preparation meeting opportunity.
Oprah Winfrey
luge - the ultimate laxative.
Otto Jelinek
lullaby - the spell whereby the mother attempts to transform herself back from an ogre to a saint.
James Fenton
lunacy - the foundation of all writing.
Edna O'Brien

lunatic - anyone surrounded by lunatics.
Ezra Pound
lunatic asylum - the place where optimism most flourishes.
Havelock Ellis
lunch - a poor compliment to breakfast and an insult to dinner.
Father Healy
luposlipaphobia - the fear of being pursued by timber wolves around a kitchen table while wearing socks on a newly waxed floor.
Gary Larson
lust - the craving for salt of a man who is dying of thirst.
Friedrich Buechner
lusting - what keeps a lot of men going into old age.
Dustin Hoffman
luxury - being alone in the bathroom.
Cy DeBoer
luxury dinner on a ship - a bad play surrounded by water.
Clive James
lying - an indispensable part of making life tolerable.
Bergen Evans
lynching - the aftermath of slavery.
Mary Church Terrell

macadam - first man born in Scotland.
Bill McGarden
macho - a man whose surplus of muscles is compensated for by his lack of brains.
Gerd de Ley
machine-gun - death's typewriter.
Ramon Gomez de la Serna
mad - a term we use to describe a man who is obsessed with one idea and nothing else.
Ugo Betti
madhouse - institution in which society locks up an some people to give the others the chance of believing they are normal.
Marc Callewaert
Madison Avenue - the Dream Street of hucksters where consumers are lulled to sleep.
Edmund H. Volkart
madman - the man who has lost everything except his reason.
G.K. Chesterton
mad money - a psychiatrist's fee.
Larry Wilde
madness - to think of too many things in succession too fast, or of one thing too exclusively.
Voltaire
Madonna - a gay man trapped in a woman's body.
Boy George
Madrid - a hole but in rainy weather, a place fit only to drown rats.
Henry Brooks Adams
maestro - Italian word meaning pianist.
Stephen Bayley
Mafia - the only company in America that does business without lawyers.
Bill Maher
(see also: mob)
magazine - simply a device to induce people to read advertising.
James Collins
magician - someone who takes off his hat to a rabbit.
Johan Bovyn

magnate - magnet for gold.
Carlos de Vriese
magnocartic - any automobile that, when left unattended, attracts shopping carts.
Rich Hall
magnum opus - a book which when dropped from a three storey building is big enough to kill a man.
Edward Wilson
majority - the best repartee.
Benjamin Disraeli
(see also: minority)
major writing - to say what has been seen, so that it need never be said again.
Delmore Schwartz
make-up - an optical illusion.
Wim Meyles
making a film - painting a picture on a railroad track with the train getting closer.
Dustin Hoffman
making love - an exploration of sadness so deep that people must go in pairs.
John Updike
making money - a hobby that will complement any other hobbies you have, beautifully.
Scott Alexander
male - a member of the unconsidered or negligible sex. The male of the race is commonly known (to the female) as Mere Man. The genus has two varieties: good providers and bad providers.
Ambrose Bierce
(see also: man)
male boutique - where you go in to buy a tie and they measure your inside leg.
George Melly
male chauvinism - a shrewd method of extracting the maximum work for the minimum of compensation.
Michael Korda
male feminists - misogynists in sheep's clothing.
Lenny Schafer
male menopause - the time when a man starts turning off the lights for economical rather than romantic reasons.
John Merino
malice - only another name for mediocrity.
Patrick Kavanagh

Mallorca - an island completely surrounded by sea...
Glyn Haydn
mallennium - a thousand years of shopping.
Troy Dickson
Malta - the only place in the world where the local delicacy is the bread.
Alan Coren
mammon - patron saint of bankers.
Juul Kinnaer
man (the male) - the second strongest sex in the world.
Philip Barry
(see also: catlike man, good man, ideal man, real man)
man (the human being) - a virus with shoes.
Bill Hicks
(see also: big man, honest man, human being, mankind, modern man, nice man, practical man)
(to) manage - to do everything except anything. (So is to imagine).
Jan-Walter de Neve
management - an organisation that makes it difficult for other people to work.
Peter F. Drucker
(see also: good management, mismanagement, participative management, top management)
management consultant - someone who tells you how to improve doing something that he or she can't do at all.
Shankar Sivanandan
management democracy - everybody agreeing what the leader wants.
John Ashcroft
manager - nitwit who is responsible for streamlining a department he knows nothing about.
Patrick de Witte
(see also: general manager, good manager, perfect fund manager, top manager)
managing - getting paid for home runs someone else hits.
Casey Stengel
man and woman - two locked caskets, of which each contains the key to the other.
Isak Dinesen
Manhattan - an island about thirteen miles long and five hours wide.
Milton Berle

maniac - privileged mortal who has only one folly.
Pierre Decourcelle
manicurist - nail technician.
George Carlin
manipulation - violence with gloves on.
Fernand Auwera
mankind - an endangering species.
Richard Greene
manners - the noise you don't make eating soup.
L.L. Levinson
(see also: good manners)
manual - a unit of documentation. There are always three or more on a given item. One is on the shelf; someone has the others. The information you need is in the others.
Ray Simard
manuscript - something submitted in haste and returned at leisure.
Oliver Herford
Maradona - the highest-paid handballer in history.
Con Houlihan
marble - the soap of the ages.
Ramon Gomez de La Serna
March - the month God created to show people who don't drink what a hangover is like.
Garrison Keillor
marijuana - no more of a medicine than homosexuality is a disease.
Jeffrey A. Schaler
market - a barometer of civilisation.
Jason Alexander
marketeers - Satan's Little Helpers.
Bill Hicks
marketing - sales with a college education.
John Freund
market research - what you call it when you already know the answer you want, but still hunt up the question that will produce it.
Robert Fuoss
marquis - a sort of four-move chess problem.
Geoffrey Madan

marriage - a form of legalized rape.
Billy Crystal
(see also: good marriage, happy marriage, Hollywood marriage, ideal marriage, marital freedom, old-fashioned marriage, perfect marriage, remarriage, wedding)
marriage announcement - the printed part of a love-affair.
Robert Lembke
marriage bells - the death bells of friendship.
Paul Heyse
marriage vow - an absurdity imposed by society.
George Sand
married woman - a prostitute under contract.
Johnny Soporno
(to) marry - to lose half your rights and double your duties.
Arthur Schopenhauer
martyr - an enthusiastic suicide with a devout alibi.
Gerd de Ley
martyrdom - the only way in which a man can become famous without ability.
George Bernard Shaw
Marx, Groucho - the Voltaire of vaudeville.
Leo Rosten
Marx, Karl - a great man. He predicted everything but Marxism.
André Frossard
Marxism - the opiate of the unstoned classes.
Arthur Kleps
Marxists - people whose insides are torn up day after day because they want to rule the world and no one will even publish their letter to the editor.
Mark Helprin
mashed figs - a foodstuff that only your grandmother would eat, and only then because she couldn't find her dentures.
Bill Bryson
masochist - a sadist, without opportunities.
Cor Gilhuis
mass - the plural of no-one.
F.J. Schmit
mass media - the wholesalers; the peer-groups; the retailers of the communication industry.
David Riesman
mass murderers - people who have had *enough*.
Quentin Crisp

master key - nightmare for crusaders.
Guy Commerman
masterpiece - the latest opus by a commercially successful author or film-maker, esp. as proclaimed by shrewd reviewers who like to see themselves quoted in national ad campaigns.
Rick Bayan
masturbation - sex with someone you love.
Woody Allen
materialism - the only form of distraction from true bliss.
Doug Horton
materialist - someone who prefers a bottle in a ship rather than a ship in a bottle.
Julien Vandiest
mathemagician - successful corporate accountant.
Willis Bird
mathematician - a device for turning coffee into theorems.
Paul Erdos
mathematics - the grammar of numbers.
Hans Lohberger
matrimony - the high sea for which no compass has yet been invented.
Heinrich Heine
matter - a convenient formula for describing what happens where it isn't.
Bertrand Russell
mature - either tumbledown or overgrown, depending on whether it refers to the building or the garden.
Peter Clayton
maturity - a high price for growing up.
Tom Stoppard
(see also: full maturity)
mausoleum - a house for mice.
John S. Crosbie
maxim - a minimum of sound to a maximum of sense.
Mark Twain
May - Mother Nature's way of apologizing for February.
William D. Tammeus
maybe - the polite form of 'no'
Marc Pairon
Mayflower - a small ship on which several million Pilgrims came to America in 1620.
Steve Allen

M.B.A. - acronym for several different but related terms: (1) Master of Business Administration; (2) Master Bull Artist; (3) Master of Blind Ambition.
Jim Fisk & Robert Barron
McJob - a low-pay, low-prestige, low-dignity, low-benefit, no-future job in the service sector.
Douglas Coupland
meal time - the only time in the day when children resolutely refuse to eat.
Fran Lebowitz
meaningless words - the only valuable slogans for the silent majority.
Gerd de Ley
meanness - the parent of insolence.
Benjamin Franklin
meat - a status dish in which the sizzle counts for more than the intrinsic nutritional worth.
Magnus Pyke
mechanic - a person who picks your pocket from underneath your car.
Colin Bowles
media - just a word that has come to mean bad journalism.
Graham Greene
(see also: mass media, multimedia)
medical examiner - a coroner with a bigger office.
Ryan James
medical profession - the only one which a man may enter at any age with some chance of making a living.
W. Somerset Maugham
medical specialist - a doctor with a smaller practice but a larger boat.
Martin A. Ragaway
medical statistician - somebody who goes into a ward and takes the average temperature of all the patients.
Shimon Peres
medical student - someone who knows less than anyone else around him, inanimate objects not included.
Howard Bennett
medicine - the art of attending to people as far as their final resting place with Greek words.
Dino di Segré
(see also: holistic medicine)

medieval studies - just a branch of the entertainment business.
Bruce McFarlane
mediocrity - one of the conditions of huge success.
Wim Wenders
meditation - a gift confined to unknown philosophers and cows.
Finlay Peter Dunne
meek - the people who will inherit the earth after the real estate has been sufficiently ravaged by the strong.
Edmund H. Volkart
meekness - the mask of malice.
R.G. Ingersoll
meeting - an event where minutes are taken and hours wasted.
James C. Kirk
megalomania - childhood disease of the dwarfs.
Stanislaw Jery Lec
Mein Kampf - the fashion Bible written by Austria's black sheep, Adolf. It literally translates as: 'My Flamboyance'.
Sacha Baron Cohen
melancholic - a cynic who is incapable of opportunism.
Theo Mestrum
melancholy - the hopeful idea that weeping is good for something.
Piet Grijs
memoirs - the back stairs of history.
George Meredith
Memorial Day - the day we honour our war dead by getting in a car and driving until one of the kids throws up.
Lewis Black
memorials - confessions of guilt.
Madzy Ford
memorial service - farewell party for someone who has already left.
Robert Byrne
memories - hunting horns whose sound dies on the wind.
Guillaume Apollinaire
memory - the jewellery box of the brain.
Manuel van Loggem
(see also: good memory, moving memory, remember)
menage-à-trois - a French term. It means "Kodak moment."
Greg Ray

mental illness - a myth, whose function is to disguise and thus render more palatable the bitter pill of moral conflicts in human relations.
Thomas Szasz
menu - a list of dishes that a restaurant has just run out of.
Erma Bombeck
meow - 'woof' in cat.
George Carlin
mercy - an attribute beloved of detected offenders.
Ambrose Bierce
merit - the opinion one man entertains of another.
Lord Palmerston
metallurgist - someone who is allergic to metal.
Leo Rosten
metaphor - the most fertile power possessed by man.
José Ortega Y Gasset
metaphysician - a blind man in a dark room - looking for a black hat - which isn't there.
Lord Bowen
metaphysics - a restaurant where they give you a thirty thousand page menu, and no food.
Robert M. Pirsig
methodism - spiritual influenza.
George Crabbe
methodology - the science that gives the impression that pupils have discovered something for themselves.
Jan Humblet
methods - the masters of masters.
Charles-Maurice de Talleyrand
metronome - a gnome that lives in the city.
Heather Hart
metrophobia - fear of poetry.
Matt Groening
metrosexual - a homosexual who is interested in shopping.
Marian Salzman
Mexican bachelor - a man who cannot play the guitar.
Lillian Day
Mexican straight flush - any five cards and a gun.
Hugh Leonard
Mexico - where life is cheap, death is rich, and the buzzards are never unhappy.
Edward Abbey

Miami - a place where 1,000 different nationalities get together and give each other the finger on I-95.
Richard Jeni
Miami Beach - where neon goes to die.
Lenny Bruce
Microsoft - the biggest virus ever created by man.
Bud Minton
Microsoft Windows - proof that P.T. Barnum was correct.
Denny Miller
microwave.- the smallest movement of the ocean.
Michael Driscoll
microwave oven - oven invented just to prove that pub food *could* get worse.
Mike Barfield
middle age - five years older than I am.
Elton John
middle-aged - the only people who really adore being young.
Pam Brown
Middle East - a region where oil is thicker than blood.
James Holland
Middle Eastern states - quarrels with borders.
P.J. O'Rourke
middleman - someone who plunders one party and bamboozles the other.
Benjamin Disraeli
middleness - the very enemy of the bold.
Charles Krauthammer
midgets - the last to know it's raining.
Larry Tucker
midlife - when you reach the top of the ladder only to find that it was leaning against the wrong wall.
Joseph Campbell
mid-wife crisis - any character in a Hollywood movie whose wife and/or kids are introduced more than an hour into the movie and who hugs and kisses any or all of them will be dead in the next 20 minutes (e.g. 'Goose' in *Top Gun*).
Edward Savio
migration - a headache birds get when they fly down for the winter.
Richard Lederer
mild heart attack - one you remember.
Jim Caffrey

militarism - armed to the teeth because above them there isn't anything.
Toon Verhoeven
military glory - the attractive rainbow that rises in showers of blood.
Abraham Lincoln
military intelligence - contradictio in terms.
Oswald G. Villard
military school - a meat machine in reverse: you put sausages in and get pigs out.
Gerd de Ley
milk-cow - stepmother to every man's baby.
Josh Billings
millionaires - people who marry their secretaries because they are so busy making money they haven't time to see other girls.
Doris Lilly
mime - a harmless public nuisance whose silence creates a pretence of profundity for crowds of onlookers who pretend to enjoy the show.
Rick Bayan
(see also: pantomime)
mind - the standard of the man.
Isaac Watts
(see also: dirty mind, focused mind, great mind, orderly mind)
mindbinding - a universal demand of patriarchal males...
Mary Daly
mine - a hole in the ground owned by a liar.
Mark Twain
mini series - an Australian fillum that doesn't know when to stop.
Barry Humphries
minister - a man who has to pray for a living.
O.A. Battista
minister of external affairs - a beautiful job if there were no internal ones.
Joseph Luns
minister of finance - a legally authorized pickpocket.
Paul Ramadier
ministry - a place where the late-comers pass by the people who go home early.
Georges Courteline
minority - the greatest half.
Jacob Israël de Haan

minor operation - one performed on someone else.
Richard Selzer
minor surgery - what other people have.
Calvin Coolidge
miracle - an event described by those to whom it was told by men who did not see it.
Elbert Hubbard
miracle drug - any drug that will do what the label says it will do.
Eric Hodgins
mirror - the only device with which to check if you are still yourself.
Herman Brusselmans
misanthropist - a bruised philanthropist.
Ward Ruyslinck
misbehave - the best way to behave.
Mae West
miscellaneous - always the largest category.
Joel Rosenberg
miser - a disagreeable contemporary, but an agreeable ancestor.
Victor de Kowa
misery - a match that never goes out.
Thomas H. Huxley
misfortune - the kind of fortune that is never missed.
Ambrose Bierce
mismanagement - the hereditary epidemic of our brood.
Lord Byron
misogynist - a man who hates women as much as women hate one another.
H.L. Mencken
misquotations - the only quotations that are never misquoted.
Hesketh Pearson
missionaries - perfect nuisances who leave every place worse than they found it.
Charles Dickens
mist - evaporated horizon.
Max Croiset
mistake - a lesson on its way to be learned.
Milton Berle
Mr. Right - nowadays a guy who hasn't been laid in fifteen years.
Elayne Boosler
mistress - something that goes between a mister and a mattress.
Joe Lewis

mistrust - the foundation of democracy. Without mistrust you have no control over politics.
Noël Slangen
misunderstanding - the most usual form of communication.
Peter Benary
mixed economy - society in the process of committing suicide.
Ayn Rand
mob - a society of bodies voluntarily bereaving themselves of reason.
Ralph Waldo Emerson
(see also: Mafia)
mobile phone - the thin line between conspicuous success and standing in the street talking to yourself like a madman.
Mike Barfield
mob violence - a riot by people you disagree with.
Thomas Sowell
(see also: demonstration)
mockaroni - imitation pasta.
John Dratwa
mockery - the easiest, laziest form of entertainment.
Jason Chayka
model - two mobile eyes in a mobile head, itself a mobile body.
Robert Bresson
model husband - one who, when his wife is away, washes the dishes - both of them.
Herbert V. Prochnow
modeling - nothing more than organized walking.
Sam Stewart
moderate - one who has rejected extremes, at least for the moment.
Mignon McLaughlin
moderation - the key of lasting enjoyment.
Hosea Ballou
moderator - one who understands the art of leading a discussion in such a way that the point is not lost.
Peter Maiwald
modern - the day before yesterday.
Oskar Kokoschka
modern architecture - the absence of style.
Quinlan Terry
modern art - a square lady with three breasts and a guitar up her crotch.
Noël Coward

modern boss - one who would replace people with a computer, if he could find one that cringes.
Milton Berle
modern centaur - half a man and half a sports car.
Edith Grobleben
modern city - a place where you go out for a walk and get a breath of fresh air-pollution.
Joel Rothman
modern composer - a madman who persists in manufacturing an article nobody wants.
Arthur Honegger
modern executive - a man who wears his clothes out at the seat of his pants.
O.A. Battista
modern home - one where a switch can control everything but the children.
Jasmine Birtles
modernism - an attempt to reconstruct the world in the absence of God.
Bryan Appleyard
(see also: post-modernism)
modernity - the will to 'heroize' the present.
Michel Foucault
(see also: postmodernity)
modern journalism - survival of the vulgarest.
Oscar Wilde
modern kitchen - where the pot calls the kettle chartreuse.
Vicky Satter
modern man - any person born after Nietzsche's edict that 'God is dead' but before the hit recording 'I Wanna Hold Your Hand'.
Woody Allen
modern music - three farts and a raspberry, orchestrated.
John Barbirolli
modern politics - civil war carried on by other means.
Alasdair MacIntyre
modern science - generally practised by those who lack the flair for conversation.
Fran Lebowitz
modern sculptor - a man who can take a rough block of stone or wood, work on it for months and make it look like a rough block of stone or wood.
Charles Kelly

modern wife - a prostitute who doesn't deliver the goods.
W. Somerset Maugham
modest - the kind of pride least likely to offend.
Jules Renard
modest thinker - someone who thinks better than he thinks.
Gabriël Laub
modesty - the desire to be praised twice.
Godfried Bomans
(see also: false modesty)
Mohammed - one of the most common Christian names in the world.
David Jensen
molehill - a mountain to the apprentice skier.
Boris Evanoff
molehill man - a pseudo-busy executive who comes to work at 9 am and finds a molehill on his desk. He has until 5 p.m. to make this molehill into a mountain. An accomplished molehill man will often have his mountain finished before lunch.
Fred Allen
Monaco - the center of the spinning industry of the world.
Oliver Herford
(see also: Monte Carlo)
monarchy - a labour-intensive industry.
Harold Wilson
(see also: king)
Monday - a depressing way to spend one-seventh of your life.
Mary Kramer
Monday morning - the best cure for insomnia.
Sandra Cooley
money - a poor compensation for all the time we lose in making it.
James Geary
(see also: enough money, extra money, gold, mad money, making money, mammon)
Mongolia - the most beautiful country in the world, for the simple reason that there is nothing to see.
Lukas de Vos
monkey - a human being, retroactively.
Piet Theys
(see also: ape)
monks - the acceptable face of hoodies.
Mark Radcliffe

monogamous - preferring to have affairs in secret.
Chaz Bufe
monogamy - an obsolete word meaning a fidelity complex.
J.B. Morton
monologue - the best conversation between two people.
Edward Dahlberg
monopolist - a fellow who manages to get an elbow on each arm of his theatre chair.
Herbert V. Prochnow
monopoly - business at the end of its journey.
Henry Demarest Lloyd
Monte Carlo - a sunny place for shady people.
Noël Coward
Montreal - the only place where a good French accent isn't a social asset.
Brendan Behan
moon - the night's laundress.
Ramon Gomez de La Serna
moonshiner - one who conducts his business in distill of the night.
Dave Krieger
moose - an animal with horns on the front of his head, and a hunting lodge wall on the back of it.
Groucho Marx
moral - what you feel good after.
Ernest Hemingway
morale - faith in the man at the top.
Albert S. Johnstone
moral indignation - jealousy with a halo.
H.G. Wells
moralists - the ones who scratch other people's itches.
Samuel Beckett
morality - largely a matter of geography.
Elbert Hubbard
(see also: absolute morality, bourgeois morality)
moral principle - a compass forever fixed and forever true.
Edward R. Lyman
moral responsibility - what is lacking in a man when he demands it of a woman.
Karl Kraus
more - the cry of the curious person.
Bette Midler

Mormon - an American expatriate with four wives and one bicycle.
Colin Bowles
morning sickness - breakfast television.
Mike Barfield
morning trains - means of transport that arrives three minutes late in your station except on the day that *you* arrive three minutes late.
Gerd de Ley
Morocco - a combination of the Bible and Hollywood.
George S. Patton
morphine - a product that was invented to let the doctors sleep peacefully.
Sacha Guitry
mortgage - from Fr. mort, death, and Eng. gag, to choke. A lawyer's invention for choking property to death.
Gideon Wurdz
mosquito - the state bird of New Jersey.
Andy Warhol
moss - the toupee worn by rocks.
Ramon Gomez de la Serna
most popular speaker - the one who sits down before he stands up.
John P. Mahaffy
mother - someone who puts you to bed when you're wide awake and wakes you up when you're fast asleep.
James M. Barrie
(see also: smart mother)
motherhood - the thrill of a wife-time.
Robert Myers
mother-in-law - anagram of 'woman Hitler'.
Les Dawson
(see also: in-laws)
mother love - the fuel that enables a normal human being to do the impossible.
Marion C. Garretty
Mother Nature - a male chauvinist pig.
Faith Hines
mother's day - an occasion which occurs twice a year: once in June and then when school reopens in September.
Lee Daniel Quinn
mother's heart - the child's schoolroom.
Henry Ward Beecher

mother's knee - the best academy.
James Russell Lowell
moths – shadows breaded with dust.
Daniel Liebert
(see also: myth)
motivation - the art of getting people to do what you want them to do because they want to do it.
Dwight D. Eisenhower
motorcar - tin overcoat.
Rochus Spiecker
motorist - a person who, after seeing a serious wreck, drives carefully for several blocks.
Jane Pickens
mountaineers - people who think it credit-worthy to risk your life for the sake of standing on top of a large piece of windswept rock and ice.
Alec Le Sueur
mountains - the beginning and the end of all natural scenery.
John Ruskin
moustache - the huge laughing cockroach on the top lip.
Osip Mandelsjtam
mouth - temporary refuge for lies.
Piet Grijs
movie - the imagination of mankind in action.
Gilbert Seldes
(see also: cinema, film, Hollywood)
movie actors - just ordinary, mixed-up people - with agents.
Freya Stark
movie business - the only business where a negative is a positive.
Menachem Golan
movie star - the only woman who can keep a maid longer than a husband.
Joey Adams
(see also: Beverly Hills, Hollywood, star)
movie studio - the best toy a boy ever had.
Orson Welles
moving memory - when the moisture from the sudden thawing of the brains is caught in a handkerchief.
Joop van Breemen
Mozart - the Victor Sylvester of his day, churning out dance music for the court.
Jeremy James

MP - the sort of job all working class parents want for their children - clean, indoors and no heave lifting.
Diane Abbott
Ms - a syllable which sounds like a bumble bee breaking wind.
Hortense Calisher
MTV - the lava lamp of the 1980s.
Doug Ferrari
muddle - the extra unknown personality in any committee.
Anthony Sampson
muesli - a dish that always looks like the sweepings from a better class table.
Frank Muir
mugwump - one of those boys who always has his mug on one side of the political fence and his wump on the other.
Albert J. Engel
multimedia - reading with the radio on.
Rory Bremner
multiple orgasm - something like a good stereo - something you see in magazines and which other people have.
Jeremy Hardy
multitasking - the ability to screw everything up simultaneously.
Jermey Clarkson
mummy - an Egyptian who was pressed for time.
Robert Orben
munchkin - what cannibals do to relatives.
Bree Schultz
murder - an extroverted suicide.
Graham Chapman
murderer - one who is presumed to be innocent until he is proved insane.
Oscar Wilde
(see also: mass murderers)
museums - graveyards of art.
Alphonse de Lamartine
music - the silence between the notes.
Claude Debussy
(see also: baroque music, chamber music, country music, jazz musician, light music, modern music, new music, pop music)
musicals - a series of catastrophes ending with a floor show.
Oscar Levant
musical comedy - the Irish stew of drama. Anything may be put into it with the certainty that it will improve the general effect.
P.G. Wodehouse

musical conductor - a man who has the distinct advantage of not being able to see the audience.
André Kostelanetz
music critics - drooling, drivelling, doleful, depressing, dropsical drips.
Thomas Beecham
musicologist - a man who can read music but cannot hear it.
Thomas Beecham
music with dinner - an insult both to the cook and violinist.
G.K. Chesterton
must - a schoolroom in the month of May.
e.e. cummings
mustang - an indocile horse of the western plains. In English society, the American wife of an English nobleman.
Ambrose Bierce
mute - your husband at a jewelry auction.
Cy DeBoer
Mylanta - my favourite southern town.
Lawrence Brotherton
mystic - a man or woman who wishes to understand the mysteries of the universe but is too lazy to study physics.
Chaz Bufe
mystical - a connection that we feel without understanding it.
Isolde Kurz
mysticism - the mistake of an accidental and individual symbol for a universal one.
Ralph Waldo Emerson
myth - a moth's sister.
Stan Laurel
mythology - the womb of man's initiation to life and death.
Joseph Campbell

N

nag - someone who pursues us with the truth.
Gregory Norminton
nagging - constructive criticism too frequently repeated.
Percy Cudlipp
nail - something you aim at before hitting your thumb with a hammer.
Peter Eldin
naïvety - modern definition of trust.
Mike Barfield
nanny - someone you employ to care for your children, wash their clothes and entertain their father.
Jasmine Birtles
nap - a brief period of sleep which overtakes superannuated persons when they endeavour to entertain unwelcome visitors or to listen to scientific lectures.
George Bernard Shaw
Naples - a polluted prince with mudded brocade, that you have to see before you die.
Simon Carmiggelt
Napoleon - mighty somnambulist of a vanished dream.
Victor Hugo
narcissist - someone better looking than you are.
Gore Vidal
narcotics - the traditional way out for many of the frustrated young in the asphalt jungle of the North.
Charlayne Hunter
narrow minded person - someone who has his brain on a fact free diet.
Charles J.C. Lyall
narrowness - the scope of fundamentalists.
Gys Miedema
nation - a society for hating foreigners.
Olaf Stapledon
national debt - America's most outstanding public figure.
Joseph B. Young

national interest - that which increases the wealth and power of the top 10 percent of the population at the expense of the other 90 percent.
Chaz Bufe
nationalism - the measles of the human race.
Albert Einstein
nationalist - a patriot with blinkers.
Fritz Francken
national pride - a modern form of tribalism.
Robert Shnayerson
national security - the chief cause of national insecurity.
Robert Anton Wilson
native - an oppressed person whose permanent dream is to become the persecutor.
Frantz Fanon
Nato - six nations in search of an enemy.
Peter Ustinov
natural selection - a mechanism for generating an exceedingly high degree of improbability.
Ronald Fisher
natural birth - a case of stiff upper labia.
Kathy Lette
natural birth control - showing your husband the contents of your first child's nappy.
Jasmine Birtles
natural death - when you die without the aid of a doctor.
Mark Twain
nature - only an immense ruin.
Paul Claudel
 (see also: Mother Nature)
naturist holiday - holiday where loss of luggage by airline presents no great problem.
Mike Barfield
nausea - sensation experienced while the body decides whether to throw up or just die.
George Thomas & Lee Schreiner
Navy - a master plan designed by geniuses for execution by idiots.
Herman Wouk
nazism - the pornography of fascism.
Robert Sabatier
(see also: neo-nazis)
necessity - the mother of attraction.
Luke McKissack

needless to say - verbal cliché used to make a superfluous statement even longer.
Mike Barfield
negligent - describes a condition in which you absent-mindedly answer the door in your nightie.
Sandra Hull
neighbour - the best part of a real-estate bargain.
Austin O'Malley
(see also: extravagant neighbour, good neighbour)
neighbourhood - a place where, when you go out of it, you get beat up.
Murray Kempton
neoconservative - a liberal who has been mugged by reality.
Irving Kristol
nerve - what we live on, after our nerves are shot.
Mignon McLaughlin
nervousness - vibrating fear.
Bill Chapko
net - the biggest word in the language of business.
Herbert Casson
net setter - a web junkie who surfs popular web sites or posts to trendy newsgroups.
Brent Glover
nett profit - the part of the balance sheet that businessmen with the best will in the world cannot hide from the shareholders.
Carl Fürstenberg
nettle - the mosquito of the plant world.
Lévi Weemoedt
neurosis - a secret you don't know you're keeping.
Kenneth Tynan
neurotic - sane but unhappy about it.
Rick Bayan
neutral country - a country that does not sell arms to a country at war. Unless they pay cash.
Coluche
neutrality - an evidence of weakness.
Lajos Kossuth
neutral men - the devil's allies.
Edwin Hubbel Chaplin
neutron bomb - a very cultural thing because it destroys the faithful and leaves the churches standing.
Kees Stip

never - a ridiculous word you should *never* use.
Simon Carmiggelt
New Age - just the old age stuck in a microwave oven for fifteen seconds.
James Randi
newlyled - a guy who tells his wife when he gets a pay raise.
Leonard L. Levinson
new morality - too often the old morality condoned.
Hartley Shawcross
new music - old music played twice as fast and half as well.
Jim Morrison
New Orleans - the only city in the world you go in to buy a pair of nylon stockings they want to know your head size.
Bill Holliday
new roads - new ruts.
G.K. Chesterton
news - what happens when there is a CNN camera in the neighbourhood.
Alain Grootaers
newspaper - a device for making the ignorant more ignorant and the crazy crazier.
H.L. Mencken
newspaper column - a letter to invisible readers.
Gerrit Komrij
New Testament - the only whodunit that clearly points to the reader as the guilty one.
Jan Hein Donner
new town - only the same town in a different place.
Susan Glaspell
New Year - the only thing we could afford that was really new.
George Burns
New Year's Day - every man's birthday.
Charles Lamb
(see also: year's end)
New York - the only city in the word where you can be awakened by a smell.
Jeff Garland
(see also: Central Park, Madison Avenue, Manhattan, Times Square, Wall Street)
New York divorce - a diploma of virtue.
Edith Wharton

New Yorker - one who gets acquainted with his neighbour by meeting him down in Florida.
Robert Myers
New Zealand - a country of thirty thousand million sheep - three million of whom think they are human.
Barry Humphries
New Zealanders - the most balanced people in the world - they have a chip on each shoulder.
Dave Allen
Niagara - pure Walt.
Robert Morley
Niagara Falls - the bride's second great disappointment.
Oscar Wilde
Nibelungen - a pornographical work for anti-semites.
Simon Carmiggelt
nice girl - one who whispers sweet nothing-doings into your ear.
James Healy
nice man - a man of nasty ideas.
Jonathan Swift
nickname - the heaviest stone that the devil can throw at a man.
William Hazlitt
nicotine - an awful curse,
It strains the heart and drains the purse.
K.T. Sarma
night - the friend of the free person.
Sophie Scholl
nightclubs - places where the tables are reserved, but the guests aren't.
Frank Caspar
nighthawk - smoker's cough.
John S. Crosbie
nightingale - a pulsating wound in the flesh of the night.
Ramon Gomez de La Serna
night-light - a safety device that allows you just enough light to see what you tripped over.
Joyce Armor
nightmares - *pillow frights.*
Robert Myers
night watchman - a man who earns his living without doing a day's work.
Douglas Helsel

no - the ultimate answer to all superfluous questions.
Herman Brusselmans
(see also: yes)
Nobel Prize - a ticket to one's funeral. No one as ever done anything after he got it.
T.S. Eliot
Nobel Prize money - a lifebelt thrown to a swimmer who has already reached the shore safely.
George Bernard Shaw
no companion - the best type of man.
Elizabeth Bowen
nod - a very hip nap.
Del Close
no exit - a sign indicating the most convenient way out of a building.
J.B. Morton
noise - what they call music in a disco-bar.
Jack de Graef
non-existent - whatever we haven't sufficiently desired.
Franz Kafka
nonsense - the end result of all sense.
Georges Bataille
nonviolence - the weapon of the strong.
Mahatma Gandhi
normal - what the herd does.
Marc Fontenel
normality - a milder form of madness.
Paul Julius Möbius
normal people - people who are different from people who are different.
PEF
(see also: abnormal person)
North Sea - a swimming pool with boats.
Arno Hintjens
Norway - the sun never sets, the bar never opens, and the whole country smells of kippers.
Evelyn Waugh
Norwegian charisma - somewhere between a Presbyterian minister and a tree.
Johnny Carson
nose - an organ that stops people understanding.
Jean Crotti

nostalgia - longing for the place you wouldn't move back to.
James Sanaker
nothing - a dreadful thing to hold on to.
Edna O'Brien
nothingness - the universe without me.
André Suarès
nouvelle cuisine - a child's portion served to an adult.
Henry Beard
novel - story that is too long and not true.
Piet Grijs
novelist - a person who lives in other people's skins.
E.L. Doctorow
novelty - the great parent of pleasure.
Robert South
now - the watchword of the wise.
Charles H. Spurgeon
nowhere - a place where rest reigns.
Piet Grijs
nuclear waste - something that can fade your genes.
Joel Rothman
nude skydiving - proof that you can be embarrassed and scared to death at the same time.
John M. Wagner
nudist camp - place where nothing goes on.
Leo Aikman
nudists - the last people you want to see naked.
David Sedaris
(see also: Buddhist nudist)
nudity - not an easy dress to wear.
Jacques Charles
numbers - the only thing mathematicians can count on.
Fulvio Fiori
nunnery - a place where nothing ever happens.
Willie Meikle
nuns - Gestapo in drag.
Dave Allen
nun's wimple - a bandage where her face was scissored from life.
Daniel Liebert
nurses - women who are full of cheerfulness over other people's troubles.
Agatha Christie
nursing - a dream job if there were no doctors.
Gerhard Kocher

nutcrackers - very tight jeans.
Johan Anthierens
nymph - a lovely young lady whom it is not desirable for a man to develop a mania for.
Edmund H. Volkart
nymphomaniac - bedseller.
Hanns-Dietrich von Seydlitz

oaths - the fossils of piety.
George Santayana
oats - a grain, which in England is generally given to horses, but in Scotland supports the people.
Samuel Johnson
obedience - the mother of success and the wife of safety.
Aeschylus
obelisk - a skinny pyramid.
Ramon Gomez de La Serna
obesity - the mother of distension.
Howard Bennett
obfuscation - the varnish of truth.
Lawrence A. Tomko
obituary - the only kind of bad publicity for a writer.
Brendan Behan
objective - being rational when you have nothing to lose.
Colin Bowles
objectivity - subjectivity, expressed statistically.
Edmund H. Volkart
objects - just data structures with an attitude.
Alex Morrow
oblivion - the offspring of silence.
Hannah More
oboe - an ill-wind that nobody blows good.
Bennett A. Cerf
obscene book - just a badly written book. Talent can never be obscene.
Raymond Poincaré
obscenity - whatever happens to shock some elderly and ignorant magistrate.
Bertrand Russell
obscurity - the refuge of incompetence.
Robert A. Heinlein
observation - activity of both eyes and ears.
Horace Mann
obsession - a search for a useful reality.
Norman Mailer

obsolescence - a factor which says that the new thing I bring you is worth more than the unused value of the old thing.
Charles F. Kettering
obstacles - challenges for winners and excuses for losers.
M.E. Kerr
obstinacy - the energy of the stupid.
Hans Habe
obvious - that which is never seen until someone expresses it simply.
Kahlil Gibran
O Calcutta - the sort of show that gives pornography a bad name.
Clive Barnes
occasional drinker - the kind of guy who goes out for a beer and wakes up in Singapore with a full beard.
Raymond Chandler
occasional vulgarity - a by-product of the vitality and passion without which there can be no great art.
Francis Toye
occult - a young horse.
Keith Nance
occupation - the necessary basis of all enjoyment.
Leigh Hunt
ocean - a place where everybody is a tourist.
Piet Grijs
(see also: Pacific Ocean)
ocean racing - something like standing under a cold shower in a howling gale tearing up ten-pound notes.
Edward Heath
ocelot - the only one who really needs a coat of ocelot fur.
Bernhard Grzimek
October - one of the particularly dangerous months to invest in stocks. Other dangerous months are July, January, September, April, November, May, March, June, December, August and February.
Mark Twain
octopus - an eight-sided cat.
Kevin Goldstein-Jackson
oddball - a third testicle.
Willie Meikle
OED database - infinite riches in a little ROM.
Erich Segal
Oedipus - dilemmama.
Hans-Horst Skupy

office - a machine for dying.
Steve Aylett
official denial - a de facto confirmation.
John Kifner
offline - where the fish-that-got-away went.
Connie Lund
Oklahoma City - probably the only city in the country where you pull a Ford Fairmont into the parking and people come out to admire your car.
Bruce Baum
old age - 15 years older than I am.
Bernard Baruch
(see also: age, being old)
old-fashioned marriage - one that outlasts the wedding gifts.
Hal Roach
old friendship - the only thing that doesn't die before we do.
Heinrich Mann
old maid - a yes-girl who didn't have a chance to talk.
Joey Adams
(see also: spinster)
old men - the neighbours of death.
Yasunari Kawabati
old people's home - the waiting-room for eternal rest.
Hugo Olaerts
old timer - a man who's had a lot of interesting experiences some of them true.
Ken Alstad
Olympic figure skating - a sport where competitors are dress as dinner mints.
Jere Longman
Olympic ideal - undetectable steroids.
Mike Barfield
Olympics - the only time you can represent America and not have to carry a gun.
George Raveling
(see also: Winter Olympics)
Omaha - a little like Newark - without Newark's glamour.
Joan Rivers
ombudsman - a person hired by the governments or news organizations to deal with troublesome matters in such a manner as to justify what went wrong.
Edmund J. Volkart

omen - a sign that something will happen if nothing happens.
Ambrose Bierce
oneself - the last person to know oneself.
Pier Paolo Pasolini
onesided - a word that mostly is defined by the other party.
Willy Courteaux
onesidedness - the worst enemy of taste.
Johan Ludvig Heiberg
on hold - what we Dial-up computer users are while waiting for that black doohickey to slowly and incrementally fill its tiny space just before displaying the "This Page Is No Longer Available" screen.
Lawrence Brotherton
onion - the only food-stuff that causes tears prior to being served.
Henry Beard
on the rebound - excellent excuse for sleeping with utterly unsuitable individuals.
Jeff Green
oomph - the sound a fat man makes when he bends over to tie his laces in a phone booth.
Ann Sheridan
oops - a noise made just prior to the Big Bang.
Cully Abrell
opening night - the night before the play is ready to open.
George Jean Nathan
open marriage - nature's way of telling you you need a divorce.
Marshall Brickman
open mind - the gateway to heaven.
Gary Barnes
openness - often a handy euphemism for "disgusting indiscretion".
Rudi Vandendaele
open relationship - he screws around; she doesn't.
Russell Ash
opera - when a guy gets stabbed in the back and instead of bleeding he sings.
Ed Gardner
(see also: going to the opera, grand opera, musical)
operation - something that takes hours to perform and years to describe.
Milton Berle
operator - a person who hates opera.
Kevin Goldstein-Jackson

operetta - a girl who works for the telephone company.
Steve Allen
opinion - the mistress of fools.
W.G. Benham
 (see also: public opinion)
opinion poll - a survey which claims to show what voters are thinking but which only succeeds in changing their minds.
Miles Kington
opium - religion for the people.
Jan Wolkers
opportunist - a person who strikes a 50-50 deal in such a way that he insists on getting the hyphen as well.
Jack Benny
opportunity - a bird that never perches.
Claude McDonald
opposition - the easiest position.
Albert Willemetz
opposition party - the party that is constantly trying not to be the opposition.
Juul Kinnaer
oppression - the mother of literary invention.
Richard Greene
optics - the geometry of light.
Claude Debussy
optimism - the art of being happy with an uncertain future.
Robert Sabatier
optimist - someone who does his crossword puzzle in ink.
Marcel Achard
oral conception - to talk your way out of it.
Pauline Lacy
oral sex - the only way most of us can get our sex partners to shut up.
P.J. O'Rourke
orator - a man who says what he thinks and feels what he says.
William Jennings Bryan
oratory - the art of making deep noises from the chest sound like important messages from the brain.
H.I. Phillips
order - what exists before you start arranging things.
Marty Rubin
orderly mind - a temple where truth condescends to appear, and delights to be worshipped.
Harriet Martineau

ordinary - a word that has no meaning.
Robin Morgan
ordinary love - the endurance of mutual foolishness.
Ramon Gomez de La Serna
oregano - the spice of life.
Henry J. Tillman
organ - a mechanical box of whistles.
Thomas Beecham
organ donor - someone who looks forward to being outlived by his liver.
Rick Bayan
organic - just another word for dirty fruit.
Ruby Wax
organic gardeners - people who till it like it is.
Joel Rothman
organised crime - just the dirty side of the sharp dollar.
Raymond Chandler
organised person - one who is too lazy to look for things.
JoAnn Thomas
organizing - what you do before you do something, so that when you do it, it's not all mixed up.
Christopher Robin
orgasm - laughter of the loins.
Mickey Rooney
(see also: multiple orgasm)
orgy - group therapy.
Joey Adams
originality - the art of concealing your source.
Franklin P. Jones
original sin - the only original thing about some men.
Helen Rowland
original writer - one whom nobody can imitate.
François-René de Chateaubriand
orism - an aphorism that isn't finished yet.
Kamagurka
ornamental fountains - the petrified toys of satyrs and nymphs.
Ramon Gomez de la Serna
orthodontics - the art of filling in the gaps.
Dave Jones
orthodontist - a guy who braces the kids and straps the parents.
Peter Darbo

orthodoxy - a corpse that doesn't know it's dead.
Elbert Hubbard
orthopaedic surgeon - someone with the strength of an ox but half the brain.
John Dorgan
ostentation - the signal flag of hypocrisy.
Edwin Hubbel Chaplin
osteopath - someone who argues that all human ills are caused by the pressure of hard bone upon soft tissue. The proof of this theory can be found in the heads of those who believe it.
H.L. Mencken
ostrich - the only animal officially endowed with political direction.
Pierre Daninos
(the) others - we, alas!
Georges Bernanos
Ottawa - a city where nobody lives, though some of us may die there.
Michael Macklen
ourselves - the people our mothers warned us against.
John Lennon
outback breakfast - a piss and a look around.
Paul Hogan
outdoors - what you must pass through in order to get from your apartment into a taxicab.
Fran Lebowitz
outer space - no place for a person of breeding.
Violet Bonham Carter
outing - a nasty word for telling the truth.
Armistead Maupin
outlying - where politicians are when campaigning.
Ken Pinkham
outspoken - when you lose a debate.
Georges Carlin
oval - bad-tempered circle.
Gerd de Ley
overestimation of men - the most expensive of all luxuries.
Hans Arndt
over-government - government of the busy by the bossy for the bully.
Arthur Seldon

overtime - time spent doing the work in the evening you never quite got around to during the day.
John Kelly
overweight - just desserts.
Robert Myers
overwork - a dangerous disorder affecting high public functionaries who want to go fishing.
Ambrose Bierce
owls - lamps on the night tables of the forest.
Ramon Gomez de La Serna
Oxford - the most dangerous place to which a young man can be sent.
Anthony Trollope
(see also: Exeter)
Oxford University - the paradise of dead philosophies.
George Santayana
oxymoron - intellectually challenged bovine.
Lawrence Brotherton
oyster - a fish built like a nut.
Peter Darbo
ozone - area in which the G-spot is located.
Irwin L. Singer

P

Pacific Ocean - a body of water surrounded on all sides by elephantiasis and other dread diseases.
Joseph Heller

pacifist - a logical person who believes that since peace is so much better than war, it is not worth fighting for.
Edmund J. Volkart

Paddington Station - two very different places depending on whether you are arriving or departing.
Geoffrey Madan

pagan - what you get when you scratch a Christian.
Israel Zangwill

pageantry - the sort of thing the British overdo so well.
Noël Coward

pain - nature's way of saying, 'Ouch!'
Greg Parrish

pain of love - the pain of being alive. It's a perpetual wound.
Maureen Duffy

painting - a fight with yourself and the material.
Karel Appel
(see also: finger painting, good painting, great work)

pair of spectacles - false teeth for the eyes.
Lévi Weemoedt

Pakistan - the sort of place every man should send his mother-in-law, for a month, with all expenses paid.
Ian Botham

Palestine - the cement that holds the Arab world together, or the explosive that blows it apart.
Yasir Arafat

Palmer, Arnold - the biggest crowd-pleaser since the invention of the portable sanitary facility.
Bob Hope

pamper - someone who breaks wind.
Willie Meikle

pandemonium - a recipe to cook demons.
Victoria Tarrani

panic - that subtle emotion you feel when you realize your business has three more salesmen than customers.
Robert Orben

panic room - the kitchen on Christmas Day.
Mike Barfield
pantheism - the doctrine that everything is God, in contradiction to the doctrine that God is everything.
Ambrose Bierce
pantomime - the smell of oranges and wee-wee.
Arthur Askey
(see also: mime)
Papacy - the Ghost of the deceased Roman Empire, sitting crowned upon the grave thereof.
Thomas Hobbes
Papaphobia - fear of the Pope.
Matt Groening
paparazzi - dogs of war.
Catherine Deneuve
paper clips - the larval stage of wire coat hangers.
Jerry Scott & Jim Borgman
papyromania - compulsive accumulation of papers.
Laurence J. Peter
papyrophobia - abnormal desire for 'a clean desk'.
Laurence J. Peter
paradise - the Luna Park of Limbo Land.
Colin Bowles
(see also: true paradise)
paradox - a tail that eats its own snake.
J. Goudsblom
paragraphing - one of the lower forms of cunning, like a way with women.
Harry V. Wade
paralysis - the first stage of wisdom.
Francis Picabia
paranoia - knowing the facts.
Woody Allen
paranoid - a sensible and well-adjusted reaction to living in Hell, where they really were all out to get you.
Terry Pratchett
paranoid-schizophrenic - someone who always thinks he is following himself.
Gene Perret
parakeet - a keet that takes care of you until the real keet arrives.
George Carlin
parasite - double vision.
Victoria Tarrani

parental love - the only real charity going. It never comes back. A one-way street.
Abbie Hoffman
parenthood - feeding the mouth that bites you.
Peter De Vries
parents - the very last people who ought to be allowed to have children.
Samuel Butler
(see also: father, love of parents, mother, perfect parent, successful parent)
Paris - a city that doesn't look kindly on poor people - contrary to what it says in the brochures.
Simon Carmiggelt
parking - street sorrow.
Herb Caen
parking lot - a place where you pay to leave your car while dents are put in the fenders.
Herbert V. Prochnow
parking space - what disappears when you make a U-turn.
R.G. Menon
parks - pavements disguised with a growth of grass.
George Gissing
parkway - a place where cars are driven, as distinguished from a driveway where cars are parked.
Edmund J. Volkart
parliament - the longest running farce in the West End.
Cyril Smith
parliamentarianism - putting political prostitution in barracks.
Karl Kraus
parody - the last refuge of the frustrated writer.
Ernest Hemingway
(see also: self-parody)
participative management - involving the right people at the right time in the decision process.
Wayne Barlow
parties - fêtes worse than death.
Barbara Stanwyck
parting - the younger sister of death.
Osip Mandelsjtam
part-time job - full-time job for half salary.
Denise D. Lynn

parturition - a physiological process - the same in the countess and in the cow.
W.W. Chipman

party - the bringing together of people who have nothing to say to each other and doing it extremely well.
Gerhard Löwenthal

parvenu - always someone else.
Anka Muhlstein

pas de deux - father of twins.
Janet Rogers

passion - the desire to take a cigarette out of one's mouth before kissing one's betrothed.
Gary Davies

passport picture - a photo of a man that he can laugh at without realizing that it looks exactly the way his friends see him.
Phyllis Diller

past - a coarse and sensual prophecy of the present and the future.
Nathaniel Hawthorne

pastime - a device for promoting dejection. Gentle exercise for intellectual debility.
Ambrose Bierce

pastis - a drink you can compare with breasts: one is not enough and three is too many.
Fernandel

pastry - the acid test of a good restaurant.
Henry Root

pâté - a French meat loaf that's had a couple of cocktails.
Carol Cutler

path - just a place that has had the life trampled out of it.
Ray Goforth

pathos - the laziness of logic.
Hans Kasper

patience - the art of caring slowly.
John Ciardi

patient man - one who can listen to his wife until she's exhausted.
O.A. Battista

patio - what your husband calls the back part of your house since the walls collapsed.
Cy DeBoer

pat on the back - the most painful kind of fee.
Heinrich Böll

patriotism - the last refuge of a scoundrel.
Samuel Johnson
patriots - people who always talk of dying for their country, but never of *killing* for it.
Bertrand Russell
(see also: real patriot)
patron - a wretch who supports with insolence and is paid with flattery.
Samuel Johnson
pauses - the most precious things in speech.
Ralph Richardson
PC - the LSD of the 90s.
Timothy Leary
peace - a brief moment between wars when people stop to reload.
James Dobson
peace of mind - the contentment of the man who is too busy to worry by day, and too sleepy to worry at night.
Woodrow Wilson
peacocks - myths which have been retired.
Ramon Gomez de La Serna
peanut butter - pâté for children.
Brigitte Bardot
pearl - an oyster tumour.
Colin Bowles
Pearl Harbor - a two-hour movie squeezed into three hours, about how on December 7, 1941, the Japanese staged a surprise attack on an American love triangle.
Roger Ebert
pedagogue - a monster with teeth of chalk.
Jeroen Brouwers
pedantry - stupidity that read a book.
Samuel Butler
pedestal - as much a prison as any small space.
Gloria Steinem
pedestrian - someone who thought he had put petrol in his tank.
Sam Levenson
pediatricians - men of little patients.
Shelly Friedman
peephole - observation port.
George Carlin
peeping Tom - a guy who is too lazy to go to the beach.
Henny Youngman

peers - a kind of eye-shade or smoked glass, to protect us from the full glare of Royalty.
Geoffrey Madan
pekes - biological freaks.
E.B. White
Peking - toilet king.
Tim Bruening
pen - a printer, hooked straight to my brain.
Dale Dauten
penalty - a cowardly way to score.
Pélé
pencil - the only thing that goes missing in Nature.
Robert Benchley
penicillin - what you give a man who has everything.
Jerry Lester
penis - a male organ commonly employed in place of the brain.
Chaz Bufe
(see also: phallus, small penis)
pension - pay given to a state hireling for treason to his country.
Samuel Johnson
Pentagon - immense monument to modern man's subservience to the desk.
Oliver Shewell Franks
people - just friends waiting to be made.
Jeffery Borenstein
(see also: normal people)
peptic ulcer - a hole in a man's stomach through which he crawls to escape from his wife.
J.A.D. Anderson
perennial - any plant which, had it lived, would have bloomed year after year.
Henry Beard
perfect bureaucrat - the man who manages to make no decisions and escape all responsibility.
Brooks Atkinson
perfect cat - one with a purr that doesn't wake you up in the middle of the night.
Alan Forman
perfect fund manager - a guy who can't pick his kids out in a police lineup.
Michael Stolper

perfect husband - a man who is convinced he has the perfect wife.
Vicky Satter
perfection - when form and content meet.
Marcel Marceau
perfectionism - the enemy of creation.
John Updike
perfectionist - someone who takes great pains to give them to other people.
Martin A. Ragaway
perfect happiness - the absence of the striving for happiness.
Henri-Frédéric Amiel
perfect lawyer - one who can persuade the jury to come in with a verdict : 'We find the defendant not guilty, but we strongly advise him not to do it again...'
Maurice Garçon
perfect love - to love the one through whom one became unhappy.
Sören Kierkegaard
perfect lover - one who turns into a pizza at 4:00 A.M.
Charles Pierce
perfect marriage - one in which "I'm sorry" is said just often enough.
Mignon McLaughlin
perfect parent - a person with excellent child-rearing theories and no actual children.
Dave Barry
perfect politician - a person who can lie to the press, then believe what he reads.
Will Durst
perfect secret - the one nobody knows.
Gerd de Ley
perfect stillness - the only perfection you will ever achieve.
Philip J. Simborg
perfume - any smell that is used to drown a worse one.
Elbert Hubbard
period - the end of a grammatical sentence and the beginning of a woman's sentence.
Cy DeBoer
permanence - a man-made fantasy smiled on by time.
Paul von Ringelheim
permissiveness - neglect of duty.
Zig Ziglar

peroxide - bleacher's pet.
Charles G. Waugh
perpetual holiday - a good working definition of hell.
George Bernard Shaw
perplexity - the beginning of knowledge.
Kahlil Gibran
persecution - the first law of society because it is always easier to suppress criticism than to meet it.
Howard Mumford Jones
perseverance - the hard work you do after you get tired of doing the hard work you already did.
Newt Gingrich
Persian furcoat - for ladies of a certain age as inevitable as menopause.
Simon Carmiggelt
persistence - what makes the impossible possible, the possible likely, and the likely definite.
Robert Half
person - that inexplicable test tube of chemical disappointments.
Howard Jacobson
personal appearance - looking the best you can for money.
Virginia Cary Hudson
personal injustice - a stronger motivation than any instinct for philanthropy.
John Irving
personality - an unbroken series of successful gestures.
F. Scott Fitzgerald
personality tithe - a price paid for becoming a couple.
Douglas Coupland
personal wealth - a badge of competence at getting someone else to pay your bills.
David Ransom
personal web pages - the equivalent of home video, except that you don't have to visit somebody else's house to fall asleep - you can do so in the comfort of your own house.
Ray Valdes
personal website - something like a refrigerator door that the whole world can look at.
James S. Huggins
personhole - not an acceptable de-sexed word.
Shirley Dean

perspective - a ghastly mistake which it has taken four centuries to redress.
Georges Braque
persuade - soft leather used to make handbags.
P.C. Swanson
perversion - whatever the speaker does not have amongst his sexual preferences.
Julien Vandiest
perversity - what begins where pleasure stops.
Jean-Claude Carrière & Pierre Etaix
perverted - having sexual preferences similar to one's own, but lacking the discretion to conceal them.
Chaz Bufe
pessimism - hobby with which the neighbours have most of the fun.
Julien de Valckenaere
(see also: optimism)
pessimist - someone who regrets what he is about to do.
J. Goudsblom
(see also: optimist)
petition - a list of people who didn't have the courage to say no.
Evan Esar
pets - the glue that holds dysfunctional families together.
Edward Thompson
petting - the study of human anatomy in Braille.
Joey Adams
phallocrat - name the impotents give to normal people.
Georges Elgozy
phallus - the bridge to the future.
D.H. Lawrence
phantoms - trifling disorders of the spirit: images we cannot contain within the bounds of sleep.
Luigi Pirandello
Pharisee - a man who prays publicly and preys privately.
Don Marquis
phewy - an intermission of gas, often silent, that makes itself known by its rank smell.
Peter Furze
Philadelphia - a metropolis sometimes known as the City of Brotherly Love, but more accurately as the City of Bleak November Afternoons.
S.J. Perelman

philanthropist - one who gives away what he should give back.
Joey Adams

philantropy - the refuge of people who wish to annoy their fellow creatures.
Oscar Wilde

philistine - one who has a problem for every solution.
Robert Zend
(see also: cultural philosopher, good philosopher, great philosophers)

philosophize - only another way of being afraid and leads hardly anywhere but to cowardly make-believe.
Louis-Ferdinand Céline

philosophy - common sense with big words.
James Madison

phobophobia - fear of fear itself.
Matt Groening

phonesia - the affliction of dialing a phone number and forgetting whom you were calling just as they answer.
Rich Hall

phoning in sick - the only winter sport at which the British excel.
Ronald White

photographs - pictures taken to please the family, bore the neighbours, and enrich the camera shops.
Edmund J. Volkart
(see also: great photograph)

photographers - the taxidermists of time.
Rein Nomm

photography - focus pocus.
Terrance Hughes
(see also: trick photography)

phrase - a clutch of words that gives you a clutch at the heart.
Robert Frost

physical pain - the only antidote to mental suffering.
Karl Marx

physician - one who pours drugs of which he knows little into a body of which he knows less.
Voltaire
(see also: medical profession)

physicist - just an atom's way of looking at itself.
Niels Bohr

physics - a form of insight and as such it's a form of art.
David Bohm

piano - a monster that screams when you touch its teeth.
Andrés Segovia
pianoforte - a harp in a box.
Leigh Hunt
picnic - a meal eaten more than 50 yards from the nearest toilet.
Henry Beard
picture - something between an thing and a thought.
Samuel Palmer
(see also: passport picture)
pier - a disappointed bridge.
James Joyce
piety - a nobler form of superstition.
Fritz Francken
pig - an animal that dreams of pig-swill and garbage and an abundance of acorns; of sunny pastures and more than its fair share of mud, of spring and the love of pigs.
Daan Zonderland
pigeon - rat with wings.
Alfred Small
pigmentation - thoughts of a swine.
Keith Nance
pigtail - a story about a pig.
Kevin Goldstein-Jackson
pillage - to plunder a pharmacy.
Johnny Hart
pimp - a man who knows what a woman's worth.
Rich Hall
pimping - a popular form of entertainment in medical centers, occasionally interrupted by teaching.
Howard Bennett
pimple - a panderer's apprentice.
Meg Sullivan
pink - the navy blue of India.
Diana Vreeland
pink elephant - a beast of bourbon.
John S. Crosbie
pioneering - basically amounts to finding new and more horrible ways to die.
John W. Campbell
pious man - one who would be an atheist if the king were.
Jean de La Bruyère

pipe smoking - the most protracted of all forms of tobacco consumption. It may explain why pipe smokers are generally regarded as patient men - and philosophers.
Jerome E. Brooks
pirouette - a whirlwind made to measure.
Gys Miedema
pistol - the sceptre of the bully.
George Meredith
pitching - the art of instilling fear by making a man flinch.
Sandy Koufax
Pittsburg - hell with the lid taken off.
James Parton
pity - a short-lived passion.
Oliver Goldsmith
(see also: self-pity)
plagiarism - to copy so clumsily that it is noticed.
Gaby vanden Berghe
plagiarist - someone who steals a writer's mental children.
Isaac Asimov
planet - a large body of matter entirely surrounded by a void, as distinguished from a clergyman, who is a large void entirely surrounded by matter.
Elbert Hubbard
planned economy - where everything is included in the plans except economy.
Carey McWilliams
planning - bringing the future into the present so you can do something about it now.
Alan Lakein
planning a wedding - not the best way to start off married life.
Kathy Nicolai
plans - inaccurate predictions.
Ben Bayol
(see also: strategic plan)
plastic surgeons - people who are always making mountains out of molehills.
Dolly Parton
plastic surgery - medicine in reverse: you go in healthy and come out as a patient.
Midas Dekkers
platform - something a candidate stands for and the voters fall for.
Gracie Allen

platitude - a truth repeated until people get tired of hearing it.
Stanley Baldwin
platonic friendship - euphemism for lack of courage.
Herluf van Merlet
platonic love - the time between the first meeting and the first kiss.
Paul Géraldy
platonic lover - a man who holds the eggshells while somebody else eats the omelette.
Robert Myers
platonic relationships - those friendships which we all know involve at least one person living a lie.
Jeff Green
play - work that you enjoy doing for nothing.
Evan Esar
play (theatre) - basically a means of spending two hours in the dark without being bored.
Kenneth Tynan
Playboy - Donald Fuck.
Toon Verhoeven
playboy - a man who believes in wine, women, and so long.
John Travolta
playgirl - a heart stimulant for elderly gentlemen.
Robert Myers
playing polo - something like trying to play golf during an earthquake.
Sylvester Stallone
playwright - a lay preacher peddling the ideas of this time in popular form.
August Strindberg
pleasure - the least hateful form of dejection.
Ambrose Bierce
plebiscite - a popular vote to ascertain the will of the sovereign.
Ambrose Bierce
pleonasm - an unsatisfied woman.
Jean Grenier
plot - the knowing of destination.
Elizabeth Bowen
plumber - a drain surgeon.
Leopold Fechtner
pluralism - that's when more people disagree with you.
Jean-François Revel

plus sign - the crucifix of capitalism.
Guy Commerman
PMS - means never wanting to say you're sorry.
Diana Jordan
poaching - the fancy word for boiling.
P.J. O'Rourke
pockets - the difference between men and women.
Susan Strasberg
poem - a prolonged hesitation between sound and sense.
Paul Valéry
(see also: good poem)
poet - a sculptor that paints music.
Clem Schouwenaars
(see also: bad poet, true poets)
poet laureate - just a bard in a gilded cage.
Raymond Cvikota
poetry - an echo, asking a shadow to dance.
Carl Sandburg
poetry books - handy implements for killing persistent irritating flies.
Geoffrey Grigson
poise - the ability to keep talking while the other fellow picks up the bill.
Michael Hodgin
poison - the coward's weapon.
Phineas Fletcher
point - the opposite of infinity.
Ed Richard
point of view - a dangerous luxury when substituted for insight and understanding.
Marshall McLuhan
poker - a tough way to make an easy living.
Bob Thompson
polar bear - rectangular bear after a coordinate transform.
Bill White
polar exploration - the cleanest and most isolated way of having a bad time which has been devised.
Apsley Cherry-Garrard
police files - our only claim to immortality.
Milan Kundera
police state - a pleonasm.
Kurt Tucholsky

politeness - the small print of the Ten Commandments.
Godfried Bomans
(see also: courtesy)
political ability - the ability to foretell what is going to happen tomorrow, next week, next month, and next year. And to have the ability afterward to explain why it didn't happen.
Winston Churchill
political asylum - any governmental office.
Johnny Carson
political campaigns - the graveyard of real ideas lies and the birthplace of empty promises.
Teresa Heinz
political convention - a chess tournament disguised as a circus.
Alistair Cooke
politically correct culture - an imitation fur coat - inhabited by real fleas.
Peter Robinson
political correctness - censorship under another name.
Peter Hall
political corruption - the toboggan to national disruption.
John A. Ward
political economy - the rich man's version of the Sermon on the Mount.
Geoffrey Madan
political election - a circus wrestling match.
Nikita Khrushchev
political history - far too criminal a subject to be a fit thing to teach children.
W.H. Auden
political influence - the cornerstone of group progress in America.
Kenny Jones
political oratory - the art of saying platitudes with courtesy and propriety.
Armando Palacio Valdés
political problem - an economical problem without a solution.
Georges Elgozy
political promises - any similarity to fiction is genuine.
Eric Piscador
political refugee - someone who votes with his feet.
Vladimir Lenin

political thinking - deciding upon the conclusion first and then finding good arguments for it.
Richard Crossman
political war - one in which everyone shoots from the lip.
Raymond Moley
politicians - people who shake your hand before an election, and your purse afterwards.
Gerd de Ley
(see also: bravest politician, consensus politician, honest politician, perfect politician)
politics - something for people who are too ugly to get into show business.
Bill Clinton
(see also: modern politics, practical politics, world politics)
pollution - grime in the streets.
Joel Rothman
polygamy - to some the opposite of monotony.
Gene Mora
(see also: bigamy)
polymath - a parrot that likes mathematics.
Kevin Goldstein-Jackson
pomposity - only the failure of pomp.
G.K. Chesterton
poodle - nothing more than a mini llama - and it's gay!
Wim Helsen
poor - the only ones who are obliged to have money.
Henri Alphonse Esquiros
poor buoyancy - the realization that one was a better person when one had less money.
Douglas Coupland
poor man - one who gets his money by earning it.
Bob Edwards
poor relation - the most irrelevant thing in nature.
Charles Lamb
pop art - the indelible raised to the unspeakable.
Leonard Baskin
popcorn - the last area of the movie business where good taste is still a concern.
Vincent Canby
pop culture - a benign growth taking over everything it touches.
Brian Eno

pope - God's ventriloquist.
Marc Pairon
(see also: Vat 69)
pop music - rock music without the sex or the soul.
Mark Fisher
popularity - the capacity for listening sympathetically when men boast of their wives and women complain of their husbands.
H.L. Mencken
population growth - the primary source of environmental damage.
Jacques-Yves Cousteau
pornographer - someone who tickles you to death with a fig leaf.
Luc van Brussel
pornographic films - Nipples cover the screen like acne on a juvenile's forehead.
Stephen Pile
pornography - the eroticism of the others.
André Breton
(see also: real pornography)
port - the milk of donhood.
Max Beerbohm
Port au Prince - a sort of slum Venice in which the canals are open drains.
Norman Lewis
portrait - a picture in which there is something wrong with the mouth.
Eugene Speicher
positive thinking - self-improvement through self-deception.
Rick Bayan
(to) possess - a verb, invented by people who are bored.
Chris Yperman
possession - friendship between men and things.
Jean-Paul Sartre
possibility - the seed of the flower.
Richard Wilkins
possibly - no in three syllables.
L.L. Levinson
posterity - the patriotic name for grandchildren.
Art Linkletter
post impressionist - a person who does impressions by mail order - or a person who dresses up as an envelope.
Tony Blackburn

post-modernism - modernism's midlife crisis.
Lori Ellison
postmodernity - the simultaneity of the destruction of earlier values and their reconstruction. It is renovation within ruination.
Jean Baudrillard
post office - the old stamping grounds.
Fibber McGee
postponement - the sincerest form of rejection.
Robert Half
postwar architecture - the accountants' revenge on the prewar businessmen's dreams.
Rem Koolhaas
potato - an Irish avocado.
Fred Allen
pottering - the most fun you can have in slippers.
Guy Browning
poultry-geist - a haunted chicken.
Clynch Varnadore
pound notes - the best religion in the world.
Brendan Behan
poverty - something that can't be bought with money.
Herman Brusselmans
(see also: honest poverty)
power - the ultimate aphrodisiac.
Henry Kissinger
(see also: true power)
power politics - the diplomatic name for the law of the jungle.
Ely Culbertson
practical man - a man who practices the errors of his forefathers.
Benjamin Disraeli
practical politics - the glad hand, and a swift kick in the pants.
Kin Hubbard
practice - the only norm for verifying truth.
Deng Xiaoping
pragmatism - brainstorming in a glass of water.
Toon Verhoeven
praise - the daughter of present power.
Jonathan Swift
(to) pray - a culturally acceptable way of complaining.
Kees Simhoffer
prayer - a wish turned heavenward.
Phillips Brooks
(see also: intercessory prayer)

preamble - warm-up before a walk.
Ray Hand
precipitous action - something you do when you're all wet.
Don Daniels
preconcieved notions - the locks on the door to wisdom.
Merry Browne
prediction - an explanation in advance.
James Carse
preface - the most important part of a book. Even reviewers read a preface.
Philip Guedalla
pregnancy - getting company inside one's skin.
Maggie Scarf
pregnant - full of love.
Johan Anthierens
prejudice - any line of reasoning that proves you are right.
O.A. Battista
premature ejaculation - a crime of passion.
Hellura Lyle
première - a large number of people standing around looking famous.
Dennis Mackail
Premier League football - a multi-million-pound industry with the aroma of a blocked toilet and the principles of a knocking shop.
Michael Parkinson
premise - a proper girl.
Victoria Tarrani
preparation - an important key to self-confidence.
Arthur Ashe
prepared childbirth - a contradiction in terms.
Joyce Armor
preposition - something you should never end a sentence with.
Jill Etherington
preppie - a human gimme pig.
Joey Adams
presence - more than just being there.
Malcolm S. Forbes
present - the history of the future.
Alecander Pola
(see also: future, past, today)

preservative - any addition to an edible product that increases the life of the food while shortening the life of the consumer.
Henry Beard
presidency - a cross between a popularity contest and a high school debate, with an encyclopaedia of clichés as first price.
Saul Bellow
press - short for pressure.
Tom Fontana
(see also: wooing the press)
press agent - a guy who hitches his braggin' to a star.
Hedda Hopper
(see also: theatrical press agent)
pressure - what you feel when you don't know what's going on.
Chuck Knoll
prestige - a bubble that bursts right away when you blow it yourself.
Heinz Hilpert
pretty girl - one who can run away with a man's imagination... and his money.
O.A. Battista
preview - that part of a theatre run which is not affected by bad reviews.
Miles Kington
price-tag hunting - a favourite indoor sport.
Renee Long
pride - the father of modesty.
Rudy Kousbroek
priests - people who create much work by not working.
Ramon J. Sender
prig - a fellow who is always making you a present of his opinions.
George Eliot
prime mate - a chimpanzee's best friend.
Michael Blickman
prime minister - the loneliest job in the world.
Stanley Baldwin
prime time - the precious evening hours of our lives that most of us spend watching television.
Rick Bayan
primitive artist - an amateur whose work sells.
Grandma Moses
Prince Edward - one of the chief flag-bearers for the Republican cause.
Will Self

princess - an accident that happened while trying to make a prince.
Manfred Gottfried
principles - a dangerous form of social dynamite.
Katherine Susan Anthony
(see also: in principle)
printer - a device that consists of three parts: the case, the jammed paper tray and the blinking red light.
Dave Barry
prison - a guest house with so many amenities that many of its patrons are quite happy to return.
Lambert Jeffries
(see also: governor, maximum security prison, warder)
prisoner of war - a man who tries to kill you and fails, and then asks you not to kill him.
Winston Churchill
privacy - keeping taboos in their place.
Kate Millett
private greed - making money by selling people what they want.
Thomas Sowell
private property - the original source of freedom. It still is its main bulwark.
Walter Lippmann
private school - a place which has all the faults of a public one, without any of its compensations.
Cyril Connolly
privileges - the greatest enemies of justice.
Marie von Ebner-Eschenbach
P.R. man - a press agent with a manicure.
Alan Gordon
probability - the greatest enemy of truth.
Abbé Sergé
problems - opportunities with thorns on them.
Hugh Miller
(see also: big problems, little problems, political problem, real problem)
procrastination - the art of keeping up with yesterday.
Don Marquis
proctologist - a doctor who starts out at the bottom and stays there.
Joe Tierney
procurer - fornicaterer.
Joey Adams

prodigy - a child who plays the piano when he ought to be in bed.
J.B. Morton
producer - an authoritarian figure who risks nothing, presumes to know public taste, and always wants to change the end of the film.
Federico Fellini
producing a school play - a simple way of qualifying for admission to a mental hospital.
Balaam
profanity - a man's way of letting off scream.
O.A. Battista
professional - someone who can do his best work when he doesn't feel like it.
Alistair Cooke
professional celebrity - the crowning result of the star system of a society that makes a fetish of competition.
C. Wright Mills
professional football - the primary cause of wife abandonment by modern males, who sit spellbound before the tube as teams of hulks try to outdo each other in offensiveness.
Rick Bayan
professional golf - the only time you will see Asians that are good drivers.
Mark Morfey
professionalism - knowing how to do it, when to do it, and doing it.
Frank Tyger
professional wrestling - just rehearsed acrobatics.
George Hackenschmidt
professional writer - an amateur who didn't quit.
Richard Bach
professions - conspiracies against the laity.
George Bernard Shaw
professor - one who talks in someone else's sleep.
W.H. Auden
(see also: college professor)
profitability - the sovereign criterion of the enterprise.
Peter Drucker
profits - part of the mechanism by which society decides what it wants to see produced.
Henry C. Wallich
(see also: nett profit)

programmer - people who, at dead of night, use unreliable hardware with totally unsuitable development packages for incompatible systems, to convert contradictory requests from incompetent operators into a program which no one will use anyway.
Joachim Graf
programming - an unnatural act.
Alan J. Perlis
(see also: diagnostic program)
programming today - a race between software engineers striving to build bigger and better idiot-proof programs, and the Universe trying to produce bigger and better idiots. So far, the Universe is winning.
Richard Cook
progress - stepping in dogshit and putting it down to experience.
John Lennon
prohibitionist - the sort of man one wouldn't care to drink with - even if he drank.
H.L. Mencken
prohibitions - signs of weakness of the democracy.
Hugo Schiltz
promiscuity - a stepping stone to love.
Edna O'Brien
promiscuous person - someone who is getting more sex than you are.
Victor Lownes
promise - an IOU.
Robert Half
(see also: broken promises, political promises)
promoters - guys with two pieces of bread looking for a piece of cheese.
Evel Knievel
promotion - new title, new salary, new office, same old crap.
Jim Fisk & Robert Barron
propaganda - patriotism as practised by our enemies.
Rick Bayan
propane filling station - tank heaven for little grills.
Sue Glover
property - organised robbery.
George Bernard Shaw
(see also: private property)
prophecy - the wit of a fool.
Vladimir Nabokov

prophet - anyone who says that anything will happen.
J.B. Morton
propriety - the least of all laws, and the most observed.
François de La Rochefoucauld
prosperity - the best protector of principle.
Mark Twain
prostitute - commercial sex worker.
George Carlin
(see also: frostitute, hooker, pimp)
prostitution - the fastfood of sex.
Matthew Graham
protestantism - a religion which has as its chief contribution to human thought the massive proof that God is a bore.
H.L. Mencken
protest song - a song that's so specific that you cannot mistake it for bullshit.
Phil Ochs
protocol - etiquette with a government expense account.
Judith Martin
proverb - one man's wit and all men's wisdom.
John Russell
providence - the Christian name of Chance.
Madame de Créqui
prude - one who is troubled by improper thoughts, as distinguished from the rest of us, who rather enjoy them.
Babe Webster
prudence - a rich, ugly old maid courted by incapacity.
William Blake
prudent investor - someone who made money in the third quarter.
Kurt Brouwer
prune - a plum that hasn't taken care of itself.
Art Linkletter
psychiatrist - a person who owns a couch and charges you for lying on it.
Edwin Brock
(see also: shrink)
psychiatry - spending $50 an hour to squeal on your mother.
Mike Connolly
psychoanalysis - that mental illness for which it regards itself as therapy.
Karl Kraus

psychoanalyst - a non-swimmer who works as a lifeguard.
Thomas S. Szasz
psychoceramics - the study of crackpots.
Benny Hill
psychologist - someone you go to when you're slightly cracked, and continue attending until you're totally broke.
Tony Hancock
(see also: experimental psychologist)
psychology - the science that tells you what you already know, in words you can't understand.
Joey Adams
psychopath - someone who lives in an ivory tower and dribbles over the battlements.
Colin Bowles
psychosis - the final outcome of all that is wrong with a culture.
Jules Henry
pteronophobia - fear of being tickled by feathers.
Matt Groening
puberty - a hair raising experience.
M. Leger
pubic hair - no substitute for wit.
J.B. Priestley
public - as an individual they might be stupid but as a group they are a genius.
Lenny Bruce
publication - the male equivalent of childbirth.
Richard Acland
public behaviour - merely private character writ large.
Stephen R. Covey
publicist - a man who bores the community with the details of the illegalities of his private life.
Oscar Wilde
publicity - the theory that no news is bad news, that neither divorce nor adultery nor sex videotapes nor checking into a clinic to dry out will stay our celebrities from swiftly cashing in on the free exposure.
Rick Bayan
public life - the paradise of voluble windbags.
George Bernard Shaw
public office - the last refuge of a scoundrel.
Boies Penrose

public opinion - a vulgar, impertinent, anonymous tyrant who deliberately makes life unpleasant for anyone who is not content to be the average man.
William R. Inge
public relations - organized lying.
Malcolm Muggeridge
public schools - the nurseries of all vice and immorality.
Henry Fielding
publishers - people that kill good trees to put out bad newspapers.
James G. Watt
publishing - a matter saying Yes and No at the right time.
Michael Joseph
puck - a hard rubber disk that hockey players strike when they can't hit one another.
Jimmy Cannon
pug - the living proof that God has a sense of humor.
Margo Kaufman
pugnacity - a form of courage, but a very bad form.
Sinclair Lewis
pull together - to avoid being pulled apart.
Bob Allisat
pulpit - the cradle of English prose.
A.G. Little
pun - the lowest form of humor - when you don't think of it first.
Oscar Levant
(see also: good pun, punning)
Punch - the official journal of dentists' waiting rooms.
J.B. Priestley
punctual - childless.
Joyce Armor
punctuality - the virtue of the bored.
Evelyn Waugh
punctual man - a fellow who doesn't own a watch.
O.A. Battista
punishment - the justice that the guilty deal out to those that are caught.
Elbert Hubbard
punk - just a way to sell trousers.
Malcolm McLaren
punk movement - a room without furniture, completely empty.
Tom Waits

punning - a talent which no man affects to despise but he that is without it.
Jonathan Swift
puppy - a little waggin' without wheels.
Robert Myers
pure love - a willingness to give without a thought of receiving anything in return.
Peace Pilgrim
puritan - an ox that thinks it is appalling that bulls exist.
Julien de Valckenaere
puritanism - the haunting fear that someone, somewhere, may be happy.
H.L. Mencken
purpose - the keystone in the temple of achievement.
James Allen
push-up bra - the equivalent of Einstein's theory of relativity.
Dolly Parton
pussyfoot - a rare female birth defect requiring the use of open-toed shoes.
George Carlin
Putin regime - capitalism with a Stalin face.
Grigory Yavlinsky
puzzle - cupboard from Ikea.
Jan Verheyen
Pyramids - a practical joke played on history.
Peter Forster

Q

QANTAS - a condom on the penis of progress.
Ian Tuxworth
quacks - the greatest liars in the world except their patients.
Benjamin Franklin
quadrasexual - someone who will do anything with anyone for a quarter.
Ed Bluestone
quality - what you get when you exclude coincidence.
Louis van Gaal
quandary - a camel with four humps.
Diane Reamy Capewell
quantity - a very poor substitute for quality - but it's the only one around.
Mignon McLaughlin
quantum mechanics - the stuff dreams are made of.
Steven Wright
quantum particles - the dreams that stuff is made of.
David Moser
quark - the sound made by an English duck.
Colin Bowles
quarrels - the dowry which married folk bring one another.
Ovid
quartet - a singing group in which all four think the other three cannot sing.
Doris Maloney
Quebec - one of the ten provinces against which Canada is defending itself.
Carl Dubuc
queen - often a crone on a throne.
Alberto Young
(see also: king)
question - often the mother of the lie.
Wilhelm Busch
(see also: silly question, stupid questions)
question mark - a tired exclamation mark.
Stanislaw Jerzy Lec

quiet - what all murdering, psychopathic neighbours prove later to have been.
Mike Barfield
quiggiligus - one of the individual holes in the mesh on most speakers.
Matthew Feinberg
quilt guilt - always hogging more than your share of the covers.
Judith Viorst
quire - a singing group.
Victoria Tarrani
quorum - a sufficient number of members of a deliberative body to have their own way and their own way of having it.
Ambrose Bierce
quotation - a line borrowed from some immortal work of the dominant culture, generally in an effort to impress one's peers.
Rick Bayan
(see also: beautiful quotation, misquotation)
quotation book - a supermarket of thoughts.
Gerd de Ley
quotations marks - handcuffs for pithy expressions.
Wolfram Weidner
(to) quote - to hire a text without paying rent.
Karel Jonckheere

R

rabbit - the *real* fast food.
Patrick de Witte
rabble - offensive term your husband uses in regard to *your* side of the family.
Cy DeBoer
rabid fan - a guy who boos a television set.
Jimmy Cannon
racehorse - an animal that can take several thousand people for a ride at the same time.
Marjorie Johnson
race track - a place where windows clean people.
Henny Youngman
racewalking - what looks like a bunch of people trying to rush to the bathroom without breaking into an embarrassing run.
Reg Henry
racial prejudice - a pigment of the imagination.
Nigel Rees
racing - 99% boredom and 1% terror.
Geoff Brabham
racism - only a form of misanthropy.
Joseph Brodsky
racist - someone who is winning an argument with a liberal.
Peter Brimelow
racket - a line you adopt to make money you don't deserve.
John Coates
radical - a man with both feet firmly planted in the air.
Franklin D. Roosevelt
radicalism - the conservatism of tomorrow injected into the affairs of today.
Ambrose Bierce
radio - broken television.
Wim Kan
(see also: transistor radio)
radio announcer - a man who talks until you have a headache, and then tries to sell you an aspirin.
Peter Darbo
radio static - the lint of sound.
Daniel Liebert

ragtime - white music - played black.
Joachim Berendt
rain - what makes flowers grow - and taxis disappear.
Hal Roach
rainbow - the apology of an angry sky.
Sylvia A. Voirol
raise - belonging to Raymond.
Cynthia MacGregor
raisin - a worried grape.
Julian Tuwim
raising kids - part joy and part guerilla warfare.
Ed Asner
rampart - what the Greek Restaurant served wrapped in grape leaves.
Ken Pinkham
rap - a pounding headache set to rhythm; a profane street sermon; the end of music as we know it.
Rick Bayan
rape - burgled love.
Pierre Dac
(see also: double rape)
rapist - a kleptomaniac of sex.
Sim
rap music - called so because the 'c' fell off the printer.
Allan Bease
rare volume - a returned book.
Harry Herschelovitzer
rational - devoid of all delusions save those of observation, experience and reflection.
Ambrose Bierce
rationalisation - getting cheese directly from the cow.
Werner Mitsch
(see also: irrationality)
rational thought - interpretation according to a scheme which we cannot escape.
Friedrich Nietzsche
rattler - a fart which is theoretically loud enough to rattle nearby cups and saucers.
Peter Furze
reactionary - a somnambulist walking backwards.
Franklin D. Roosevelt

reader - someone who fills his time with what the author kills his with.
Julien de Valckenaere
reading - to look through the eyes of an author.
Okke Jager
reading of proofs - the art of avoiding misprints.
Miles Kington
Reagan, Ronald - a triumph of the embalmer's art.
Gore Vidal
real - that which is always already reproduced.
Jean Baudrillard
real adventurer - someone who travels through the four disciplines of life: the mind, the body, the soul and sex.
Ernesto Barba
real antichrist - he who turns the wine of an original idea into the water of mediocrity.
Eric Hoffer
real artists - those who don't repeat themselves.
Joanna Russ
real atheist - the one who solemnly believes that God does believe in Himself.
Pierre Dac
real book - one that reads us.
W.H. Auden
real bores - those who start to list their ailments the moment you ask how they are.
Jô Soares
real comedian - one you laugh at before he opens his mouth.
George Jean Nathan
real elation - when you feel you could touch a star without standing on tiptoe.
Doug Larson
real estate - the closest thing to the proverbial pot of gold.
Ada Louise Huxtable
real estate agents - God's curse on mankind when locusts are out of season.
Lewis Grizzard
real friend - one who walks in when the rest of the world walks out.
Walter Winchell
real generosity - doing something nice for someone who'll never find it out.
Frank A. Clark

real genius - nothing else but the supernatural virtue of humility in the domain of thought.
Simone Weil
real gentleman - someone who doesn't insult people he has no respect for.
Louis Ferron
real happiness - when you marry a girl for love and find out later she has money.
Bob Monkhouse
real heroes - men who fall and fail and are flawed, but win out in the end because they've stayed true to their ideals and beliefs and commitments.
Kevin Costner
real hunger - when one man regards another man as something to eat.
Tadeusz Borowski
real hypochondriac - someone who only goes on holidays accompanied with his doctor.
Gerhard Uhlenbruck
real integrity - doing the right thing knowing nobody's going to know whether you did or not.
Oprah Winfrey
really intelligent man - one who recognises how stupid he is.
Kamagurka
real knowledge - everything we don't know.
Leonid S. Sukhorukov
real leaders - ordinary people with extraordinary determinations.
John Seaman Garns
real life - the annoying time between computer crashes.
Steven Stephens
real love - not to love *because of,* but *in spite of.*
Gilbert Cesbron
really plain woman - one who, however beautiful, neglects to charm.
Edgar Saltus
real man - someone who can ski through an avalanche - and still manage not to spill any beer.
Bruce Feirstein
real patriot - the fellow who gets a parking ticket and rejoices that the system works.
Bill Vaughan
real pornography - movies starring Doris Day.
Al Alvarez

real problem - what to do with the problem solvers after the problems are solved.
Gay Talese
real riches - the riches possessed inside.
B.C. Forbes
real secret - something which only one person knows.
Idries Shah
real wealth - to afford to work without being paid.
Mireille Cottenjé
real winners - the losers that don't give up.
Stefaan Lievens
real woman - a young, pretty, sexy, tender woman who is no taller than five feet six who adores you.
Françoise Parturier
real xenophobe - one who hates foreigners so much that, when he travels to their country, he just can't stand himself.
Raymond Devos
realism - a corruption of reality.
Wallace Stevens
(see also: socialist realism, true realism)
realist - someone who paints what other people don't paint.
R.J. Richardson
reality - just a crutch for people that can't handle CyberSpace!
Hank Duderstadt
really original woman - the one who first imitates a man.
Italo Svevo
reason - an emotion for the sexless.
Heathcote Williams
rebel - a man who says no.
Albert Camus
receding hare line - a row of 50 rabbits walking backwards.
Lorraine A. Bellis
receiver - someone appointed by the court to take what's left.
Robert Frost
reception - a sherry-go-round.
Eric van der Steen
receptionist - someone who is by definition underpaid to lie.
Karen Brodine
recession - what the government calls a depression that spares the rich.
Rick Bayan

recipe - a series of step-by-step instructions for preparing ingredients you forgot to buy in utensils you do not own to make a dish the dog will not eat the rest of.
Henry Beard
recording artist - someone that makes music but who cannot be called a musician.
Jim Poserina
rectal exam - that part of the physical examination that illustrates the true meaning of the Yuletide maxim, "It is better to give than to receive."
Howard Bennett
rectitude - the formal, dignified demeanor assumed by a proctologist immediately before he examines you.
Kyle Bonney
recycling - the meticulous separation of one's rubbish into its fundamental components, so as to conserve precious natural resources like glass and plastic.
Rick Bayan
reducing diet - the taming of the chew.
Shelly Friedman
redundancy - an air-bag in a politician's car.
Larry Hagman
refinance - a debt warmed up.
Lee Elliot
reformer - someone who will ruin the neighbour to his right just to leave a small tip for the neighbour to his left.
Jan Greshoff
refrigerator - a place where you store leftovers until they're old enough to throw out.
Al Boliska
(to) refuse awards - another way of accepting them with more noise than is normal.
Peter Ustinov
regeneration - what every generation needs.
Charles H. Spurgeon
reggae music - one of them stones that was refused by the builders.
Charlie Ace
regionalism - patriotism in less than 500 acres.
Pierre-Robert Leclercq
regret - something you have when you don't have something.
Geert Galle

regulation - the substitution of error for chance.
Fred J. Emery
rehabilitation - magic words said before releasing criminals.
Thomas Sowell
reincarnation - an ideology that's making a comeback.
Simon O'Connor
reintarnation - coming back as a hillbilly.
Barry Blyveis
rejection - the greatest aphrodisiac.
Madonna
relations - a tedious lot of people who don't know how to live or when to die.
Oscar Wilde
(see also: poor relation)
relationship - the mirror in which you discover yourself.
Krishnamurti
reliable computer – one who crashes less than the competition.
Stephen Manes
relics - the loose parts of a saint.
Fons Jansen
religion - what people had before television.
Dylan Moran
religious cultist - a holy roller.
Richard Lederer
religious maniac - someone who believes in God.
Colin Haycraft
religiousness - the wine fermentation of the developing and rotting of the disintegrating mind.
Franz Grillparzer
remarriage - the triumph of hope over experience.
Samuel Johnson
remarrying - sometimes posthumous cheating.
Decouly
(to) remember - to take revenge on time.
Fernand Auwera
(see also: memory, recollection)
remembrance - a form of meeting.
Kahlil Gibran
remorse - a violent dyspepsia of the mind.
Ogden Nash
remote - a place with only one big modern hotel. See also 'off the beaten track'.
J.B. Morton

rent - an economical result as certain and as inevitable as the harvest is a natural result after the seed-time.
Benjamin Disraeli
renunciation - an inconspicious variation on treason.
Bernhard Schlink
repartee - what a person thinks of after he becomes a departee.
Dan Bennett
repentance - another name for aspiration.
Henry Ward Beecher
repetition - the last law of learning.
John Wooden
reporter - something between a whore and a bartender.
Wallace Smith
repression - the seed of revolution.
Woodrow Wilson
reprieve - a better word for triumph.
Gregory Norminton
Republicans - the party that says government doesn't work and then gets elected and proves it.
P.J. O'Rourke
reputation - character minus what you've been caught doing.
Michael Iapoce
rescuing idea - one that disagrees with your habitual nature but which agrees with truth.
Vernon Howard
research - a way of taking calculated risks to bring about incalculable consequences.
Celia Green
(see also: scientific research)
research men in advertising - really blind men groping in a dark room for a black cat that isn't there.
Ludovic Kennedy
resemblances - the shadows of differences.
Vladimir Nabokov
resentment - resting on one's quarrels.
Vida Shiffrer
reservations - what a Jewish princess makes for dinner.
Maureen Lipman
reserve - an artificial quality that is developed in most of us but as the result of innumerable rebuffs.
W. Somerset Maugham
resignation - egoism in dressing gown.
Jan Vercammen

resolute - obstinate in a course that we approve.
Ambrose Bierce
resolutions - cheques that men draw on a bank where they have no account.
Oscar Wilde
respect - the only respectable form of stupidness.
Jan Greshoff
respectability - the dickey on the bosom of civilization.
Elbert Hubbard
responsibility - a detachable burden easily shifted to the shoulders of God, Fate, Fortune, Luck or one's neighbour.
Ambrose Bierce
(see also: self-responsibility)
rest - the cellulitis of the mind.
Pierre Daninos
restaurant - the only place where people are happy to be fed up.
Hal Roach
(see also: great restaurants)
restraining order - just nature's way of saying, "Take marksmanship classes."
Jim Bannon
restraint - the better part of beauty.
Frances Gray Patton
resume - a balance sheet without any liabilities.
Robert Half
resurrection - God's way of getting our attention.
Peter J. Gomes
(to) retire - to begin to die.
Pablo Casals
retirement - the transition from Who's Who to Who's He.
Eddie George
(see also: early retirement)
retirement age - the point at which time is not important anymore and your boss gives you a gold watch.
Peter Darbo
retirement dinner – the very last opportunity an employee has to be fed up by the company.
Robert Orben
retirony - retirement irony.
John Hind
retro-style - last refuge in case of a lack of imagination.
Robert Sabatier

reunions - the conveyor belts of our individual histories.
Alex Haley
revelation - the daughter of refusal.
André Breton
revenge - a dish which people of taste prefer to eat cold.
Dennis Price
(see also: getting revenge)
reverie - thought's Sunday.
Henri-Frédéric Amiel
reviewmanship - to show that it is really you yourself who should have written the book, if you had had the time.
Stephen Potter
Revised Prayer Book - an attempt to suppress burglary by legalising petty larceny.
William R. Inge
revisionist - revolutionary who likes to become a secretary of state.
Jean-Jacques Marie
revolution - a small stop to change drivers.
Carlos de Vriese
(see also: successful revolution)
revolutionary - an oppressed person waiting for the opportunity to become an oppressor.
Rick Bayan
revolutionary party - a contradiction in terms.
Richard Crossman
reward - no part of the definition of duty.
Robert Brault
rhetoric - a poor substitute for action.
Theodore Roosevelt
rhinoceros - an animal with a hide two feet thick, and no apparent interest in politics. What a waste.
James C. Wright
rich - to own too much.
Frédéric Dard
rich country - a country that succeeded in hiding its poor people.
Philippe Bouvard
riches - the savings of many in the hands of one.
Eugene Debs
(see also: wealth)
richest love - that which submits to the arbitration of time.
Lawrence Durrell

richest man - one whose pleasures are the cheapest.
Harold J. Smith
rich man - someone who doesn't know how poor he is.
Theo Herbst
(see also: real riches, truly rich man)
rich people - the scum of the earth in every country.
G.K. Chesterton
rich widows - only secondhand goods that sell at first-class prices.
Benjamin Franklin
ridicule - the tribute paid to the genius by the mediocrities.
Oscar Wilde
right - easy to be, difficult to get, impossible to give.
Piet Grijs
righteous indignation - your own wrath as opposed to the shocking bad temper of others.
Elbert Hubbard
riot - the language of the unheard.
Martin Luther King
risk - the drug of successful people.
Sigmund Graff
rituals - the formulas by which harmony is restored.
Terry Tempest Williams
rivers - roads which move, and which carry us whither we desire to go.
Blaise Pascal
road house - a place where you can fill the car and drain the family.
Clyde Moore
roaster - the guy who's making the boat move.
Kim Soriano
robbery - redistribution of wealth.
Leonard Rossiter
rock and roll - music for the neck downwards.
Keith Richards
rock-climbing - ballet in a vertical idiom.
John Cleare
rock concert - a place where you go to mangle with the crowd.
Jeff Rovin
rock journalism - people who can't write interviewing people who can't talk for people who can't read.
Frank Zappa
rock music - music frequently played by those who are stoned.
Joey Adams

rock musicians - hung up, neurotic, over-weight hippies with sex problems.
David Lee Roth
rodeoing - about the only sport you can't fix. You'd have to talk to the bulls and the horses, and they wouldn't understand you.
Bill Linderman
romance -a nice little tale where you have everything As You Like It, where rain never wets your jacket and gnats never bite your nose and it's always daisy-time.
D.H. Lawrence
(see also: historical romance)
Roman literature - Greek literature written in Latin.
Heinrich von Treitschke
Romanoff's Restaurant - a place where a man can take his wife and family and have a lovely seven-course meal for $3,400.
George Jessel
Romans - a people who, while they were poor, robbed mankind; and as soon as they became rich, robbed one another.
Samuel Johnson
romantic - old Rome.
Sofie Geenen
romanticism - to make grapes again from wine.
Toon Verhoeven
romanticist - an artist whose great dissatisfaction with himself makes him productive.
Friedrich Nietzsche
romantic love - mental illness. But it's a pleasurable one. It's a drug. It distorts reality, and that's the point of it. It would be impossible to fall in love with someone that you really saw.
Fran Lebowitz
Rome - an example of what happens when the buildings in a city last too long.
Andy Warhol
room - a place where you hide from the wolves outside.
Jean Rhys
room clerk - guest service agent.
George Carlin
root - a flower that disdains fame.
Kahlil Gibran
rope - rungless ladder.
Les Coleman
rose - the good conscience of its thorns.
Hans Kudszus

routine - an early stage of decay.
Hans Kudszus
Royal Commission - a broody hen sitting on a china egg.
Michael Foot
royal flush - when a king goes to the bathroom.
Douglas Helsel
rubberneck - what you do to relax your wife.
Edward Thompson
rudeness - the weak man's imitation of strength.
Eric Hoffer
rugby - a good occasion for keeping thirty bullies far from the centre of the city.
Oscar Wilde
ruin - the destination toward which all men rush.
Garrett Hardin
rules - solutions to yesterdays problems.
Kelvin Throop
rum - generically, fiery liquors that produce madness in total abstainers.
Ambrose Bierce
rumour - a baby myth.
Colin Bowles
running - the greatest metaphor for life, because you get out of it what you put into it.
Oprah Winfrey
rush hour - that hour when the traffic is almost at standstill.
J.B. Morton
Russia - the only country of the world you can be homesick for while you're still in it.
John Updike
(see also: Moscow)
Russian communism - the illegitimate child of Karl Marx and Catherine the Great.
Clement Attlee
Russian novel - a story in which the main character sulks for 600 pages.
Colin Bowles
Russian roulette - one of those games in which the winner the loser too.
Jan J. Pieterse
Russians - sort of combination of evil and incompetence - like the Post Office with tanks.
Emo Philips

S

s - the fish-hook of the alphabet.
Ramon Gomez de La Serna
Sabbath - a carwash for Swedish autos.
Joseph Leff
sacrifice - the root of the flower.
Richard Wilkins
sadist - someone who is nice to masochists.
Vincent McHugh
sadness - a form of fatigue.
André Gide
sado-masochism - the employment of chains, handcuffs, whips, blindfolds, bedposts and/or Nazi uniforms as instruments of love.
Rick Bayan
safe - a term employed by tobacco and chemical company "scientists" to describe products that they themselves would never, ever use.
Chaz Bufe
safe car - one that doesn't go faster than its driver.
Robert Lembke
safe sex - doing it when your wife is abroad.
Gerd de Ley
safety - period in which danger takes a break.
Karel Boullart
sage - the instructor of a hundred ages.
Ralph Waldo Emerson
sailing - the fine art of getting wet and becoming ill while slowly going nowhere at great expense.
Henry Beard
sailor - a person who is grounded by the sea.
Dr. Mardy
(see also: coarse sailor)
saints - dead sinners revised and edited.
Ambrose Bierce
St Valentine - patron saint of rose growers, restaurant owners and divorce lawyers.
Jeff Green

salesmanship - the difference between rape and ecstasy.
Roy Herbert Thomson
(see also: good salesman)
sales talk - trade wind.
Jacob Braude
saloon - the poor man's club run with intent to make the poor man poorer.
Kin Hubbard
sandal - shoe in a bathing-suit.
Piet Grijs
sandbar - pub on the beach.
Joseph Leff
San Francisco - the city that never was a town.
Will Rogers
sanity - an illusion caused by alcohol deficiency.
N.F. Simpson
(see also: insanity)
Santa - Satan spelled inside out.
George Carlin
Santa Claus - the only catholic who can sit children on his lap without facing a trial.
Jo van Damme
sarcasm - the greatest weapon of the smallest mind.
Alan Ayckbourn
sardine - a little fish with no head that lives in oil.
Léo Campion
satiety - a mongrel that barks at the heels of plenty.
Minna Antrim
satire - tragedy plus time.
Lenny Bruce
satirist - the fool who sets a mousetrap to catch an elephant.
Adolf Nowaczynski
satisfaction - the greatest enemy of creativity.
Raymond van het Groenewoud
satisfactory - where they make Viagra.
Willie Meikle
Saturday - the day of the week that determines how sick a little boy was on Friday.
O.A. Battista
saturnine - baseball team that plays on weekends.
William Safire
sauntering - the gastronomy of the eye.
Honoré de Balzac

sausages - breadcrumbs in battle dress.
Tommy Handley
savage - simply a human organism that has not received enough news from the human race.
John Ciardi
savage nation - one that doesn't wear uncomfortable clothes.
Finlay Peter Dunne
(to) save - to gather and to keep nuts till the day you have no more teeth.
Jan Schepens
savers - the ones who do most to unite generations.
Johan Albrecht
saving - a way of spending money without having the pleasure of it.
Robert Lembke
savings bank - one that generates little interest.
Hugo Raes
saxophone - an ill woodwind that nobody blows good.
Steve Allen
scandal - the manure of democracy.
Dario Fo
scare spray - what witches put on their hair.
Clynch Varnadore
scars - the definitive make-up.
Herman Brusselmans
sceptic - someone who once lost his wallet in a church while standing between a policeman and a nun.
Colin Bowles
scepticism - the beginning of faith.
Oscar Wilde
schadenfreude - not just the pleasure derived from the misfortunes of others, it's the pleasure derived from the misfortune of others who are thinner than you are.
Ellen Goodman
Scheherazade - the classical example of woman saving her head by using it.
Esme Wynne-Tyson
schizophrenia - illness with an even amount of patients.
Piet Grijs
schizophrenic - someone who never comes alone.
Gerd de Ley

schizofrenic behaviour - a special strategy that a person invents in order to live in an unlivable situation.
R.D. Laing
schnapps - the crack of alcohol.
Denis Leary
scholar - an idler who kills his time with study.
George Bernard Shaw
scholarship - polite argument.
Philip Rieff
school - just a jail with educational opportunities.
Robertson Davies
(see also: grade school, ideal school, private school, skydiving school)
school bus driver - someone who thought he liked children.
John Rooney
schoolchildren - hostages to red tape and fiscal insufficiency.
Rosellen Brown
school days - among the happiest days of your life, provided, of course, that your children are old enough to attend.
Sam Ewing
school food - the piece of cod which passeth understanding.
Geoffrey Willans & Ronald Searle
school run - the thirty-second dash between your illegally parked car to the school door and back again.
Jasmine Birtles
schools nowadays - parking places for children.
Greet Boon
school trip - the shortest distance between two amusement parks.
René Turkry
school year - a long, painful period of time consisting of twenty months for students, thirty for teachers.
Edmund J. Volkart
Schwarzenegger, Arnold – an actor who looks like a condom full of walnuts.
Clive James
science - the art of explaining predictable noise.
Fabien Benetou
(see also: modern science, truth in science)
Science Fiction - fairy tales for nerds.
Rick Bayan
(see also: hard SF)
scientific jargon - superior slang.
Sandra Raphael

scientific man - a further development of the artistic man.
Friedrich Nietzsche
scientific progress - milestones or millstones?
Gerhard Uhlenbruck
scientific research - the only form of poetry that may be rewarded by the state.
Jean Rostand
scientific thought - saying in hard words and involved sentences what could better be said in easy ones.
Samuel Butler
scientist - a strange bird: first he broods but eventually he lays his egg.
H. Ferwerda
(see also: true scientist)
scissors - trained storks.
Ramon Gomez de La Serna
Scotland - land of the omnipotent No.
Alan Bold
(see also: Glasgow)
Scotsmen - people that wear kilts because sheep can hear zippers a mile away.
Blanche Knott
scoundrel - every man over forty.
George Bernard Shaw
scoutmaster - an idiot dressed like a little boy, followed by little boys dressed like idiots.
Maurice Biraud
scrap book - a graveyard for lost thoughts.
Ramon Gomez de la Serna
scratching - one of nature's sweetest gratifications, and the one nearest to hand.
Michel de Montaigne
scream - the first human statement.
Robin Skelton
scream queen - an actress who eeks out a living.
Aaron Allston
screenwriters - schmucks with Underwoods.
Jack Warner
screenwriting - an opportunity to fly first class, be treated like a celebrity, sit around the pool and be betrayed.
Ian McEwan
screwin' around - foolin' around without dinner.
Maurine Dallas Watkins

script-doctor - a man with no original ideas of his own but specializes instead in ruining the original ideas of others.
Thomas Beller

scriptures - the sacred books of our holy religion, as distinguished from the false and profane writings on which all other faiths are based.
Ambrose Bierce

scuba diving - the closest you can come to going through the back of the wardrobe into a more fabulous world.
Norman Tebbit

sculpture - just a drawing you fall over in the dark.
Al Hirschfeld

sea - the best thing I know between France and England.
Douglas W. Jerrold

sea horse - an embryo that gave up.
Paul Rodenko

Seattle - the only place in the world, excepting New York, where you can park your car, walk two blocks, then find your own tires on sale.
Richard McRae

seaweed - something you don't want your neighbours to do when they look in your garden.
Art Linkletter

second place - the first loser.
Dale Earnhardt

second youth - mostly first old age.
Alexander Pola

secrecy - the freedom tyrants dream of.
Bill Moyers

secret - what you tell someone else not to tell because you can't keep it to yourself.
L.L. Levinson
(see also: perfect secret, real secret)

secret in the Oxford sense - you may tell it to only one person at a time.
Oliver Shewell Franks

(the) secret of success - making your vocation your vacation.
Mark Twain

secretary - someone you pay to learn to type while she hunts for a husband.
Jim Davidson

secure - safe from attack by a hacker under six.
Stephen Manes

security - a smile from a headwaiter.
Russell Baker
seduction - the art of genital persuasion.
John S. Crosbie
 (see also: verbal seduction)
seersucker - one who spends all her money on fortune-tellers.
Peter de Vries
seesaw - tool used by Moses to cut a passage in the Red Sea.
Gail S. Angel
segregation - the offspring of an illicit intercourse between injustice and immorality.
Martin Luther King
(the) self - every person's true enemy.
Ding Ling
self-abnegation - a rare virtue that good men preach and good women practice.
Oliver Wendell Holmes
self-abuse - the devil's telephone booth.
Edward Barker
self-approval - joy accompanied with the idea of one's self as the cause.
Benedictus de Spinoza
self-confidence - the result of a successfully survived risk.
Jack Gibb
self-contemplation - infallibly the symptom of disease.
Thomas Carlyle
self-criticism - a mark of social maturity.
Gore Vidal
self-decapitation - an extremely difficult, not to say dangerous, thing to attempt.
W.S. Gilbert
self-defense - the clearest of all laws, and for this reason: the lawyers didn't make it.
Douglas W. Jerrold
self-delusion - pulling in your stomach when you step on the scales.
Paul R. Sweeney
self-denial - the effect of prudence on rascality.
George Bernard Shaw
self-destruction - the effect of cowardice in the highest extreme.
Daniel Defoe

self-discipline - when your conscience tells you to do something and you don't talk back.
W.K. Hope
self-education - the only kind of education there is.
Isaac Asimov
self-esteem - the reputation we acquire with ourselves.
Nathaniel Branden
self-evaluation - the skin rash of the emotionally insecure.
John D. MacDonald
self-improvement - a dangerous form of vanity.
Alan Watts
self-interest - a mirage that is blown away by the winds that penetrate the fortress built to protect it.
David Aaronovitch
selfishness - that detestable vice which no one will forgive in others and no one is without in himself.
Henry Ward Beecher
self-knowledge - the beginning of all wisdom and the end of many illusions.
Gerd de Ley
selflessness - only selfishness on another level.
Margaret Landon
 self-love - the only truthful and effective form of human love.
Jan Greshoff
(see also: being in love with yourself)
self-made man - the living proof of the horrors of unskilled labour.
Ed Wynn
self-parody - the first portent of age.
Larry McMurtry
self-pity - the only pity that counts.
Oscar Levant
self-possession - one of the very best of all earthly possessions.
George D. Prentice
self-praise - better than no praise at all.
Gust Gils
self-preservation - the first principle of our nature.
Alexander Hamilton
self-reflection - the school of wisdom.
Baltasar Gracià n Y Morales
self-respect - the secure feeling that no-one, as yet, is suspicious.
H.L. Mencken

self-responsibility - the core quality of the fully mature, fully functioning, self-actualizing individual.
Brian Tracy
self-restraint - feeling your oats without sowing them.
Shanon Fife
self-righteousness - a loud din raised to drown the voice of guilt within us.
Eric Hoffer
self-sacrifice - usually contains an unspoken demand for payment.
Mason Cooley
self-satisfaction - the state of mind of those who have the happy conviction that they are nit as other men.
Margery Allingham
self-trust - the belief that one is more than one is.
F.J. Schmit
self-willed person - somebody who doesn't share your opinions.
Juul Kinnaer
selling - an espionage game.
Joe Girard
semantics - the propagandist's worst friend.
Stuart Chase
seminar .- a gathering of purportedly intelligent people who sit around pooling their ignorance until group findings emerge.
Bryan Wilson
Senate - a place filled with goodwill and good intentions, and if the road to hell is paved with them, then it's a pretty good detour.
Hubert H. Humphrey
senator - person who makes laws in Washington when not doing time.
Mark Twain
senile - what elderly tourists do in Egypt.
Tim Bruening
senility - memopause.
Hugo Olaerts
senior moment - a euphemism to indicate a temporary loss of marbles to anyone over 50.
Bill Sadgarden
sensations - rapid dreams.
George Santayana
sense of humour - just common sense, dancing.
Clive James

sensitive man - the one who orders white wine and a salad for lunch while all his buddies order a beer and a burger.
Lewis Grizzard
sensuality - the vice of young men and of old nations.
William Edward Hartpole Lecky
sentiment - the sick half-brother of thought.
Tom Lanoye
sentimental irony - a dog that bays at the moon while he pisses on a grave.
Karl Kraus
sentimentalism - the working off on yourself of feelings you haven't got.
D.H. Lawrence
sentimentalist - one who desires to have the luxury of an emotion without paying for it.
Oscar Wilde
sentimentality - the sentiment we don't share.
Graham Greene
September - the month when a lot of people discover what a good time the moths had while they were on vacation.
O.A. Battista
septic tank - poo keeper.
Charles G. Waugh
sequel - evidence that more is usually too much.
Rick Bayan
serenity - complete self-abnegation and enormous understanding.
Eleanora Duse
serenity of age - a euphemism for the fading power to feel the sudden shock of joy or sorrow.
Arthur Bliss
serenpedity - searching for a needle in a haystack and instead finding a farmer's daughter.
Hermann Bondi
seriousness - stupidity sent to college.
P.J. O'Rourke
serious sport - war minus the shooting.
George Orwell
sermons - one of the last forms of public discourse where it is culturally forbidden to talk back.
Harvey Cox
servant - someone who can play the master but never be one.
Heere Heeresma

serve - the device of all those who like to command.
Jean Giraudoux
service - the rent you pay for room on this earth.
Shirley Chisholm
settlement - a device by which lawyers obtain fees without working for them.
D. Robert White
seventy - when your vital juices are prune.
Robert Orben
7 Up - Snow White's favourite drink.
Dave Allen
sex - the only human activity in which professionals do worse than amateurs.
Midas Dekkers
(see also: oral sex, safe sex, unlimited sex, unnatural sexual act)
sex appeal - what a man can only describe with his hands.
Uschi Glas
sex crime - not getting any.
Stephen Peters
sex drive - a physical craving that begins in adolescence and ends in marriage.
Robert Byrne
sexism - the foundation on which all tyranny is built.
Andrea Dworkin
sexit - exit from a brothel.
Gerd de Ley
sex-shop - the only shop that sells parts we already have.
Paul van Vliet
sexton - a heavy relationship.
Willie Meikle
sexual act - one of the most primitive methods of mooring oneself at least temporarily to something or someone.
Rosemary Stoyle
sexual climax - as close as we get to God before our ultimate climax: death.
Phil Marquist
sexual drive - the motor memory of previously remembered pleasure.
Wilhelm Reich
sexual freedom - freedom from having to have sex.
Jane Wagner

sexual harassment - a reprehensible act that occurs when, in the war between the sexes, the male advances and the female retreats; or vice versa.
Edmund H. Volkart
sexual harassment at work - a problem for the self-employed.
Victoria Wood
sexual intercourse - kicking death in the ass while singing.
Charles Bukowski
sexuality - the basis of all friendship.
Jean Cocteau
sexual modesty - masculine shame attributed to women.
Céline Renooz
sexual passion - the cause of war and the end of peace, the basis of what is serious... and consequently the concentration of all desire.
Arthur Schopenhauer
sexual pleasure - a passion to which all others are subordinate but in which they all unite.
Marquis de Sade
Sexual Revolution - conquest of the last frontier, involving the efficient management and manipulation of reproductive organs for the purpose of establishing the New Puritanism.
Bernard Rosenberg
Shakespeare - a dramatist of note
Who lived by writing things to quote.
H.C. Bunner
shame - the social side of guilt.
John P. Grier
sham rock - a Counterfeit Irish Diamond.
James Harris
shape - something that a bathing suit takes, when there is a beautiful girl in it.
Louis Verbeeck
sharing - sometimes more demanding than giving.
Mary Catherine Bateson
sharp knives - the secret of a successful restaurant.
George Orwell
sharp tongue - the only edged tool that grows keener with constant use.
Washington Irving
sheer hose - a sieve for the beauty of a woman's legs.
Ramon Gomez de La Serna

shelf-gratification - thumbing through the men's magazines at a newsstand.
Chris Doyle
shells - the flowers of the seabed.
Jeroen Brouwers
sherpas - the elevators of the Himalayas.
Tomi Ungerer
shin - a device for finding furniture in the dark.
Michael Hogin
shitcom - scatological TV-series.
Gerd de Ley
shitting - one thing the rich have to do for themselves.
Lindsey Davis
shoes - the first adult machines we are given to master.
Nicholson Baker
shoplifter - a shopper with the gift of grab.
John S. Crosbie
shopping - sex without an orgasm.
Paul Mazursky
shopping malls - liquid TV's for the end of the twentieth century. A whole micro-circuity of desire, ideology and expenditure for processed bodies drifting through the cyber-space of ultracapitalism.
Arthur Kroker
shortcut - the longest distance between two points.
Charles Issawi
shortsightedness - the foster mother of gossip.
Haines
short-term goals - the stepping stones to the bigger ones.
Beth Pugh
show business - sincere insincerity.
Benny Hill
shrink - a person who will listen to you as long as you don't make sense.
Joey Adams
(see also: psychiatrist)
Shrinkenstein - a monster's psychiatrist.
Jackie Holle
shyness - egotism out of its depth.
Penelope Keith
side effects - symptoms of a cure that induce nostalgia for the original disease.
Rick Bayan

sigh - an amplifier for people who suffer in silence.
Robert Orben
sight seeing - looking at a lot and seeing nothing.
Henk Kooyman
signals - the empty cries of silence.
Herman Brusselmans
silence - a hole in the noise.
Bert Schierbeek
silent majority - usually the noisiest minority since the Salvation Army got brass bands.
Katharine Whitehorn
silicone - a substance for making mountains out of molehills.
Colin Bowles
Silicon Valley - the Florence of the late 20th century.
Francis Fukuyama
silk - material invented so women could go naked in clothes.
Muhammad Ali
silk handkerchief - the goodbye of a caress.
Ramon Gomez de La Serna
silk stockings - the last things a woman discards - when she is economising.
Sidney Tremayne
silly - you in a natural state.
Mike Myers
silly question - the first intimation of some totally new development.
Alfred North Whitehead
silocone - putty for the holes in your ego.
Rob Urgert
silver-wedding party - the happy occasion during which a married couple celebrates the fact that 25 years of marriage are over.
Joan Harrison
simple - difficult to explain.
Guy Commerman
simple ideas - the perfect breeding ground for fanaticism.
Eric-Emmanuel Schmitt
simplicity - the soul of efficiency.
R. Austin Freeman
simplistic - argument you disagree with but cannot answer.
Thomas Sowell

sin - a preference not shared by others.
Jean Lorrain
(see also: unforgivable sins)
sincerity - the easiest virtue to fake.
Simon May
(see also: insincerity)
(to) sing - to touch people with your happiness.
Vera Coomans
Singapore - Disneyland with the death penalty.
Eve Jones
singing - basically a form of pleasant, controlled screaming.
George Carlin
singing mouth - an annoying thing to keep open.
Gust Gils
single's bar - meet market.
Syman Hirsch
sink - the great symbol of the bloodiness of family life.
Julian Mitchell
sister - a best friend you can't get rid of.
Amy Li
Sisyphus - the only one for whom it was a myth.
Mignon McLaughlin
sitcom - what television does best: put witticisms in the mouths of performing types and remind us when to laugh.
Rick Bayan
sixty - a wonderful age, especially if you're 70.
Sam Ewing
6.9 - a delightful activity interrupted by a period.
Richard Lederer
skeleton - the proof of flesh.
Gys Miedema
skiing - wearing three thousand dollars' worth of clothes and equipment and driving for two hundred miles in the snow in order to stand around a bar an get drunk.
P.J. O'Rourke
ski jacket - the larval stage of a blimp.
Henry Beard
skillful listening - the best remedy for loneliness, loquaciousness and laryngitis.
William A. Ward
ski teacher - someone who is mostly occupied with fallen women.
Markus M. Ronner

skin - that which keeps the human form in the human form.
Leonard Rossiter
skinheads - men with as much on the skull as under it.
Gerd de Ley
sky - the daily bread of the eyes.
Ralph Waldo Emerson
skydiving school - one in which you *must* be a dropout to graduate.
Marsha Coleman
(see also: nude skydiving, stunt skydiving)
skyscraper - a boast in glass and steel.
Mason Cooley
Sky television - a bit like the *Sun* on video.
Prince Charles
slander - to lie or tell the truth about someone.
Peter Darbo
slang - a language that rolls up its sleeves, spits on its hands and goes to work.
Carl Sandburg
slavery - government without the consent of the governed.
Jonathan Swift
slaves - the best slaveguards.
Cor Gilhuis
(see also: happy slaves)
sleep - an eight-hour peep show of infantile erotica.
J.G. Ballard
(see also: daytime sleep, nap)
sleeplessness - a desert without vegetation or inhabitants.
Jessamyn West
slogan - a good old American substitute for the facts.
Jacob Braude
slot machine - crack for old people.
Keenan Ivory Wayans
slum - the measure of civilization.
Jacob Riis
slurm - the slime that accumulates on the underside of a soap bar when it sits in the dish too long.
Rich Hall
slut - woman with the morals of a man.
Mari Heikkinen
S/M - high technology sex.
Pat Califia

small penis - the leprosy of homosexuals.
Andrew Holleran
small town - a place where there is little to see or do, but what you hear makes up for it.
Ivern Ball
(see also: village)
smart doctor - one who can diagnose the ailment of a patient who doesn't smoke or drink and isn't overweight.
Al Haywood
smart girl - one who has enough willpower to resist a man's advances and enough willpower to block his retreat.
O.A. Battista
smart insect - spelling bee.
Linda Williams
smart mother - one who knows an ounce of prevention is worth a pound of cure.
Lee Daniel Quinn
smart society - a body of autocrats in deadly warfare against plutocrats.
Minna Antrim
smart woman - one who can keep her husband pursuing her after she lets him catch her.
O.A. Battista
smell - breath's brother.
Patrick Süskind
(to) smell - foreplay of taste.
Marc Pairon
smile - half a kiss.
Kornel Makuszynski
smog - the air apparent.
Joel Rothman
smoke - fire's sleight of hand.
Ramon Gomez de La Serna
smoker - a drug addict who believes that he has the right to annoy and poison those around him. Unlike the user of non-addictive drugs, the smoker is to be pitied and tolerated rather than spied upon, entrapped, and imprisoned.
Chaz Bufe
(see also: inveterate smoker)
smokers' rights - the right of smokers to annoy and to damage the health of nonsmokers in public places.
Chaz Bufe

smoking - the main cause of statistics.
Fletcher Knebel
(see also: cigarette, tobacco)
snackmosphere - the air in a bag of potato chips.
Marie Johnson
snacktrek - the peculiar habit, when searching for a snack, of constantly returning to the refrigerator in hopes that something new will have materialized.
Rich Hall
snake - Adam's first pet after the fall.
Franz Kafka
sneak preview - a place where four or five men, making for or five thousand a week, go watch a pimply-faced kid write "It stinks" on a card.
Nunnally Johnson
sneer - often the sign of heartless malignity.
Johann Kaspar Lavater
sneezing - much achoo about nothing.
John S. Crosbie
snob - someone who sends his dog to London in order to learn to bark.
Philippe Jullian
(see also: society snob)
snobbery - the pride of those who are not sure of their position.
Berton Braley
snooker - just chess with balls.
Clive James
snoring - the nicest sound in the world. Ask any widow.
L. Polak
snow - powdered water.
Slawomir Mrozek
snowboarding - an activity that is very popular with people who do not feel that regular skiing is lethal enough.
Dave Barry
snowdrift - a beautiful thing - if it doesn't lie across the path you have to shovel or block the road that leads to your destination.
Hal Borland
snowflakes - one of nature's most fragile things but just look what they can do when they stick together.
Vista M. Kelly
snuggle - an act of warmth that your husband will inevitably interpret as foreplay.
Tom Carey

snuggling - sex for the soul.
Kim Christensen
soak - what tax plans may attempt to do to the rich, when the usual sources of revenue have run dry.
Edmund J. Volkart
soap opera - the only place in our culture where grown-up men take seriously all the things that grown-up women have to deal with all day long.
Gloria Steinem
soccer - a game in which everyone does a lot of running around. Twenty-one guys stand around and one guy does a tap dance with the ball.
Jim Murray
soceraphobia - fear of parents-in-law.
Matt Groening
Social Democrats - the heterosexual wing of the Liberal Party.
George Foulkes
socialism - a fairy tale that still believes in people.
Toon Verhoeven
socialist - someone who thinks his neighbour earns too much.
W.F. Hermans
socialist realism - a solemn pledge to abstain from truth.
Alexandr Solzhenitsyn
social life - a form of do-it-yourself theatre.
Muriel Oxenberg Murphy
social policy - the desperate surgical decision to remove corns from a cancer patient.
Karl Kraus
social work - a band-aid on the festering wounds of society.
Alexander Chase
society - public limited company with an unlimited irresponsibility.
Georges Elgozy
(see also: great society, ideal society, smart society)
society snob - a person who craves equality - but only with his superiors.
Joey Adams
sociologists - people who prove you that it will go dark when you switch off the light.
Jan Blokker
sociology - the study of people who do not need to be studied by people who do.
E.S. Turner

sock - a highly sensitive conjugal object.
Jean-Claude Kaufman
softball - the single greatest organizing force in lesbian society.
Alix Dobkin
software - the successful attempt to make the most of the errors of computer hardware and to add new errors through development.
Joachim Graf
(see also: hardware)
software engineering - that part of computer science which is too difficult for the computer scientist.
F.L. Bauer
software industry - unique industry where selling substandard goods is legal and you can charge extra for fixing the problems.
Duncan Simpson
softwear analyst - clothing inspector.
David Todd
soldiers - involuntary blood-donors.
Zarko Petan
solemnity - a device of the body to hide the faults of the mind.
François de La Rochefoucauld
solicitor - a man who calls in a person he doesn't know to sign a contract he hasn't seen to buy property he doesn't want with money he hasn't got.
Dingwall Bateson
solicitous wife - one who is so interested in her husband's happiness that she hires a detective to find out who is responsible for it.
Joey Adams
solitaire - the only thing in life that demands absolute honesty.
Hugh Wheeler
solitude - the playfield of Satan.
Vladimir Nabokov
solutions - the chief cause of problems.
Eric Sevareid
solvency - making enough money to pay the taxes you wouldn't have to pay if you weren't making so much money.
Vern McLellan
sons - the anchors of a mother's life.
Sophocles
song - poetry frustrated with music.
Freek de Jonge

sophisticate - a man who thinks he can swim better than he can and sometimes he drowns.
Oscar Hammerstein II
sophistication - the ability to yawn without opening your mouth.
Herbert V. Prochnow
soporific - the effect of eating too much lettuce.
Beatrix Potter
sorrow - one of the vibrations that prove the fact of living.
Antoine de Saint-Exupéry
Soul - the way Black folks sing when they leave themselves alone.
Ray Charles
soul - the wife of the body.
Paul Valéry
sound-hole - a petomaniac's ass.
J. Vandaal
southern gentleman - a redneck with money in the bank.
Joey Adams
space - the widest open of all mouths.
Malcolm de Chazal
space travel - the only presently known way of leaving this world without dying.
J.P. Stapp
Spain - a country that can be saved only by a series of earthquakes.
Cyril Connolly
(see also: Madrid, Mallorca)
spare ribs - what everybody else has except Adam.
Johnny Hart
sparklers - the gay cousins of the fireworks family.
Dave Attell
sparrow - an eagle in the eyes of a louse.
Nico Scheepmaker
(to) speak - to write in the air.
Ramòn Gòmez de la Serna
(to) speak ill of others - a dishonest way of praising ourselves.
Will and Ariel Durant
specialist - one who knows more and more about less and less.
Charles H. Mayo
(see also: expert)
speculation - news you can use, eventually.
Jon Stewart
speculator - one who bought stocks that went down.
Malcolm S. Forbes

speech - a picture of the mind.
John Ray
speed - the one genuinely modern pleasure.
Aldous Huxley
speed limit - the velocity one must exceed by approximately 10 mph on a motorway or risk being run off the road.
Rick Bayan
sperm - a bandit in its pure state.
E.M. Cioran
sperm bank - only a place whose come has time.
Milton Berle
sperm donor - the only job for which no woman is or can be qualified.
Wilma Scott Heide
spice - the plural of spouse.
Christopher Morley
spin doctor - just another kind of quack.
Richard Greene
Spinoza - the only one who didn't read Spinoza.
Francis Picabia
spinster - the bachelor's widow.
André Prévot
(see also: old maid)
spirituality - the last refuge of a failed human. Just another way of distracting yourself from who you really are.
George Carlin
spirtle - the fine stream from a grapefruit that always lands right in your eye.
Rich Hall
spit out the plum - to abandon an English accent.
Barry Humphries
sponges - the skulls of the waves of the sea.
Ramon Gomez de La Serna
sponsor - Maecenas who wants something in return.
Jan Blokker
spontaneity - only a term for man's ignorance of the gods.
Samuel Butler
spook - something everyone is afraid of and no-one believes in.
Colin Bowles
sport - the opiate of the masses.
Russell Baker
(see also: serious sport)

sportsman - generally a bookmaker who takes actresses to night clubs.
Jimmy Cannon
(see also: amateur sportsman, top sportsman)
sports writer - someone who would if he could, but he can't, so he tells those who can how they should.
Cliff Temple
spotted - notice Theodore.
Joseph Leff
spouses - impediments to great enterprises.
Francis Bacon
spreadsheet - telling lies in columns.
D.J. Fleming
spring - nature's way of saying, "Let's party!"
Robin Williams
squash - boxing with racquets.
Jonah Barrington
squirrels - just rats with cuter outfits.
Darren Star
stage - just a platform shoe.
Bono
stalagmites - miniature German prison guards.
Spike Milligan
Stalinism - a wound which is still bleeding.
Anatoli Rybakov
stand-up comedian - an artist who cannot speak, cannot sing and stands on the stage with his shirt hanging out.
Bert Verhoye
stand-up comedy - the art of letting an audience laugh by simulating spontaneity.
Lee Glickstein
star - a performer who makes more than his or her agent.
Rick Bayan
(see also: movie star)
stars - the lamps of the ages.
Ramon Gomez de La Serna
stardom - a gilded slavery.
Helen Hayes
starlet - the name for any woman under thirty not actively employed in a brothel.
Ben Hecht
start up disk - the one disk you *always* manage to lose.
Mike Knowles

state - that great fiction by which everyone tries to live at the expense of everyone else.
Frédéric Bastiat
state legislators - politicians whose darkest secret prohibits them from running for higher office.
Dennis Miller
state run lotteries - tax breaks for the intelligent.
Evan Leibovitch
statesman - a politician who has been dead ten or fifteen years.
Harry S. Truman
(see also: constitutional statesman, true statesman)
statesmanship - housekeeping on a great scale.
John Simon
(see also: honest statesmanship, true statesmanship)
stateswoman - a woman who meddles in public affairs.
Samuel Johnson
statistician - somebody that thinks that the average person has one breast and one testicle.
Aidan Moran
(see also: medical statistician)
statistics - a bunch of numbers running around looking for an argument.
George Burgy
status - a gauge people use to measure what isn't important.
Richard Wilkins
status quo - Latin for the mess we're in.
Marshall Keeble
status symbol - anything you can't afford, but did.
Harold Coffin
stay - a charming word in a friend's vocabulary.
Louisa May Alcott
steak - my favourite animal.
Fran Lebowitz
steak out - a cow spying on another cow.
Douglas Helsel
stealing - a glorious occupation, particularly in the art world.
Malcolm McLaren
stealth bomber - a bomber that doesn't show up on radar and you can't see it. Then we don't need one.
Robin Williams
stereo - the device teenagers use for their experiments on how many decibels it takes to reach the pain level.
Joyce Armor

stereotypes - behaviour patterns you don't want to think about.
Thomas Sowell
steward - stewardess without tits.
Luk Wyns
stewardess - a girl who asks you what you want, then straps you in the seat so you can't get it.
Jimmy Edmondson
stick - a boomerang that doesn't work.
Bill Kirchenbauer
stiff apology - a second insult.
G.K. Chesterton
stiff attitude - one of the attributes of rigor mortis.
Henry S. Haskins
stigma - something to beat a dogma with.
Philip Guedalla
stockbroker - someone who invests other people's money until it's all gone.
Woody Allen
stomach - a slave that must accept everything that is given to it, but which avenges wrongs as slyly as does the slave.
Emile Souvestre
stool - ejaculation of the 'third'-age.
Karel Jonckheere
stopwatch - improved version of the whip.
Julien Vangansbeke
story - something that happens to characters you care about.
Raymond Chandler
story-telling - an instinct to come to terms with mystery, chaos, mess.
Graham Swift
straight line - the most stupid distance between two points.
Pietro Silvio Rivetta
stranger - a bastard you haven't met yet.
Rich Garella
strapless gown - a dress that has visible means of support.
O.A. Battista
strategic plan - the cookery book of a top manager.
Pieter Klaas Jagersma
Stravinsky - Bach on the wrong notes.
Sergei Prokofiev
strength - the capacity to break a chocolate bar into four pieces with your bare hands - and then eat just one of the pieces.
Judith Viorst

stress - the handcuffs of the heart.
Helmut Qualtinger
stretch pants - the garment that made skiing a spectator sport.
Peter Darbo
strike - a more or less long period preceding a return to work.
Yvan Audouard
string - a kite's umbilical cord.
Les Coleman
string quartet - the most perfect expression of human behavior.
Jeffrey Tate
Strip Club - another form of safe sex.
Sparkle Moore
strip poker - the only game where the more you lose, the more you have to show for it.
Henny Youngman
strip teaser - a busy body.
Joey Adams
stroll - a roundabout way of arriving at a pub.
Wim Kan
strong man - the one who is able to intercept at will the communication between the senses and the mind.
Napoleon Bonaparte
stud - a slut with chest hair.
Rick Bayan
students - people who throw stones through the windows of established firms of which they hope to become directors later on.
Wim Kan
(see also: medical student)
stunt skydiving - every newsreader's nightmare.
Angus Deayton
stupid - anyone able to draw incorrect conclusions from sufficient data.
T.G. Browning
stupidity - the basic building block of the universe.
Frank Zappa
(see also: gross stupidity)
stupid questions - the beginning of all news.
Jan Blokker
stutterer - the only person who may break his word.
August Leunis
style - being yourself, but on purpose.
Quentin Crisp

styling - the elevation of reality to a nicer place.
Patricia Fields
subscriber - someone who wants to read the same every morning, but on freshly printed paper.
Battus
substitoot - a second-string trumpeter in the school band.
Doug Larson
suburb - an attempt to get out of reach of the city without having the city be out of reach.
Mason Cooley
suburbia - where the developer bulldozes out the trees, then names the streets after them.
Bill Vaughan
subway - the warm wedlock of the rush hours.
Christopher Morley
success - the result of taking a misstep in the right direction.
Al Bernstein
(see also: secret of success, true success, ultimate success)
successful doctor - one who can keep his patients alive long enough for nature to heal them.
Doc Blakely
successful executive - one who delegates all the responsibility, shifts all the blame, and takes all the credit.
William Heads
successful investing - anticipating the anticipations of others.
John Maynard Keynes
successful lawsuit - the one worn by a policeman.
Robert Frost
successful man - one who can lay a firm foundation with the bricks others have thrown at him.
David Brinkley
successful parent - one who raises a child who grows up and is able to pay for their own psychoanalysis.
Nora Ephron
successful people - the individuals who form the habit of doing what the failing person doesn't like to do.
Donald Riggs
successful revolution - an affair with a bad ending.
Georges Ribemont-Dessaignes
successful salesman - someone who has found a cure for the common cold shoulder.
Robert Orben

successful salesmanship - 90% preparation and 10% presentation.
Bertrand R. Canfield
successful suicide - a cry for help which hasn't been heard in time.
Graham Greene
successful tool - one that was used to do something undreamed of by its author.
S.C. Johnson
successful woman - one who doesn't have to work as hard after marrying a man as she did trying to catch him in the first place.
O.A. Battista
(see also: successful man)
suffering - the main condition of the artistic experience.
Samuel Beckett
suicide - the only perfect crime that remains unpunished.
Warren Manzi
(see also: successful suicide)
suicide blonde - a blonde dyed by her own hand.
Saul Bellow
suicide bomb - the nuclear weapon of the poor.
Robert Fisk
suicide hotline - where they talk to you until you don't feel like killing yourself. Exactly the opposite of telemarketing.
Dana Snow
suitable - the last thing we ever want.
Ellen Glasgow
summer - the season in which tourists relieve themselves of their manners and their pets.
Dimitri Verhulst
summer afternoon - the two most beautiful words in the English language.
Henry James
summer holidays - when parents realize that teachers are grossly underpaid.
Herm Albright
sun - the nipple in the Milkway.
Guido van Heulendonk
sunbather - a target for the artillery of the sun and a filling station for the mosquitos.
Vittorio de Sica

Sunday - the day God took off from creating the world to take Mrs. God around IKEA.
Jeff Green
Sunday school - a prison in which children do penance for the evil conscience of their parents.
H.L. Mencken
sunlight - the world's best disinfectant.
William Proxmire
Superbowl - our great national campfire around which we cluster.
George F. Will
superego - that part of the personality which is soluble in alcohol.
Harold Lasswell
superficial - a really good referee.
William Safire
superfluous - a very necessary thing.
Voltaire
superhighway - a prison in motion.
Clifton Fadiman
superior man - the one who is free from fear and anxieties.
Confucius
supermarket - a place where you can find anything... except your children.
Leopold Fechtner
supernatural - the natural not yet understood.
Elbert Hubbard
supernaturalism - the mysticism of the materialist.
William R. Inge
superstition - someone else's religion.
J.C. Bloem
superwoman - someone who scrubs her own floors.
Bette Midler
Supper Ten - the biggest gluttons in town.
Gerd de Ley
surfer - an American lemming.
Jacob Bronowski
surgeons - physicists that wear gloves so as not to leave fingerprints.
Patrick Timsit
surgery - the ready motion of steady and experienced hands.
Claudius Galen
surprise - the greatest gift which life can grant us.
Boris Pasternak

surrealism - merely the reflection of the death process. It's one of the manifestations of a life becoming extinct, a virus which quickens the inevitable end.
Henry Miller
survival - the ultimate revenge.
Vincent Browne
suspicion - the beginning of wisdom, and of madness.
Mason Cooley
swearing - a compromise between running away and fighting.
Finley Peter Dunne
sweat - the perfume of a hard working man.
E. Constant Sr.
sweater - a garment worn by a child when his mother feels chilly.
Nora Ephron
Sweden - country where they commit suicide and the king rides a bicycle.
Alan Bennett
Swedes - fake Norwegians.
Greg d'Alessio
Swift, Jonathan - an occasional poet who sings lightly about dandruff, drains, body odour, dirty underclothes and comic farts.
Tom Paulin
swimming - a confusing sport: sometimes you do it for fun, other times you do it to not die.
Demetri Martin
swimming pools - what children often confuse with a restroom.
Joyce Armor
swinger - a well-built guy in the nude.
Milton Berle
Swiss - a very mountainous people.
Johann Georg August Galetti
Switzerland - a bloody country, even the cheese has got holes in it!
Tom Stoppard
Sydney - confusion surrounded on three sides by water and on the fourth by the hospital.
Kylie Tennant
symbolism - a facade of respectability to hide the indecency of dreams.
Mason Cooley
symmetry - a graveyard with a British accent.
Edmund J. Volkart

sympathizer - a fellow that's for you as long as it doesn't cost anything.
Kin Hubbard
sympathy - between shit and syphilis in the dictionary.
R. McGinley
sympatica - the touchstone that leads to talent's highest altitude.
Minna Antrim
symphony - a stage play with the parts written for instruments instead of for actors.
Colin Wilson
symptoms - nothing but the cry from suffering organs.
Jean Martin Charcot
synonym - a word you use when you can't spell the word you first thought of.
Burt Bacharach
syntax - all the money collected at the church from sinners.
Douglas Helsel
syphilis - a sociable disease.
Peter de Vries
sysadmin - a device for converting a mixture of pizza and caffeine into uptime.
Unca Ullu
system - nothing more than the subordination of all aspects of the universe to any one such aspect.
Jorge Luis Borges

T

t - the hammer of the alphabet.
Ramón Gómez de la Serna
Tabasco sauce - the only good vegetable.
P.J. O'Rourke
table - the only place where a man is never bored during the first hour.
Anthelme Brillat-Savarin
tabloids - the price we pay for freedom of the press.
Gerard Schuijt
tact - knowing how far we may go too far.
Jean Cocteau
tactful boss - someone who never kisses his wife in the presence of his secretary.
Wolfgang Gruner
tactical nuclear weapon - an atomic bomb that says "Sorry".
Battus
tactics - doing what you can with what you have.
Saul Alinsky
tail-gunner - petomaniac.
J. Vandaal
take my wife - the wrong answer to the wrong question.
Gerd de Ley
taking cocaine - dropping an atomic bomb on your brain.
Arnold M. Washton
taking leave - the most earnest form of human togetherness.
Hans Kudszus
taking part - sometimes more ridiculous than winning.
Dominique Stove
talent - one of those sad roads that lead to everywhere.
André Breton
talented actor - someone as rare as an arse on a face.
Thomas Bernhard
(to) talk - a trick to say nothing.
Simone de Beauvoir
talkative woman - one who does talk as much as a man.
Cheris Kramarae

talking - excellent exercise for the mouth's all-important oral sex muscles.
P.J. O'Rourke
talk is cheap - assertion refuted by lawyers and mobile telephone companies.
Mike Barfield
talk show - to talk bullshit with an alibi.
Jan Lenferink
talking to myself - the only way I can be assured of intelligent conversation.
Richard Curtis
tambourine - the drum's lively daughter.
Ramon Gomez de La Serna
tango - a dance in which faces are bored and rear ends amuse themselves.
Georges Clemenceau
tapas – sandwich fillings with pretensions.
Philippe Geubels
tape player - what they do to an athlete after he sprains his ankle.
Steve Jacobson
tap-in - a putt that is short enough to be missed one-handed.
Henry Beard
tapioca - the only known dessert that produces leftovers.
Henry Beard
taste - the enemy of creativeness.
Pablo Picasso
(see also: good taste, bad taste)
tautology - the alarm bell of the mind.
Robert Sabatier
tavern - a place where madness is sold by the bottle.
Jonathan Swift
tavern chair - the home of human felicity.
Samuel Johnson
tax collector - a taxidermist who stuffs you and keeps the skin.
Colin Bowles
taxes - a form of capital punishment.
Eddie George
(see also: art of taxation, equitable tax, income tax returns)
taxi - vehicle that always seems to dissolve in the rain.
Dan Bennett
taxi driver - a man who drives away customers.
Henry Cate

taxpayer - someone who works for the federal government but doesn't have to take a civil service examination.
Ronald Reagan
tax reform - taking the taxes off things that have been taxed in the past and putting taxes on things that haven't been taxed before.
Art Buchwald
tea - the champagne of the poor.
Hugh Leonard
(see also: hotel tea)
(to) teach - to learn twice.
Joseph Joubert
teacher - someone who doesn't know it either, but gets paid for it.
Piet Grijs
(see also: best teacher, good teacher)
teaching - the process by which the notes of the professor become the notes of the student without passing through the mind of either.
Woody Allen
team effort - a lot of people doing what I say.
Michael Winner
team spirit - an illusion that you only glimpse when you win.
Steve Archibald
teamwork - wasting half of one's time explaining to others why they are wrong.
Wolinski
tear gas - the only surefire method of getting children away from the television set.
Joyce Armor
tears - the melting ice of the soul.
Herman Hesse
(see also: women's tears)
technicality - a point of principle which we have forgotten.
Elwyn Jones
technical objection - the first refuge of a scoundrel.
Heywood Broun
technique - what you fall back on when you run out of inspiration.
Rudolf Nureyev
technocrats - bureaucrats who are technically better equipped.
Zarko Petan
(see also: European technocrat)

technology - a way of organizing the universe so that man doesn't have to experience it.
Max Frisch
technology today - the campfire around which we tell our stories.
Laurie Anderson
technocrat - young man with no power, who abuses it.
Georges Elgozy
tech support - a fine art which, once mastered, virtually ensures loss of sanity.
Joe Thompson
tedium - the bane of immortality.
Neil Lowe
teenage borrowing – a polite form of theft.
Jack Dee
teenage girl - a diet waiting to happen.
Jasmine Birtles
teenager - stereo-type.
Aldo Cammarota
(see also: adolescents)
teeth - bars for our thoughts.
E. Constant Sr.
teetotaller - someone who will never know what he missed.
Marcello Mastroianni
telephones - appliances that displace bodies immersed in water.
Martin S. Kottmeyer
televangelists - the professional wrestlers of religion.
Rick Overton
television - a weapon of mass distraction.
Larry Gelbart
(see also: American television, cable television, Sky television, TV, watching TV)
television criticism - something like describing an accident to an eye-witness.
Jackie Gleason
television remote control - the most effective birth-control device in history.
Jay Leno
television set - a watching machine.
Jacob Braude
television sponsor - a guy who watches the commercials and goes to the fridge during the show.
Stanley Davis

temper - the one thing you can't get rid of by losing it.
David Dorfman
temperance - the nurse of chastity.
William Wycherley
temporary insanity - breaking into someone's home and ironing all their clothes.
Sue Kolinsky
temptation - an irresistible force at work on a moveable body.
H.L. Mencken
tenderness - the body language of the soul.
Marc Pairon
tennis - the same as ping pong except that the players stand on the table.
Coluche
tenor - not a man but a disease.
Hans von Bülow
terror - the fiercest nurse of cruelty.
Josiah Henson
terrorism - armed propaganda.
Frank Kitson
terrorist - someone who is prepared to give his ideals for other people's lives.
Alexander Pola
testicle - a humorous question on an exam.
Paul Kocak
testing - paying people to find the defects that you paid people to create so that you can pay people to fix them so that you can pay people to test again.
James S. Huggins
tests - the Programmer's Stone, transmuting fear into boredom.
Kent Beck
Texas breakfast - a two-pound hunk of steak, a quart of whisky, and a hound dog. If you're wondering why you need the dog - well, somebody has to eat the steak.
Texas Bix Bender
text - a group of words that are all surprised to meet each other.
Battus
thanks - the highest form of thought.
G.K. Chesterton
Thanksgiving - so called because we are all so thankful that it only comes once a year.
P.J. O'Rourke

theatre - the aspirin of the middle classes.
Wolcott Gibbs
theatre critic - a skulking submarine that can sink an entire production with one well-aimed torpedo.
Rick Bayan
(see also: drama critic)
theatre director - a person engaged by the management to conceal the fact that the players cannot act.
James Agate
theatrical press agent - a resilient amalgam of glue and guile, chutzpah and heartburn, optimism and imagination.
Robert Berkvist
theologist - someone who tells you how God has to be according to him.
Fons Jansen
theology - an effort to explain the unknowable by putting it into the terms of the not worth knowing.
H.L. Mencken
theory - often just practice with the hard bits left out.
J.M. Robson
thesaurus - a dinosaur with a highly developed vocabulary.
Nick Siegler
They Say - the biggest liar in the world.
Douglas Malloch
thing - a thing without a name.
Marc van Halsendaele
(to) think - to deny what one believes.
Alain
thinking - one thing no one has ever been able to tax.
Charles F. Kettering
(see also: lateral thinking)
third world development - a cannibal using a knife.
Stanislaw Jerzy Lec
thirty - a nice age for a woman - especially if she happens to be forty.
Phyllis Diller
thirty-five - a wonderful age and an flexible idea that can last for more than ten years.
Renate Rubinstein
thought - the sound of silence.
Gys Miedema
(see also: rational thought, true thoughts)

three - an unlucky number if one is the third.
Sidney Tremayne
three-year-old-child - a being who gets almost as much fun out of a fifty-six-dollar set of swings as it does out of finding a small green worm.
Bill Vaughan
thriller - an extension of the fairy tale.
Raymond Chandler
throat - place where lies and bread meet.
Piet Grijs
throne - only a bench covered with velvet.
Napoleon Bonaparte
thug - a lost man in disguise.
Common
thunder - the sound of God moving his beer barrels across the floor of the sky.
Cyril Fletcher
thunderstorm - the rage of a god that weeps.
Ben Cami
thunderwear - what Thor wears under his armour.
Tiff Wimberly
tiger - a large-hearted gentleman with boundless courage.
Jim Corbett
µtime - the longest distance between two places.
Tennessee Williams
(see also: killing time, wasted time)
timefoolery - setting the alarm clock ahead of the real time in order to fool yourself into thinking you are not getting up so early.
Rich Hall
timelessness - a watchmaker's nightmare.
Gys Miedema
timer - adjustable clock that rings or otherwise signals when a particular dish is overcooked.
Henry Beard
times of crisis - golden times for false prophets.
Bas Heijne
Times Square, New York - neon-classical.
Nicola Zweig
timing - the essential ingredient of politics.
Pierre Trudeau
tinsel - snake mirrors.
Steven Wright

tip - a small sum of money you give to someone because you are afraid he wouldn't like not being paid for something you haven't asked him to do.
Ann B. Caesar
tired businessman - one whose business is usually not a successful one.
Joseph R. Grundy
tired locomotive - one that lies down in a derailment because they would not let it sit and rest on a bench in the station.
Ramon Gomez de la Serna
titles - a form of psychic compensation.
Robert Townsend
toastmaster - a man who eats a meal he doesn't want so he can get up and tell a lot of stories he doesn't remember to people who've already heard them.
George Jessel
tobacco - my favourite vegetable.
Frank Zappa
(see also: cigarette, smoking)
today - the last day of the first part of your life.
John Hovancsek
(see also: present, tomorrow)
today's literature - prescriptions written by patients.
Karl Kraus
toddler - someone who survived the abortion wave.
Jan Lambin
toe - a part of the foot used to find furniture in the dark.
Rilla May
Tokyo - a city confected from quotations.
Peter Conrad
tolerance - the result of boredom.
Quentin Crisp
(see also: intolerance)
tombstone - about the only thing that can stand upright and lie on its face at the same time.
Mary Wilson Little
tomorrow - actually the last day of the first part of my life.
Michael McCuiston
tomorrow night - nothing but one sleepless wrestle with yesterday's omissions and regrets.
William Faulkner

tongue - the meanest piece of meat in the world.
Jan Mens
(see also: fluent tongue, sharp tongue)
tool - an object that enables you to take advantage of the laws of physics and mechanics in such a way that you can seriously injure yourself.
Dave Barry
tooth fairy - a gay dentist.
Colin Bowles
topless bar - a place where you can always find a friendly face - and nobody watching it.
Joey Adams
top management - supposed to be a tree full of owls hooting when management heads into the wrong part of the forest. I'm still unpersuaded they even know where the forest is.
Robert Townsend
top manager - someone who solves problems of which other managers are not aware.
Pieter Klaas Jagersma
top sportsman - he who must have an aggressive mind in an aggressive body.
Koen Meulenaere
Toronto - a kind of New York operated by the Swiss.
Peter Ustinov
tortoise - the only animal that can make love to a hedgehog, but seldom has the urge to do that.
François Cavanna
Tory - a term derived from an Irish word meaning "savage".
Samuel Johnson
totalitarianism - the interruption of mood.
Norman Mailer
touch - the meaning of being human.
Andrea Dworkin
toupee - top secret.
Robert Myers
tourism - the art of seeing as many things as possible without seeing anything.
Jan Greshoff
(see also: disaster tourism)
tourist - someone who wants to be bored in a strange country.
Karel Jonckheere
tout - a guy who has nothing to lose and makes sure you do too.
Milton Berle

towel - the only thing that gets wet as it dries.
Peter Darbou
town - something you love when you leave it.
Jos Daelman
(see also: city, hick town, new town, small town)
toxteth - a combination of 'toxic' and 'death'.
Paul Hoggart
trade - the skill of selling things before they become worthless.
Jan Schepens
trade secrets - what women do.
Robert Meyers
trade unions - islands of anarchy in a see of chaos.
Aneurin Bevan
tradition - the most sublime form of necrophilia.
Hans Kudszus
traditionalist - a pessimist about the future and an optimist about the past.
Lewis Mumford
tragedy - situation in which both parties are right.
Simon Carmiggelt
(see also: comedy)
tramp - a ragged individualist.
Jane Ace
trampoline - dance floor for optimists.
Gys Miedema
tranquility - the old man's milk.
Thomas Jefferson
transaction - cash-cash.
Tomi Ungerer
transistor - a girl who used to be your brother.
Mitch Murray
transistor radio - the modern leper's bell.
Ian Fleming
translating - the ultimate act of comprehending.
Alberto Manguel
translation - reproduction of Rembrandt in black and white.
Johan Huizinga
transsexual - someone who loves women so much he wants to join them.
Renée Richards
transvestite - stalagmite that likes to hang around.
Jan Hyde

Transylvania - Dracula's terror-tory.
Jeff P. Symonds
(to) travel - to discover that everyone is wrong about other countries.
Aldous Huxley
travelling - the process of journeying thousands of miles away from people to avoid them, and then sending them a card saying, 'Wishing you were here'.
E.C. McKenzie
(see also: best travel, true traveler)
tray - a portable mess.
Henry Beard
Treasury Bill - an ominously worded demand for payment issued by the U.S. Treasury.
Kurt Brouwer
trees - the main cause of Forest Fires!
Billy Connolly
trial lawyer - an adversary of justice.
Robert Myers
tribe - a group of people who honor the same perceptions.
Carolyn Myss
trickle-down theory - the less than elegant metaphor that if one feeds the horse enough oats, some will pass through to the road for the sparrows.
J.K. Galbraith
trick photography - focus-pocus.
Doris Dolphin
trigonometry - a weapon of math destruction.
Jeff MacNelly
trip - just what is needed to spoil a vacation.
Edmund J. Volkart
triple jump - only jumping into a sandpit.
Jonathan Edwards
triplets - small journeys.
Kevin Goldstein-Jackson
trombone - a trumpet in uniform.
Jacques Brel
tropical nights - hammocks for lovers.
Anaïs Nin
trot - the foundation of the gallop.
Richard Berenger

Trotskyist - someone who believes in the working man because he never saw one.
Tom Lanoye
troubles - the brooms and shovels that smooth the road to a good man's fortune.
Saint Basil
trout - a fish known mainly by hearsay. It lives on anything not included in a fisherman's equipment.
H.I. Phillips
true affluence - not needing anything.
Gary Snyder
true celebrity - someone identifiable by name only.
Liz Smith
true champion - someone who wants to make a difference, who never gives up, and who gives everything she has no matter what the circumstances are. A true champion works hard and never loses sight of her dreams.
Dot Richardson
true charity - the desire to be useful to others with no thought of recompense.
Emanuel Swedenborg
true critic - the man who becomes your personal enemy on the sole provocation of a bad performance, who will only be appeased by good performances.
George Bernard Shaw
true cynic - one who expects nothing more from life than confirmation of his disappointments.
Simon May
true Dubliner - a man who can peel an orange in his pocket.
Niall Toibin
true egotist - the one who is only thinking of himself as he talks about other people.
Pierre Dac
true friend - the one that stabs you in the front.
Oscar Wilde
true friendship - self-love at second-hand.
William Hazlitt
true genius - one who can admit at times to being ignorant.
Jerry C. Elliott
true gratitude - thanking God for everything when you've got everything.
O.A. Battista

true happiness - to be dissolved into something completely great.
Willa Cather
true gentleman - a man who treats a woman like a lady no matter how pretty she isn't.
O.A. Battista
true hypocrite - the one who ceases to perceive his deception, the one who lies with sincerity.
André Gide
true Irishman - a fellow who would trample over the bodies of twelve naked women to reach a pint of porter.
Sean O'Faolain
true irreverence - disrespect for another man's god.
Mark Twain
true leadership - the art of changing a group from what it is to what it ought to be.
Virginia Allan
true loser - the one everybody expected to win.
Claude Lelouch
true love - to keep playing Adam and Eve.
Piet Theys
true paradise - the one we have lost.
Marcel Proust
true poets - the guardians of the state.
Wentworth Dillon
true power - knowing that you can, but you don't.
Juliet Alicia Jarvis
true realism - consists in revealing the surprising things which habit covered and prevents us from seeing.
Jean Cocteau
true scientist - one who never loses the faculty of amazement.
Hans Selye
true solitude - a din of birdsong, seething leaves, whirling colors, or a clamor of tracks in the snow.
Edward Hoagland
true statesman - the one who is willing to take risks.
Charles de Gaulle
true statesmanship - the art of changing a nation from what it is into what it ought to be.
W.R. Alger
true success - the experience of the miraculous.
Deepak Chopra

true terror - to wake up one morning and discover that your high school class is running the country.
Kurt Vonnegut
true thoughts - those which do not understand themselves.
Theodor W. Adorno
true traveler - he who goes on foot, and even then, he sits down a lot of the time.
Colette
truly free man - the one who will turn down an invitation to dinner without giving an excuse.
Jules Renard
truly happy person - one who can enjoy the scenery on a detour.
Tim Middleditch
truly rich man - one who has paid all of his taxes.
O.A. Battista
trust - the precursor to betrayal.
Dave Krieger
 (to) trust people - a luxury in which only the wealthy can indulge; the poor cannot afford it.
E.M. Forster
truth - what one is obliged to tell policemen.
Bertrand Russell
(see also: great truth)
truthful - dumb and illiterate.
Ambrose Bierce
truth in science - the working hypothesis best suited to open the way to the next better one.
Konrad Lorenz
trying - the first step towards failure.
Matt Groening
t-shirts - the going form of immortality.
John Crosby
tuba - the most intestinal of instruments - the very lower bowel of music.
Peter de Vries
tumescence - the period between pubescence and senescence.
Robert Byrne
tumor - an extra pair.
Mike McKinley
turbulence - the best laxative known to man.
Billy Connolly
turd - a fart's assault on immortality.
Gerd de Ley

Turkey - the Mecca of the mocca.
E. Constant Sr.
turkey - living proof that an animal can survive with no intelligence at all.
Harvey Comstock
Turkish food - edible Greek food.
A.A. Gill
tv critic - a man forced to be literate about the illiterate, witty about the witless and coherent about the incoherent.
John Crosby
tv station - an unbeatable mechanism for accumulating debt.
Clive James
twentieth century - the innovative century that brought you WW I, WW II, and WWW.
Bill Higgins
twentieth-century man - one who lives within his means, but has to borrow the money to do it.
Colin Bowles
twenty-five - the best age to live like an animal.
Pieter Aspe
twenty-four-hour room service - generally refers to the length of time it takes for a club sandwich to arrive. This is indeed disheartening, particularly when you've ordered scrambled eggs.
Fran Lebowitz
twilight - a time of pause when nature changes her guard.
Howard Thurman
twins - four hands in one belly.
Karel Jonckheere
(see also: birth of twins)
two weeks - about the ideal length of time to retire.
Alex Comfort
tyranny - the death of history.
Greg Bear
tyrant - a mixture of cowardice, narrow-mindedness, high-handedness, irresponsibility and conceit. He is truly representative of the majority of people.
Gabriël Laub

U

ubermensch - a drunken German, with a lisp.
Laurie A. Murray
ugliness - the safest contraceptive.
Hervé Bazin
ugly women - the misprints of creation.
Peter Sirius
ukelele - the missing link between music and noise.
E.K. Kruger
ultimate indignity - to be given a bedpan by a stranger who calls you by your first name.
Maggie Kuhn
ultimate success - enjoying the pleasure of learning from constant improvement.
Lorrin L. Lee
ultimatum - in diplomacy a last demand before resorting to concession.
Ambrose Bierce
umbrella - a webbed palmtree.
Piet Grijs
uncertainty - the normal state.
Tom Stoppard
unconventionality - the most conventional convention.
Robert Hugh Benson
under-consumption - the root-evil of depressed trade.
John Atkinson Hobson
undercook - where they caught the waitress in the storeroom.
Ken Pinkham
underlay - missionary position.
Willie Meikle
(to) understand - to give meaning to suffering.
Antoine de Saint-Exupéry
understanding - the difference between data and information.
Charles J.C. Lyall
undeserved praise - satire in disguise.
Alexander Pope
undertaker - the last man to let you down.
Jimmy O'Dea

uneasy conscience - a hair in the mouth.
Mark Twain
unemployment - capitalism's way of getting you to plant a garden.
Orson Scott Card
unethical researcher - anyone who gets more grants than you do.
Howard Bennett
unfair competition - selling cheaper than someone else.
Ralph Harris
unfaithful - having nothing to say to your husband because you've already said everything to someone else.
Françoise Sagan
unforgivable sins - those we didn't commit when we had the chance.
Julien de Valckenaere
unfurnished - recently burgled.
Mike Barfield
ungrateful - a person who has nothing to expect anymore of the victim of his ingratitude.
Robert Sabatier
unhappiness - the difference between our talents and our expectations.
Edward de Bono
unhappy love - the only kind of love that endures.
Emanuel Wertheimer
unhealthy - what thin people call fat people - and vice versa.
Sandra Bergeson
unilateral withdrawal - a concept which, if nothing else, will at least help to solve the world's population problem.
Joel Rothman
unkindness - the displeasure that one has in oneself.
Adrienne Monnier
unknown - the largest need of the intellect.
Emily Dickinson
unlimited sex - the adult's version of owning a candy store.
Earl Pomerantz
union-leader - someone who will do everything for the working man, except to become one himself.
Alfredo La Mont
unique - a nutless Frenchman.
Richard Lederer

United Nations - an organization for countries that cannot tolerate injustice and oppression - except at home.
Joey Adams
United States - a nation of one hundred fine, mob-hearted, lynching, relenting, repenting millions.
Vachel Lindsay
(see also: America, USA)
unity - organised hatred.
John Jay Chapman
universal suffrage - the government of a house by its nursery.
Otto von Bismarck
universe - a big place, perhaps the biggest.
Kilgore Trout
university - a place where rich men send their sons who have no aptitude for business.
Kin Hubbard
Unix - the answer, but only if you phrase the question very carefully.
Belinda Asbell
unmarried man - an example of the failure of Care in the Community.
Jasmine Birtles
unnatural sexual act - the one which you cannot perform.
Alfred Kinsey
unsolicited advice - the junk mail of life.
Bern Williams
unused intelligence - a primary source of unhappiness.
Bryan Appleyard
upper crust - a bunch of crumbs held together by dough.
Joseph A. Thomas
urban development - the laying of areas of asphalt interspersed with new houses.
Herman Moscoviter
urinal - the one place where all men are peers.
Rick Bayan
urine - the reward for the drink.
Tomi Ungerer
urratem - the ultimate misprint.
Johan Anthierens
US Senate - an old sow which doesn't move very fast, but never sinks.
Everett Dirksen

USA - how the West was wounded.
John Theyssens
 (see also: America, United States)
Usenet - essentially a huge group of people passing notes in class.
R. Kadel
user - the word computer professionals use when they mean "idiot."
Dave Barry
Utopia - a term of abuse for every good idea put forward by a political opponent.
Lévi Weemoedt
Utopian - a poet who has gone astray.
William R. Inge
utter waste - a coachload of lawyers going over a cliff with three empty seats.
Lamar Hunt

vacation - what you take when you can't take what you've been taking any longer.
L. Frank Baum
(see also: holiday)
vacation time - when you spend days looking for a place to avoid next year.
Milton Berle
vaccination - the medical sacrament corresponding to baptism.
Samuel Butler
vaccine - a microbe with its face washed.
Frank Scully
vacuum - a hell of a lot better than some of the stuff that Nature replaces it with.
Tennessee Williams
vagina - inasmuch as this is the beginning for everybody there is a misunderstanding that it is also the end.
Battus
Valentine's Day - Extortion Day.
Jay Leno
valour - a soldierly compound of vanity, duty and the gambler's hope.
Ambrose Bierce
valuable executive - one who can tell you exactly how much money his job is saving the company.
O.A. Battista
values - tapes we play on the Walkman of the mind: any tune we choose so long as it does not disturb others.
Jonathan Sacks
vampire - a cannibal that stops after the apéritif.
Gerd de Ley
Van Gogh, Vincent - the only one I know of who could sleep on both his ears.
Frédéric Dard
vanish - fade accompli.
Charles G. Waugh
vanity - other people's pride.
Sacha Guitry

variability - one of the virtues of a woman.
G.K. Chesterton
varicose veins - the result of an improper selection of grandparents.
William Osler
variety - the only known aphrodisiac.
Mark Connolly
varnishing - the only artistic process with which the Royal Academicians are thoroughly familiar.
Oscar Wilde
vasectomy - the kindest cut of all.
Laurence J. Peter
vases - the means for passing all the family quirks from one generation to the next.
Ramon Gomez de la Serna
Vatican - house of pill refute.
Henry Root
Vat 69 - the Pope's telephone number.
John S. Crosbie
(see also: Pope)
vegetarian - someone who gives peas a chance.
Colin Bowles
vengeance - a lazy form of grief.
Martin Stellman & Brian Ward
Venice - *a fine city if only it were drained.*
Ulysses S. Grant
Venus de Milo - a good example of what happens to somebody who won't stop biting her fingernails.
Will Rogers
verbal diarrhoea - number one in the list of common diseases.
Gerrit Komrij
verbal seduction - the surest road to actual seduction.
Marya Mannes
verse - a special illness of the ear.
W.H. Auden
vers libre - a device for making poetry easier to read and harder to write.
H.L. Mencken
very close family - one with relations who have relations.
Cynthia MacGregor
Vesuvius - Italy's arse.
Marcel Mariën

veteran - old actor you thought was dead.
Russell Ash
veto - an insidious tool to subvert democratic rule.
Samuel Oak Chilliwack
vibrator - electrical milkman.
Kees van Kooten & Wim de bie
vice - a pleasure you didn't taste yet.
Louis Aragon
Vice Presidency - sort of like the last cookie on the plate. Everybody insists he won't take it, but somebody always does.
Bill Vaughan
Vice-President - someone who presides over the Senate and sits around hoping for a funeral.
Harry S. Truman
vicious circle - the one and only perpetuum mobile.
Marie Claire Loupard
victim - a person to whom life happens.
Peter McWilliams
Victorian Apartment - place where the bedrooms have only enough space for one tightly bound woman.
Wes Smith
victory - a matter of staying power.
Elbert Hubbard
village - a charming little place where the neighbours make them themselves responsible for keeping an eye on your wife.
Jean Richard
(see also: small town)
villains - people who do the same things that we do, but we have the right reasons.
Mignon McLaughlin
viola - the hermaphrodite of the orchestra.
Thomas Beecham
violence - the last refuge of the incompetent.
Isaac Asimov
(see also: domestic violence)
violin - bad hotel.
Richard Lederer
violinist - that peculiarly human phenomenon distilled to a rare potency-half tiger, half poet.
Yehudi Menuhin
virgin - no man's land.
Karel Jonckheere

virginity - nothing more but a child's disease.
Frédéric Dard
virility - an illness which is best avoided.
Nicholas Goodison
virtual reality - the use of head-mounted displays and graphics to induce nausea.
Stephen Manes
virtue - vice tired out.
Josh Billings
(see also: great virtues, vice)
virtuous king - a king who has shirked his proper function to embody for his subjects an idea of illustrious misbehaviour beyond their reach.
Logan Pearsall Smith
virus - a Latin word used by doctors, meaning, 'Your guess is as good as mine.'
E.C. McKenzie
vision - often what somebody turns to when it gets hard doing what's required.
Louis V. Gerstner
visionary - the only true realist.
Federico Fellini
visualization - daydreaming with a purpose.
Bo Bennett
Vivaldi - a man for all seasons.
Juul Kinnaer
vocation - the backbone of life.
Friedrich Nietzsche
voice - a second face.
Gérard Bauer
voice mail - the technological upchuck of the age.
Herb Caen
vol-au-vent - the single nastiest thing ever invented as a food that doesn't involve an initiation ceremony.
A.A. Gill
voloptuous woman - one who has curves in places where some girls don't even have places.
Henny Youngman
volume - a defense to error.
Richard A. Leahy
vote - the instrument and symbol of the Freeman's power to make a fool of himself and a wreck of his country.
Ambrose Bierce

voter's block - the attempt, however futile, to register dissent with the current political system by simply not voting.
Douglas Coupland
voting - a process of standing in line to decide which party will waste your money.
Babe Webster
vulgarity - the conduct of other people.
Oscar Wilde
(see also: occasional vulgarity)
vulnerability - the gateway to strength.
Bill Chapko

waffles - pancakes with syrup traps.
Mitch Hedberg
wages - the measure of dignity that society puts on a job.
Johnnie Tillmon
Wagner - the Puccini of music.
J.B. Morton
waist - a terrible thing to mind.
Tom Wilson
waistband - device to uphold one's honour.
André Vansteenbrugge
(to) wait - to stare at eternity for a while.
Eduard Acda
waiter - a man who believes that money grows on trays.
Tommy Cooper
waiting - the hoofs of time.
Kahlil Gibran
Waiting For Godot - a play in which nothing happens, twice.
Vivian Mercier
Wales - a country where the only concession to gaiety is a striped shroud.
Gwyn Thomas
(see also: Welsh)
walking - a form of exercise that loses some appeal when done behind a lawnmower.
Gary Fletchall
wall - the safeguard of simplicity.
Alice Meynell
wallets - the fabricated items into which we put our fabricated money, which most people believe to be their possession of the realest value.
T. Sachs
wallowing - sex for depressives.
Jeanette Winterson
Wall Street - the only place people ride to in a Rolls-Royce to get advice from people who take the subway.
Warren Buffett

want (noun) - a growing giant whom the coat of Have was never large enough to cover.
Ralph Waldo Emerson
(to) want - to have a weakness.
Margaret Atwood
war - capitalism with the gloves off.
Tom Stoppard
(see also: peace)
war between the sexes - the only one in which both sides regularly sleep with the enemy.
Quentin Crisp
war crimes - a pleonasm.
Kees Stip
ward clerk - the hospital's version of the appendix - every ward has one, but it's not clear what they do.
Howard Bennett
warden - the only man who should not be judged by the company he keeps.
Joey Adams
warder - a prisoner who is free.
Miguel Zamacoïs
warming trend - when a cold develops into a fever.
Linda Williams
Washington - the only place where sound travels faster than light.
Carl Thompson
wasp - the Nazi of the insect world.
John Cleese
wastebasket - a writer's best friend.
Isaac Bashevis Singer
wasted time - the biggest waste of all.
Marie Leszcynska
watch - the handcuff of time.
Sigismund von Radecki
(see also: clock)
watching TV - the most stupid way of looking for emptiness.
Ronald Giphart
water - the most important ingredient in the English kitchen.
Daniel Darc
Watergate - the only brothel where the madam remained a virgin.
Mort Sahl
water lily - a flower that escaped from the trees to navigate the waters.
Ramon Gomez de la Serna

Waterloo - a battle of the first rank won by a captain of the second.
Victor Hugo
watermelon - good fruit: you eat, you drink, you wash your face.
Enrico Caruso
water pollution - cirrhosis of the river.
Joel Rothman
we - the I of a schizophrenic.
Gerd de Ley
weaker sex - the kind you have after the kids have worn you out.
John Henry
weakness - force of habit.
Leonid S. Sukhorukov
wealth - any income that is at least 100 dollars a year more than the income of one's wife's sister's husband.
H.L. Mencken
(see also: great wealth, personal wealth, riches)
wealth tax - capital punishment.
Leonard Rossiter
weapon - a device for making your enemy change his mind.
Lois McMaster Bujold
weariness - the shortest path to equality and fraternity.
Friedrich Nietzsche
weather - the climate of an hour.
Ambrose Bierce
weather forecaster - the only profession where you can consistently be wrong and still get paid.
David Feherty
Web - not a mass medium, but a medium for the masses, who are already well along in the process of making it their own.
Denise Caruso
weblog - a location of vanity.
Gerrit Komrij
(see also: blogger)
wedding - a necessary formality before securing a divorce.
Oliver Herford
(see also: marriage, golden wedding, I do, planning a wedding, silver-gold wedding)
wedding anniversary - the celebration of love, trust, partnership, tolerance and tenacity. The order varies for any given year.
Paul R. Sweeney
wedding cake - the most dangerous food.
James Thurber

wedding rings - the diminutive of handcuffs.
Piet Agoras
wedlock - a lane where there is no turning.
Dinah Mulock Craik
weed - a plant with a star of David.
J.C.F. Kessler
(to) weep - the ejaculation of the impotent.
Fernand Auwera
weight gain - moving into a larger slacks bracket.
Jacob Braude
Welch, Raquel - one of the few actresses in Hollywood history who looks more animated in still photographs than she does on the screen.
Michael Medved
welcome visitor - one you hate to see leave.
O.A. Battista
well-adjusted executive - one whose intake of pep pills overbalances his consumption of tranquilizers just enough to leave him sufficient energy for the weekly visit to the psychiatrist.
Arthur H. Motley
well-adjusted person - someone who can play golf as if it were only a game.
Sandy Parr
well-balanced person - someone with a drink in each hand.
Billy Connolly
well-being - productivity plus justice.
Helmut Nahr
well-composed book - a magic carpet on which we are wafted to a world that we cannot enter in any other way.
Caroline Gordon
well educated girl - the only living person that blushes when she sees a banana.
François Cavanna
well governed people - usually a people that doesn't think.
André Siegfried
well-informed employee - the best salesperson a company can have.
Edwin J. Thomas
well-raised child - the one that, because the guest brought him sweets, confesses in time that he did a pee in the white port.
Pierre Perret
well-timed silence - is the most commanding expression.
Mark Helprin

Welsh - a people who are insistent that local names must not be pronounced as they are spelt.
John Tickner
(see also: Wales)
Welsh (the language) - the only language you learn to be able to talk to fewer people.
A.A. Gill
Wensleydale - the Mozart of cheeses.
T.S. Eliot
West, Mae - a plumber's idea of Cleopatra.
W.C. Fields
Western - a universal frame within which it's possible to comment on today.
Sam Peckinpah
wet baby - the only person who likes change.
Roy Z.M. Blitzer
whaling - a sacrament of the ocean for us.
Micah McCarty
wheels - the thoughts of legs.
Harry Mulisch
whim - the plural of woman.
Kathy Lette
whining - anger through a small opening.
Stephen Stewart Smalley
whip - terror for little boys, hope for old men.
Romain Coolus
whiskey - the most popular of the remedies that won't cure a cold.
Jerry Vale
whisky-making - the art of making poison pleasant.
Samuel Johnson
White House - the finest jail in the world.
Harry S. Truman
whodunit - none of the kids that live in your house.
John Henry
whom - just womb with a breeze.
George S. Kaufman
wickedness - a myth invented by good people to account for the curious attractiveness of others.
Oscar Wilde
widow - a girl that has nothing to fear anymore.
Robert de Flers
(see also: being widowed, rich widows)

widower - the only man who can make more money than his wife can spend.
O.A. Battista
widowhood - the only good thing some women get out of marriage.
Jasmine Birtles
wife - a woman who tries to turn an old rake into a lawn-mower.
Jack Benny
 (see also: good wife, loving wife, solicitous wife)
wife-swapping - sexual fourplay.
John S. Crosbie
wilderness - the raw material out of which man has hammered the artifact called civilization.
Aldo Leopold
will - a dead giveaway.
Milton Berle
willpower - only the tensile strength of one's own disposition.
Cesare Pavese
willy-nilly – impotent.
Beth Benson
wind - the product that is the most expensive on the free market.
Johan Struye
Windows - the only operating system that you switch off with the 'start' button.
Japie
(see also: Microsoft Windows)
windscreen wipers - the eyelashes of rain.
Johan Anthierens
wine - the Mozart of the mouth.
Gérard Depardieu
(see also: fine wine, good wine)
wings - a poor substitute for thrust.
Alan Anderson
wink - a temptation in rompers.
O.A. Battista
winkle - just a bogey with a crash helmet on.
Mick Miller
winners - losers with a new attitude.
David Byrne
(see also: real winners)
winter - nature's way of saying, "Up yours".
Robert Byrne
(see also: English winter)

Winter Olympics - a celebration of amateur athletes, frostbite and unpronounceable Russian surnames.
Ryan Murphy
win-win situation - a frame of mind and heart that constantly seeks mutual benefit in all human interactions.
Stephen Covey
wisdom - a collection of platitudes.
Norman Douglas
wise - he who gathers the wisdom of others.
Juan Guerra Càceres
wisecrack - something we think of 24 hours too late.
George Burns
wisecracking - calisthenics with words.
Dorothy Parker
wise man - nothing more than a fool with a good memory.
Ryan Monroe
wisest man - only a boy who regrets growing up.
Vincenzo Cardarelli
wish - the mother of disappointment.
Alexander Pola
wit - educated insolence.
Aristotle
woman - a thing of beauty and an expense forever.
Leopold Fechtner
(see also: bad woman, body of a woman, career woman, clever woman, costliest women, cunning woman, decent woman, dirty woman, fair woman, female woman, ideal woman, learned woman, liberated woman, liberation woman, really plain woman, real woman, really original woman, smart woman, superwoman, ugly women)
woman driver - one who drives like a man and gets blamed for it.
Patricia Ledger
woman in love - a slave who lets her lover carry her chains.
Etienne Rey
woman of thirty - a woman of twenty who isn't forty yet.
Philippe Labro
woman's body - a clock that runs down very rapidly.
Sharman MacDonald
woman scorned - a woman who quickly learns her way around the courtroom.
Colette Mann
woman's heart - a deep ocean full of secrets.
James Cameron

woman's hand - the softest balsam.
Marc Andries
woman's intuition - often nothing more than man's transparency.
George Jean Nathan
woman's movie - one where the woman commits adultery all through the picture, and, at the end, her husband begs her to forgive him.
Oscar Levant
woman's refusal - rather evidence of her experience than of her virtue.
Ninon de Lenclos
woman's strength - the unresistable might of weakness.
Ralph Waldo Emerson
woman's work - shitwork.
Gloria Steinem
women's fashion - a euphemism for fashion created by men for women.
Andrea Dworkin
women's liberation - the liberation of the feminine in the man and the masculine in the woman.
Corita Kent
women's rights - men's duties.
Karl Kraus
woman's shoulders - the frontline of her mystique.
Jonathan Lenkin & Tony Gilroy
women's bodies - the first environment for all of us.
Sandra Steingraber
women's tea - giggle, gobble, gabble.
Oliver Wendell Holmes
women's tears - the world's greatest water power.
J. Kenfield Morley
women's virtue - man's greatest invention.
Cornelia Otis Skinner
women wrestlers - the only real attempt at culture on American television.
Robert Morley
wonder - the effect of novelty on ignorance.
Samuel Johnson
wooing the press - an exercise roughly akin to picnicking with a tiger. You might enjoy the meal, but the tiger always eats last.
Maureen Dowd
word-creation - a journey by ear.
Marina Tsvetayeva

words - a wonderful form of communication, but they will never replace kisses and punches.
Ashleigh Brilliant
(see also: meaningless words)
work - the curse of the drinking classes.
Oscar Wilde
(see also: hard work)
workaholic - someone who says, "Thank God It's Monday!"
Jerry Banks
workers' control - the castration of the trade union movement.
Arthur Scargill
working - fine for those with nothing to do.
Henri Jeanson
working girl - one who quit her job to get married.
Edmund J. Kiefer
work of art - an uncommitted crime.
Theodor W. Adorno
world - proof that God is a committee.
Bob Stokes
world politics - village politics on a higher scale.
Noldus Kee
worm - the greatest fan of fly fishing.
Patrick McManus
worry - today's mouse eating tomorrow's cheese.
Larry Eisenberg
worship - deepfreeze-love.
Françoise Sagan
worst - enemy of the bad.
Arthur Bloch
wowser - an ineffably pious person who mistakes the world for a penitentiary and himself for a warder.
C.J. Dennis
Woy-Woy - the only above-ground cemetery in the world.
Spike Milligan
wrap race - the day before Christmas.
Joseph Leff
wrath - the anger of the upper classes.
Jacqueline Gurnari
wrinkles - human annual rings.
Hugo Olaerts
(to) write - to try out sentences to see what they can mean.
P.F. Thomése

writer - a reader turned inside out.
John Updike
(see also: good writer, great writers, literary men, original writer)
writer's block - the cure for writer's cramp.
Inigo DeLeon
writing - a kind of conversation between yourself and someone you don't know.
Hugo Claus
(see also: good writing, major writing)
writing biography - a paradoxical enterprise, at once solitary and communal.
Penelope Niven
writing books - the closest men ever come to childbearing.
Norman Mailer
writs - the Oscars of my profession.
Nigel Dempster
wunderbar - a bar where you sit and daydream.
John S. Crosbie
WWW - the MS-DOS of hypertext systems.
Erik Naggum
WYMI - the all-philosophy radio station.
Mike Dugan

x - the folding chair of the alphabet.
Ramón Gómez de la Serna
xenophobia - a love of Australia.
Barry Humphries
Xerox - a trademark for a photocopying device that can make rapid reproductions of human error, perfectly.
Merle L. Meacham
X-rated movie – an underdeveloped plot with an overdeveloped cast.
Robert Orben
x-ray - inside information.
Hal Stebbins
xylophone - instrument developed at the request of Daniel Webster so there would be a word beginning with X in his dictionary.
Cy DeBoer

Y

Y - the champagne glass of the alphabet.
Ramon Gomez de La Serna
yacht - the stretch limo of the seas.
Rick Bayan
yak - a lovely long-haired animal, like a cow on the way to the opera.
Paul Theroux
yawn - a silent shout.
G.K. Chesterton
year - a period of 365 disappointments.
Ambrose Bierce
yearning - not only a good way to go crazy but also a pretty good place to hide out from hard truth.
Jay Cocks
year's end - neither an end nor a beginning but a going on, with all the wisdom that experience can instill in us.
Hal Borland
yes - the last word of the free life.
Piet Grijs
(see also: no)
yes, but... - the refined 'no'.
Hans Kasper
yesterday - the deadline for all complaints.
Robert Anthony
Yes, Your Honor - witty rejoinder by lawyer to judge.
Miles Kington
Yiddish - the Robin Hood of languages.
Leo Rosten
yinkel - a person who combs his hair over his bald spot, hoping no one will notice.
Rich Hall
yodelling - hogcalling with frost on it.
George M. Cohan
yoghurt - the only poisoned drink that lengthens life.
Fernand Auwera
young - an adjective used by men to describe a woman who is under eighteen or a man who is under eighty.
Nancy Linn-Desmond

young lady - a female child who has just done something dreadful.
Judith Martin
youth - that part of society that hasn't got time yet to prove they are wrong.
C. Buddingh'
(see also: fountain of youth, happy youth, second youth)
yuppie - someone who believes it's courageous to eat in a restaurant that hasn't been reviewed yet.
Mort Sahl

Z

zeal - the necessary condition for becoming a zealot, which is remarkably close to being an idiot.
Edmund H. Volkart
zealot - a woman who irons her husband's socks.
Cy DeBoer
zealotry - the enemy of idealism.
Neil Kinnock
zebra - a bar-coded horse.
Mike Barfield
Zen - the unsymbolization of the world.
Reginald H. Blyth
Zen martini - a martini with no vermouth at all. And no gin, either.
P.J. O'Rourke
zero defects - the result of shutting down a production line.
Kelvin Throop
007 - the only bond that never fails.
D. Alster
zest - the secret of all beauty.
Christian Dior
Zeus - the God of wine and whoopee.
Garrison Keillor
zig zag - the shortest distance between two bars.
L.L. Levinson
zig-zag-line - the shortest distance between two joints.
Robert Myers
Zimbabwe - a suburb pretending to be a country.
Alan Coren
zinc - the element needed to maintain good sexual function. Found in oysters and tin baths.
Jeff Green
zip code - a numerical system introduced by the U.S. Postal Service to make sure that prompt delivery of mail will be further delayed.
Edmund H. Volkart
zipper - two rows of unsmiling teeth that often induce laughter in others, es. when inadvertently left open following a trip to the toilet.
Rick Bayan

zoo - an excellent place to study the habits of human beings.
Evan Esar
zulu - an elephant's toilet.
Willie Meikle
zygote - a gamete's way of producing more gametes.
Robert A. Heinlein

ABOUT THE AUTHOR

Gerd de Ley was born in 1944 in Ghent, Flanders and is now a resident of Antwerp. A former teacher of English, he has been a professional writer and actor since 1975.

From his youth he has been an avid collector of original quotations and proverbs from all over the world and had had more than 450 works published in Holland, Belgium, USA, UK, India, Finland, Vietnam & China.

www.ingramcontent.com/pod-product-compliance
Lightning Source LLC
LaVergne TN
LVHW052257070426
835507LV00036B/3098